Local Governance and Regional Development:
Current Perspectives

Fatih Ayhan (ed.)

Local Governance and Regional Development: Current Perspectives

PETER LANG

Bibliographic Information published by the Deutsche Nationalbibliothek
The Deutsche Nationalbibliothek lists this publication in the Deutsche Nationalbibliografie; detailed bibliographic data is available online at http://dnb.d-nb.de.

Library of Congress Cataloging-in-Publication Data
A CIP catalog record for this book has been applied for at the Library of Congress.

ISBN 978-3-631-84201-0 (Print)
E-ISBN 978-3-631-84371-0 (E-PDF)
E-ISBN 978-3-631-84372-7 (EPUB)
E-ISBN 978-3-631-84373-4 (MOBI)
DOI 10.3726/b17917

Peter Lang – Berlin · Bern · Bruxelles · New York · Oxford · Warszawa · Wien

This publication has been peer reviewed.

www.peterlang.com

Preface and Acknowledgements

The economic development is crucial for all countries in order for the individuals who make up the society to live a decent life. To ensure social development in current economies, it is necessary to reduce the development differences between regions. An opportunity is provided to increase the level of social welfare by reducing development disparities among the regions. The importance of regional development has increased with the experience of the industrialization process in the world and the effects of globalization. While the increase in industrialization triggers migration from rural to urban, it also reveals the importance of local governance by causing urbanization problems. Therefore, common goals are achieved with the interaction of regional development and local governance concept. Local governments accelerate the industrialization and development moves in the region by using local resources in the most rational way. It will enable the development of the country as a whole by eliminating regional development differences from local administration to regional development. In this book, current perspectives on the regional development and local governance, which are two important concepts for the development of societies, increasing welfare and overall development goal, are presented.

In this book, different and up-to-date perspectives have been developed. Moreover, the recent publication, which will make a significant contributions to the field, has emerged with the researches made by experts in the field on local governance and regional development.

I would like to thank all authors, participants and researchers who are experts in their field for their dedication and meticulous and hope that this work will help our readers. We offer our endless gratitude to our families and children, who are the source of motivation for our authors, with their patience and support in the execution of these valuable works.

All chapters in this publication were implemented blind-review process.

Respectfully

Editor: Assoc. Prof. Fatih Ayhan.

Contents

List of Contributors

Dr. Arif İğdeli
Aksaray University, Turkey

Dr. Başak Gök
Gazi University, Turkey

Dr. Çağlar Burak Burtan
Bandirma Onyedi Eylul University, Turkey

Elias Esteban Silva Lecuna
Bandirma Onyedi Eylul University, Turkey

Emine Fırat
Canakkale Onsekiz Mart University, Turkey

Assoc. Prof. Fatih Ayhan
Bandirma Onyedi Eylul University, Turkey

Dr. Faruk Mike
Hakkari University, Turkey

Prof. Dr. Filiz Balta Peltekoğlu
Marmara University, Turkey

Dr. Gürçem Özaytürk
Niğde Omer Halisdemir University, Turkey

Prof. Dr. Hadi Gökçen
Gazi University, Turkey

Dr. Mehmet Ali Polat
Malatya Turgut Ozal University, Turkey

Assoc. Prof. Nadia Loukil
Université Tunis-EL Manar, Tunisia

Dr. Hasan Acar
Gendarmerie and Coast Guard Academy, Turkey

Dr. Muhammet Arucu
Bandirma Onyedi Eylul University, Turkey

Dr. Olivier Gajac
Galatasaray University, Turkey

Dr. Omca Altın
Kastamonu University, Turkey

Assoc. Prof. Ouidad Yousfi
University of Montpellier, France

Dr. Peyman Uysal
Antalya Bilim University, Turkey

Dr. Salih Ziya Kutlu
Canakkale Onsekiz Mart University, Turkey

Dr. Selin Pelek
Galatasaray University, Turkey

Dr. Taner Kalaycı
Bandirma Onyedi Eylul University, Turkey

Yunus Karaağaç
Istanbul Arel University, Turkey

Dr. Zuhal Akbayır
Marmara University, Turkey

Dr. Zuhal Önez Çetin
Usak University, Turkey

Part 1 Local Governance

Dr. Çağlar Burak Burtan

1.1 Justification of Administrative Procedures and Evaluation of Implied Refuses on the Axis of Local Governments

Abstract: Administrative transactions have an efficiency that serves to explain the will of the administration. This situation also makes the administrative procedures stronger as they are realizing the provisions and results from the moment they are made. When administrative transactions are evaluated together with the five elements they have, it is clear that these transactions should have a causal link in terms of cause and effect. The existence of the specified cause-effect relationship brings along the obligation of the administrative act to be justified. Therefore, the administration should be able to explain the reason for the preparation of the said transaction while creating its administrative transactions. When we look at the axis of the Turkish administrative organization, we come across the concept of implied refusal, which the administration uses in some cases. In particular, in municipal administrations, which are a type of local government in practice, responding to the applications made by individuals through tacit refusal is a quality that needs to be examined. Although there are benefits of decentralization elements; the implicit refusal through silence can be interpreted together with the disadvantages of decentralization. In this case, the result arises that the period of responding to the application made to the administration can be extended in favor of the administration with sixty days, which is the general litigation period in the administrative court (but against the applicant, within the framework of the freedom to obtain information and to seek remedies). Making amendments in the Administrative Jurisdiction Procedure Law on the tacit rejection of the application and introducing regulations in accordance with the justification principle, which must be in administrative proceedings, will also ensure the transparency of the administration.

Keywords: Turkish administration, Local administrations, Municipal administration, Administrative procedures, Justification, European Law of Good Administrative Behavior, Implied refusal.

Introduction

The administration creates public services in order to achieve the purpose of public benefit. In this framework, administrative actions that the administration carries out in line with the rules of public law are encountered in its daily operations. Accordingly, the administration announces its will with the administrative actions it has brought about to have legal consequences. Since the administrative act is a declaration of the will that constitutes a legal result, the administration should also be able to express the justification for creating the said administrative act.

The Turkish administrative organization has a structure that is basically divided into central and decentralized management. One of the biggest differences between central and decentralization is that the decision-making bodies of local government organizations (decentralized in terms of location), especially under the heading of decentralization, are elected by the people as a rule.[1] This situation enables the people to participate directly in the administration more than the central management principles. The stated result is also seen as a superiority within the framework of comparing decentralization organization with central government organization. In local governments, there are some damages against the stated superiority principle (Akgüner, 2017 : 224). Due to the local conditions and the employment preferences developing accordingly, the presence of people who will take part in areas requiring expertise in local governments is less than central government units. In my opinion, this damage is directly reflected in the establishment of administrative proceedings. Because, the administration's ability to execute the administrative act together with its justification requires both knowing the technical features of the application subject to the administrative act that constitutes the justification, and preparing it in accordance with the law in accordance with the five elements of the administrative act.

In addition, like every formation in the Turkish administrative organization, local governments undoubtedly carry out administrative action with the aim of realizing the public interest. Moreover, since the administrative act serves a superior purpose such as the public interest and aims to meet the daily needs of the society, it must be in accordance with the law in accordance with the five elements it includes. Implied refusal,[2] which is our subject of study, is clearly defined in IYUK (2577). In the first paragraph of Article 10 of the IYUK[3] titled "Silence of administrative authorities", it is regulated that anyone who has a valid and acceptable link of interest can apply to administrative offices for the purpose of carrying out an administrative action or administrative action that may be the subject of

---

1. The reason why the expression is used here as a rule is that the Governor, who is at the head of the provincial special administration under the heading of decentralization, is directly appointed by the central administration.
2. Another situation that should be criticized on the subject is the existence of foreign words in Turkish. Implied Refusal is named as "Zımni Red" in Turkish and this phrase (Zımni Red) is an Arabic word and, in my opinion, the derivation of Abstract Turkish words and sentences by making a change in the way of using implicit rejection instead of the concept of implied refusal in law and practice is in a structure that needs to be examined carefully. For criticism, see also Burtan, 2019: 1.
3. Official Gazette No. 17580 and dated 20.1.1982

an administrative action. In the continuing second paragraph of the article, if the administration does not respond to the concerned person who made his application in accordance with the method within 60 days, which is the period of filing a general lawsuit in the administrative jurisdiction. It was stated that the request for the application would be deemed to have been rejected.[4] Therefore, in order to be able to evaluate the concept of implied refusal, which is an administrative act, it is useful to briefly explain the administrative procedures together with their elements.

1 Elements of Administrative Transactions

Administrative transactions have a structure that affects both those who are directly affected by its terms and results, and everyone who has an interest. Therefore, they can be sued by anyone who has a legitimate, current and personal interest claiming that they are unlawful. The annulment cases filed in the administrative jurisdiction will be to fulfill a purely legal inspection that the administrative judicial bodies in charge should do, since one or more of the authority-form-reason-subject-purpose elements of the administrative act are filed with the claim that they are unlawful. In this context, the administrative judicial body, where concrete dispute is seen, will not be able to "check the appropriateness" in any way; That is, it will not be able to make a decision to replace the administration that carried out the administrative action and take a new decision. In fact, when an action for annulment is filed against an administrative act that has been tacitly rejected, the administrative judicial body must be able to fully control the legal compliance with the justification of the administrative act in question.

In the filing of annulment cases consisting of the evaluation of compliance with the law in the five elements of the administrative act, the condition of merely infringing the interest instead of violating personal rights can be considered as sufficient for the decisions made as a result of the annulment action, not only for the parties, but for everyone concerned. Therefore, it is once again understood that administrative acts, which may concern more than one person at the same time within the framework of a current interest, are justified. In my opinion, bringing an administrative act created by tacit refusal to the realm of law without any justification will also contradict the condition of being in the public interest. The execution of the cancellation decisions given as a result of the annulment case has a characteristic that concerns the public order and must be implemented immediately by the administration. The Administration cannot delay the execution of these decisions and cannot escape from its duty to fulfill the annulment decisions.

---

4. see at https://www.mevzuat.gov.tr/MevzuatMetin/1.5.2577.pdf, (Accessed date: 3.8.2020)

This will be expected from the administration subject to the law. In this context, it can be thought that an administrative act whose justification is unknown or not understood will be far from achieving the desired result in legal and public terms.

1.1 Authority Element of the Administrative Procedure

The authority element of the administrative process may be in terms of person, place, subject or time. Namely, the ability to make a declaration of will on behalf of the administration in administrative law depends on the fact that the relevant authorities are clearly authorized in accordance with the provisions of the legislation. Thus, transactions made by unauthorized persons may be a reason for cancellation. The dimensions of the authority element and the domain of sovereignty may also be considered in terms of location of jurisdiction in terms of location will also constitute a reason for cancellation, since it can be clearly foreseen in which geographical areas a public official can exercise his authority. For example, the powers of the governor of a province will only be valid within the boundaries of that province. Authority element is also examined in terms of subject. As often repeated; the powers of public officials are specified in the legislation. Especially in statutory professions such as civil servant, a person who wants to enter the public office is included in a structure whose boundaries are predetermined. These limits indicate which powers can be used together with personal rights. Therefore, the act of a public official out of the authority granted to him by the legislation will cause a situation of inability to arise in terms of the subject and will result in the cancellation of the transaction made within this framework. Finally, the authority element can also be evaluated over time. Granting the given authorization for a certain period of time will cause the authorization to terminate due to the expiration of the period, and the administrative action that is made as if the authorization is still continuing even though the period has expired may be canceled due to lack of authorization in terms of time.

The appearance of the authority element on administrative transactions manifests itself in three different situations in administrative law: The first is the usurpation of function. The usurpation of function refers to the interchangeability of the three basic powers, whose powers and limits are declared by the 1982 Constitution, and which have a civilized division of labor. These transactions are legally invalid. For example, marriage procedures are completed by the couples who want to get married to apply to the marriage office of the relevant municipality and get their official wedding by the marriage officer with the authority given by the mayor. This process is carried out by the municipalities,[5] which

5. In societies that accept a secular and contemporary life standard, the official marriage of couples who want to get married by religious officials will result in the dominance of religious rules over social life and in the state administration.

are a local government organization within the decentralization elements of the Turkish administrative organization. The fact that the marriage is carried out by the marriage offices affiliated to the municipalities will not indicate that the marriage offices working under the municipalities are authorized to terminate the same marriage. Because, according to the existence of the necessary conditions only family courts (where there are no family courts, civil courts of first instance as family courts) will be able to decide the divorce situation regulated between articles 161 and 184 of the Turkish Civil Code. Therefore, if the marriage department can decide to marry or want to carry out divorce, this will lead to a usurpation of function[6] and the transaction will be null and void.

The second situation is the violation of authority. A breach of authority consists of the execution of a transaction by a person who is not authorized to perform that transaction. Namely, the person authorized to make a statement of will on behalf of the administration may have taken an administrative action on an issue that does not fall within the scope of his/her duty, or an administrative action may have been taken by a person who is not in charge of the public service. In both cases, the use of a power that is not within the scope of its jurisdiction by its use or the use of authority by establishing an administrative act as if someone who is not in charge of the administrative organization in any way will be an administrative act caused by an authority that does not exist. Here, the administrative action taken as a result of this situation, which is called as a violation of authority, will be deemed invalid.

The third case is authority encroachment. Power encroachment is the bringing of an administrative action in matters that fall under the jurisdiction of another public official who is outside his/her field of duty but also within the administrative organization. For example, one of the important examples of jurisdiction violations in administrative law is that the subordinate acts by substituting the superior subordinate (Derdiman, 2014: 207).

1.2 Form Element of Administrative Procedure

The second element in evaluating whether the administrative acts subject to the annulment case are in compliance with the law is the form. In fact, the manner in which administrative acts will be made is stated in the relevant legislation. In general, when administrative transactions are examined in terms of form element, the existence of several important issues stands out. Administrative procedures should

6. Extortion of function (duty), State's action on a matter that falls within the function of the legislative or judicial body (severe and obvious encroachment of power), Council of State 7.D, E. 2009/5247, K. 2011/1460, Council of State İDDGK, E. 2010/2072, K. 2010/1467, Date: 4.11.2010, Retrieved from: Hukuk.istanbul.edu.tr, (Date of Access: 10.6.2020)

be created in writing first of all in terms of the style element. The fact that the transaction is in writing will provide the way for an action for annulment against that transaction; because it is not possible to file an action for annulment against the verbal acts of the administration. According to the case law of the Council of State, verbal decisions can only be sued when they are put in written form (Derdiman, 2014: 217). Moreover, the Council of State, in favor of the plaintiff who was deemed unsuccessful as a result of the oral examination and who applied for the annulment of the relevant decision, *the basis of which the examination board formed its observations and thoughts as a result of the oral examination, and if it is a result based on concrete information and documents, what concrete information and He has to prove his existence with documents and put forward his reasons* and decided to refuse the appeal request of the defendant administration.[7] In this respect, in terms of the form element of the administrative acts, it can be stated as a mandatory element that they are justified as well as being written and signed. The declaration of will that constitutes the content of the administrative process and explains the transaction can be written and verbal; As we have examined in our study, it may also be implicitly revealing that the administration has rejected the present application because it did not respond to the applications made to it within sixty days, which is the general litigation period in the administrative jurisdiction.

1.3 Reason Element of Administrative Procedure

The third element in the examination of the legal compliance of administrative transactions is the reason. The reason element of the administrative act refers to the issue that prompts the administration to carry out the said transaction and causes the administration to perform the specified transaction. Within the framework of the reason element, the administration may show the reason for the transaction it has made, or the same administration may have carried out the administrative act without showing any reason, in accordance with its discretionary power. The administration establishes its operations with the superiority of public power and it will be within the discretion of the administration to establish an administrative act without showing reasons. The administration has to use its discretionary power in accordance with the legislation, justified and equally for everyone in the same cases. Undoubtedly, the superiority of the public interest also requires this. If the administration acts outside these points while exercising its discretionary power, it means that it acts in an arbitrary manner.

7. Council of State 2. D, E. 2014/8821, K. 2015/1537, Date: 19.2.2015, Retrieved from: www.kazanci.com.tr, (Access Date: 10.6.2020)

According to the Council of State, it was stated that the administration should exercise its discretionary power not in absolute and unlimited manner, but in accordance with the principles of public interest and public service, and that the administrative acts created in line with the discretionary power should be based on legally valid reasons, are known principles of the law. It was determined that the plaintiff, who was subjected to a live appointment for attending a meeting of a political party, did not attend the mentioned meeting as a result of the response from the relevant police headquarters regarding the absence of a video recording of the meeting. In fact, even if he attends, it was concluded that it was necessary to investigate the content of the meeting, and in this context, as a result of the lack of reason, the transaction regarding the transfer of the plaintiff's decision on the plaintiff should be canceled in terms of the cause.[8] Again, the Council of State has ruled that there will be no compliance with the law in the proceedings subject to the case, which are created without a full and clear explanation for an administrative decision.[9] Therefore, the transactions performed by the administration by showing an invalid and unjustified reason and the transactions that cannot be explained when the reason is requested and therefore arbitrarily performed will be against the law in terms of the cause element. In this context, situations that constitute unlawfulness under the cause element are (Kalabalık, 2016: 164-165);

a) Although the reason is clearly stated in the legislation, the administrative action taken is not the reason in question;
b) Failure of the administration to explain in a precise and justified manner the reason related to the administrative proceedings in cases where the reasons are stated with ambiguous statements;
c) If the reason is not shown at all, it has been stated by the administration in the framework that it cannot be declared that the transaction carried out in this way is suitable for the public interest.

1.4 Subject Element of the Administrative Procedure

The fourth of the five elements of the administrative process is the subject element. After the execution of the administrative procedures, the result that the administration has done as a result of the reason that led the administration to

8. Council of State 5. D, E. 1997/2136, K. 1997/2986, Date: 11.12.1997, Retrieved from: www.kazanci.com.tr, (Access Date 12.6.2020)
9. Council of State 3. D, E. 2014/5065, K. 2015/6813, Date: 13.10.2015, Retrieved from: www.kazanci.com.tr, (Access Date: 12.6.2020)

create that administrative act and the result it gave birth constitutes the "subject element" of that administrative act. The subject matter, which is dealt with within the scope of the legal consequence resulting from the execution of the administrative act, also creates a change in the legal status of the concerned parties on which it has resulted, based on a certain method and rules. The power of the administrative process that will cause a change on a person will be revealed and enlightened with the subject element (Yayla, 2010: 132). Administrative proceedings should have a *causal link* between the cause element and the subject element, and the result generated based on the reason for the administrative act should be compatible. This conformity is to constitute the subject element of the transaction made based on the cause in legal terms by adhering to the legislation. For example, the reason for giving disciplinary punishment to the officer after the administration initiated a disciplinary investigation is that the officer violates the prohibitions specified in the legislation. It is clear which sanctions will be applied against the prohibitions that have been broken, or more precisely, which disciplinary penalty will be given against the disciplinary offense committed as a result of a disciplinary rule that has been broken. Moreover, it was also stated whether the administration could reduce the penalty by using its discretionary power. As a result, the sanctions specified separately for each disciplinary penalty in the legislation should be imposed and the disciplinary penalty corresponding to the action should be imposed. Otherwise, the causal link that should exist between the cause and the subject will be broken and the administrative act will have to be canceled when it is determined that it is illegal in terms of the subject element (Yaman, 2018: 25).

1.5 Purpose Element of the Administrative Procedure

The last element of the administrative process is the goal element. The administration always acts in the public interest by observing the general interests of the society. Therefore, it is not possible for all transactions and actions of the administration to serve any purpose other than the public interest. The purpose element includes a structure that prevents the administration from acting arbitrarily, making decisions for the benefit of third parties, for political reasons or for personal benefits. Arguing that administrative proceedings are not in the public interest also brings the necessity of proving the assumption in question and obliges to discuss the purpose of the administrative act in order to prove possible illegality (Korkut, 2006: 78).

The concept of public interest has an ambiguous meaning. Because, as it may vary from period to period, it may consist of decisions taken in accordance with local and universal conditions by the legislative body that makes laws in line with the needs of the society and the executive body that undertakes the government of the country. Therefore, public interest is an open-ended concept without exception and it is shaped within the framework of the demand and necessity that prevail in its time period. The concept of public benefit is the benefit that the government seeks for the State in the balance of power and people, or is it the social benefit it seeks for the people? It would be correct to interpret the public interest in a way that includes both elements and thus not take the definition in a narrow framework. The public interest, which is the concept sought in return for the purpose element from the five elements of the administrative process, is also specified as one of the basic elements of the rule of law by the Constitutional Court (Saraç, 2002: 20).

In fact, in the explanation of the concept of public benefit, it is stated that there is a determination according to the concrete conditions in each case rather than a single definition, and therefore, the concept of public benefit has been given flexibility beyond a rigid and narrow framework (Akıllıoğlu, 2011: 21). It should be noted that even the discretionary power of the administration is limited to the public interest, and this boundary of the administration binds itself in the objective element of the administrative act. Thus, although the administration does not have discretion over the purpose element of the administrative act, there is an absolute limit to the public interest. If the administrative actions taken in order to ensure the public interest are clearly intended to violate individual rights rather than reach the social benefit in the background, the administration will go beyond the boundaries drawn to it, and the relevant transactions may be canceled by the administrative judicial bodies since they do not have the purpose of public benefit. Because, the public interest, which is also a reason for limitation for various rights and freedoms, constitutes the general purpose of administrative acts (and, it should be added, actions). For this reason, its uncertain and abstract quality is a situation that should always be considered (Tombaloğlu, 2014: 355).

Articles (43), (44), (45), (46) and (47) of the 1982 Constitution are regulated under the title of public interest. The titles of these articles are "coastal exploitation", "land ownership", "agriculture, animal husbandry and protection of those working in these production branches", "expropriation", "nationalization" and "privatization", respectively. The fact that a separate regulation has been made under the title of public benefit in the Constitution also points to the necessity of determining the method and management suitable for the public benefit, which is the concept that should be considered primarily in the implementation of the specified articles. Therefore, it can be understood that the limit of the kind of regulation desired to be made regarding the articles mentioned by the administration will also be in the public interest. Moreover, it is stated in Article 1 of the Additional Protocol No. 1[10] of the *Convention on the Protection of Human Rights and Fundamental Freedoms* approved by law no (6366) that, man can only be deprived of his possessions for the public benefit.[11]

In the Constitutional Court, in its decision published in the Official Gazette dated 9.5.2014 and numbered 28995, the restrictions on fundamental rights and freedoms, regardless of the purpose pursued in democratic constitutional states, cannot be more than the intended purpose with the restriction, and the expropriation taken in accordance with the concept of public benefit the second sentence of paragraph (3) of the 8th article of the "Tourism Encouragement Law" numbered 2634, article 13 titled restriction of fundamental rights and freedoms, article 35 titled property right on the grounds that it is unconstitutional, pursuant to Article 36 titled freedom to seek rights and Article 125 regulating the possibility of a judicial remedy against all kinds of acts and actions of the administration.[12] Thus, it has been stipulated that decisions taken in line with the public interest should be subject to legal control at the point of existence of public interest and should be questionable.

The Council of State examined and concluded the existence of the public interest in many of its decisions. For example, it is stated that, considering that the site decisions were made in order to protect the natural environment in the public interest, the subject parcel should be evaluated together with its surroundings as a part of the whole, not alone, in resolving concrete disputes.[13] In a decision made by the Council of State regarding the promotion of public officials working in the administrative organization, since the service carried out by religious officials is not related to the main service areas of the administration, the personnel in the clergy positions are promoted and appointed as the provincial director, provincial deputy director and establishment manager. Personnel of the General Directorate of Services and Child Protection Agency has decided that the provisions of the "Regulation on Promotion and Change of Title" are not in compliance with the law in terms of public interest and service requirements.[14] Moreover, although the administration is given a

10. Official Gazette. 8662, dated 19.3.1954.
11. Retrieved from; http://www.echr.coe.int/Documents/Convention_TUR.pdf, (Access Date: 15.6.2020)
12. Constitutional Court, E. 2013/108, K. 2014/15, Dated: 29.1.2014, accessed at www.kazanci.com.tr, (Access Date: 16.6.2020)
13. Council of State 14. D, E. 2011/5290, K. 2011/266, Dated: 22.6.2011, Accessed at: www.danistay.gov.tr, (Date of access: 17.6.2020)
14. Council of State 5. D, E. 2010/4944, Dated: 25.11.2010, Accessed at: www. kazanci.com.tr, (Access Date: 17.6.2020)

discretionary power regarding the appointment of public officials, this power can only be used in a limited way to the public interest and service requirements, and whether the appointments are made within the scope of public interest and service requirements will be subject to judicial review.[15] Again, in another decision, the Council of State stated that the plaintiff's waiver from the case was from his individual interests, but in the event that the unlawfulness of the administrative act was determined, the plaintiff's waiver was not possible after the decision was made by the local court after the decision was made by the local court.[16] In addition, the Council of State sometimes evaluates the existence of the public interest within the framework of whether it is dominant, and in cases where the public interest is not dominant, It has decided that the rightful expectations of individuals should not be impaired, hoping that they can reach a result for their interests, whether relying on a commitment of the administration or a practice that has been going on for a long time.[17]

In determining the public interest, more precisely, in determining which activity carries public benefit, decentralization elements as well as the legislature are authorized, and they have the right to turn the activity of public interest into a public service (Gözler, 2009: 227). In my opinion, the fact that the concept of public benefit has a meaning that differs from period to period makes it indispensable to clearly understand the reasons for administrative proceedings. Knowing the current justification will also reveal how effective the relevant administrative action is in achieving the public interest. Therefore, the lack of clarity of the reasons for the administrative acts created by tacit refusal should be regarded as a deficiency in the interpretation of the purpose element of the administrative act.

2 The Problem of Justification of Administrative Transactions Created by Implied Refusal by Local Governments

The implied refusal, which is one of the administrative actions that occur with the silence of the administration, can undoubtedly be fulfilled by everybody in the Turkish administrative organization. However, the purpose of evaluating such a

15. Council of State 5. D, E. 2008/6724, K. 2010/3642, Dated; 26.5.2010, Accessed at; www.kazanci.com.tr, (Access Date: 17.6.2020)
16. Council of State 6. D, E. 1994/484, K. 1994/1873, Dated; 9.5.1994, Accessed at; www.danistay.com.tr, (Access Date: 17.6.2020)
17. Council of State 5. D, E. 2003/3647, K. 2006/1140, Dated; 14.3.2006, Accessed at; www.danistay.com.tr, (Access Date: 17.6.2020)

concept with such a wide area of use within the framework of local governments is different. The implied refusal regulated in the IYUK has a consequence that should be criticized as it lacks justification as an administrative act. In addition, besides not knowing the justification of an administrative act created by silence leads to failure in calculating the time to file a lawsuit.[18] It may cause a negativity, namely loss of rights. It should be noted that; the view of the Council of State against those who will apply against the tacit refusal to miss the judicial remedy by spending the 60-day lawsuit period is negative. The Council of State takes into account the derogative nature of the periods accepted in the administrative judiciary against the miscalculation of the time for filing a lawsuit as a result of tacit refusal.[19] However, this point of view is achieved by majority vote and not by consensus in general. In fact, when looking at the letters of opposing votes of some sample decisions stated in the footnote it is stated that the abolition of the right to file a lawsuit as a result of the error that people experience during the filing period is contrary to the Constitution. Article (11) titled binding and superiority of the Constitution, Article (36) titled freedom to seek rights, Article (40) titled protection of fundamental rights and freedoms, petition, the right to obtain information and to apply to the ombudsman (74) 'third article, the judicial remedy title (125)'

Therefore, when the mentioned constitutional articles and the law numbered (2577) are interpreted together, the implied refusal should be criticized both because of the unknown justification and the negativities it creates in the calculation of the duration of litigation for individuals. Especially, from the point of view of local governments, the unclear reason for the implied refusal can be evaluated by the fact that local governments are open to local pressure and effects. This situation is a serious drawback for the public service. Moreover, with the applicant's inability to learn the justification of the administrative act in the

18. As it is known, there are also regulations that the administration accepts through silence, therefore silence means acceptance. Thus, the concept of tacit acceptance can be considered to be free from criticism. Because, in the presence of an administrative act formed by tacit acceptance, there is now an application made to the administration and its approval. Here, the justification of the administrative act can be understood from the tacitly accepted application petition. However, in the case of implied refusal, the reason for rejection by the administration will not be known.
19. Council of State 15. D, E. 2016/718, K. 2016/1440, Dated: 7.3.2016, Accessed at: www.danistay.gov.tr; Council of State 15. D. E. 2016/536, K. 2016/1906, Dated: 21.3.2016, Accessed at: www.danistay.gov.tr; Council of State 15. D. E. 2015/7603, K. 2016/1907, Dated: 21.3.2016, Accessed at: www.danistay.gov.tr, (Date of access: 25.6.2020)

form of implied refusal without resorting to administrative jurisdiction to annul the transaction, Failures in the calculation of the time of filing a lawsuit upon the transaction denied implicitly will cause a clear violation of the freedom to seek rights and the principles of equity, which we have tried to explain above. Moreover, the failure of the administration to respond within the 60-day period is considered as a tacit refusal, while the response given by the administration after 60 days is regulated and accepted in the form of a proper and valid administrative procedure is open to criticism. This situation can mostly hinder public service responsibility. Therefore, the public official is left independent from the obligation to fulfill his duty within a certain period of time. It can be predicted that the stated result will adversely affect the public merit element. Because the concept of merit is an important principle sought not only in appointment but also in the continuation of the task (Akgüner, 2017: 37).

It can be stated that the specified possible defects will be in clear contradiction with the European Law of Good Administrative Behavior and hence the principle of good administration.

Conclusion

The silence of the administration cannot be interpreted positively in terms of negative administration for individuals. Moreover, to think otherwise means to accept or ignore the disruption of the responsibilities of the persons in charge of the Turkish administrative organization within the framework of the constitution and laws. Moreover, this situation will cause much bigger problems on the axis of local governments. In local governments, the fact that it is more difficult to provide expert personnel in their field compared to the central administration will turn the tacit rejection into a harmful power for the public. The requirement to state the justification for the administrative act is delayed by the presence of implied refusal. On the other hand, in the annulment action filed against the implied rejection, the possibility of the lack of expert officials in local governments will be encountered within the framework of explaining the reason. In this context, the regulation in IYUK regarding the concept of implied rejection is inadequate in my opinion and its effectiveness has become questionable today. The administrative transactions that occur in the method that the administration disguises through silence do not carry the element of justification that they should have. It should be accepted that the lack of justification for the administrative procedures resulting from the silence of the administration also constitutes an obstacle to the realization of the principle of good administration. Moreover, in a public administration that functions faster and more efficiently with the developing technical possibilities, it is not correct to expect results to be obtained with the silence of the administration, or rather to interpret this in an administrative center. Moreover, in many European Union member countries, silence of the administration is interpreted in favor of the individual (Bonomo, 2019: 966).

In this context, with an amendment to the IYUK, the second paragraph of article (10) regulating the implied rejection should be changed in this format: *"If no response is given within sixty days, the request is considered rejected. Those concerned may request in writing the justification of the tacit rejection made to the administration as of the end of sixty days. The administration is obliged to explain the grounds for the rejection of the application tacitly rejected within 10 days. From the day following the notification of the justification to the concerned parties, within the period of filing a lawsuit, they can file a lawsuit to the Council of State, administrative and tax courts depending on the subject "*. With this amendment, an application in favor of the individual will be accepted by learning the justification of the transaction created with implied refusal; Moreover, it will be possible to prevent public officials from having a relief in public service whose merit is questioned by relying on the concept of silence of the administration. This will enable more effective and lawful decisions to be taken in public services, especially in local governments that sometimes face the risk of being under the influence of local pressures.

References

Akgüner, T. (2017). Public Personnel Administration. Istanbul: Der Publishing.

Akgüner, T., and Kahraman, B. (2017). Administrative Law. Istanbul: Der Publishing.

Akıllıoğlu, T. (2011). Thoughts on the Concept of Public Benefit. Administrative Law and Sciences Journal, 9(1–3): 11–22.

Bonomo, A. (2019). Good Governance Principle and Silence of the Administration: A Problematic Relation (Interpreter: Nuray Sümer). Dokuz Eylul University Faculty of Law Journal, 21(2): 953–975.

Burtan, Ç. B. (2019). Competency and Hostility in Administrative Justice. İstanbul: Der Publishing.

Council of State Official Site, www.danistay.gov.tr, (Date of Access: 17–25.6.2020).

Derdiman, C. (2014). General Principles of Administrative Justice. Bursa: Alfa Aktüel Publishing.

European Court of Human Rights Official Site, www.echr.int, (Date of Access: 15.6.2020).

Gözler, K. (2009). Administrative Law Vol: II. Bursa: Ekin Printing Publication Distribution.

Kalabalık, H. (2016). Administrative Jurisdiction Law. Konya: Sayram Publishing.

KazancıKararwebsite,www.kazanci.com.tr,(DateofAccess:10-12-16-17.6.2020).

Korkut, L. (2006). Concept of Public Benefit as a Reason for Restricting Fundamental Rights and Freedoms. Liberal Thought Journal, (44): 77–98.

Legislation Information System, www.mevzuat.gov.tr, (Date of Access: 3.8.2020).

Saraç, O. (2002). Concept of Public Benefit. Finance Magazine, (139): 16–26.

Tombaloğlu, N. (2014). Concept of Public Benefit in Constitutional Court Decisions. Journal of Inönü University Law Faculty, 5(1): 353–388.

Yaman, M. (2018). A Guide to Court and Administrative Justice. Ankara: Adalet Publishing.

Yayla, Y. (2010). Administrative Law. İstanbul: Beta Publishing.

Dr. Hasan Acar and Yunus Karaağaç

1.2 Impact on Urban Governance of Local Politics and Terror Relationship: The Case of Turkey

Abstract: In Ancient Greek, the concept of democracy, which means "government of the people", is the basic element of defining the modern world, where fundamental rights and freedoms are acquired innately, and the principle of justice and the equal citizen is spread to the general. In a democratic regime, public participation in management takes place based on general and local government. While issues such as basic welfare, justice, and security are under the responsibility of the general government, in provinces, districts, towns, and villages; local services such as infrastructure, transportation, food, clean water, cleaning, and burials are performed. The fact that the municipalities, which are the center of local politics and functioning, have the authority and responsibility as a legal person, is the result of a democratic system, but it can also be seen as units that should be seized and engaged for armed attacks and terrorist organizations that cannot reach their targets.

Having carried out its first armed action in 1984, PKK (Partiya Karkeren Kurdistan) has been carrying out terrorist acts in line with the independent Kurdistan target for nearly 40 years and can renew its tactics and strategies periodically in achieving its goal. The PKK carried out rural-based terrorist activities until the political parties with which it had an organic bond strengthened within the framework of the local government and during this period caused the death of 40000 people. Political parties (Democratic Regions Party-DRP, Peoples' Democratic Party-PDP), who expressed their ties with the PKK at every opportunity, changed the concept of the PKK and changed to urban terrorism as a result of the fact that the PKK changed the concept and converted to city terrorism.

The delivery of weapons and ammunition to the organization with municipal vehicles, the municipalities providing financing to the organization from their allowances, giving priority to the companies that have a relationship with the PKK in municipal tenders and being the reference of the PKK with recruitments, after the organization's self-management call, the municipalities of DRP (Şırnak, Silopi, Cizre, Nusaybin and Yüksekova's 16 municipalities), such as the declaration of autonomy and the city war called "trench war", reveal the relationship between local government and terrorism.

This chapter aims to show that democratic developments can be manipulated by terrorist organizations and draw attention to the fact that local governments can act under the aim of terrorist organizations under a so-called democratic view.

Keywords: Local politics, Democracy, Municipal administration, Terrorism, Urban Guerrillas.

Introduction

Local governments representing the social presence in a particular region and providing political, economic, cultural, social, and service functions in the region within its jurisdiction are a product of decentralized structure and the inability of the central authority to solve all the problems of the country. In this system, while the unitary structure of the country is preserved, local governments come into play in line with the understanding of decentralization.

Municipalities, which are a local government unit and have an autonomous legal personality in the region they represent, are the main element of the decentralization regime. Mayors can be elected independently by the public, or they can also be elected as candidates of the country's political parties in general. The mayors elected as independent candidates or candidates for political parties and the municipalities under their administration, in the region they represent; infrastructure, development, transportation, water distribution, fire and police duties, and training. While the reason for the existence and jurisdiction of the municipalities are in theory, some problems may arise in the practical part of the work. One of these problems is that municipalities act under the guidance of a certain structure or terrorist organization, apart from the understanding of service, and use their political power and autonomy by the instructions of the terrorist organization.

Entering the terrorist organization led by the municipality of terrorizing and act in line with the target of terrorist organizations, it draws attention to a phenomenon that can be seen in Turkey. The determined actions of the political parties and municipalities that have organic or direct links with the terrorist organization PKK reveal cooperation between local governments and the phenomenon of terrorism.

The actions of the parties (DRP and PRP) and municipalities that have close relations with the PKK; it can be expressed as recruiting a terrorist organization, providing logistical support to the organization with municipal vehicles, realizing the propaganda of the organization, financing the terrorist organization and seeking membership or sympathy in recruitment.

This study was prepared to reveal a negative example of terrorist relations with local governments and to demonstrate that local governments can be manipulated by terrorist organizations, and the study focused on the PKK terrorist organization and its municipalities.

1 Conceptually Local Politics and Terrorism

Politics, etymologically derived from the word 'police', has been used to make decisions about the management of the city in the Ancient Greek and the issues that are public, that is, for everyone (Yayla, 2019: 25). The purpose of politics is not to use individuals and the masses by using power or to rule over scarce resources. The purpose of politics is society; to ensure its well-being, happiness, justice and freedom (Akdoğan, 2008: 10).

According to David Easton, politics is the distribution of values through authorities, and according to Andrew Heywood, it is the process of establishing, protecting or changing the general rules that enable people to live together (Taşkın, 2017: 23). The derivation of the concept of politics from a city-centered approach draws attention to the local dimension of politics. The functioning, called local politics, fills in areas where a central authority cannot be included in every subject and creates regional and local politics.

Although local politics is a local power struggle, which is carried out by the people and institutions that carry out political activities based on city and district, by considering the issues of the local people, it includes the use of the resources and opportunities of the region for the benefit of the local people (Akdoğan, 2008: 10). Local politics is used as a concept that refers to the municipal administration in a narrow sense, but in its broad sense it covers the deputies of the region in question, the local administration structure, public bureaucracy, unions and pressure groups (Alkan and Çiftçioğlu, 2007: 2).

Local politics is the result of an understanding of decentralization. The most important features of local politics, which have a decentralized structure; autonomy is the only authority in its functioning (Ertan, 2018: 27) and they are the management units closest to the citizen (Çelik et al, 2008: 90). In short, the reason and purpose of local politics are to ensure that public services reach the citizens and to represent the will of the people (Ndreu, 2016: 5).

In this study, where the relationship between local politics and terrorism is centered, the conceptual content of the phenomenon of terrorism needs to be handled holistically.

Terrorism, derived from the Latin word 'terrere', means "unexpected fear and destruction" (Semercioğlu, 2016: 100), defined as an "attempt to impose political and ideological demands of an organized group through violence or threat of violence" (Kuçuradi, 2002: 343).

Although the history of terrorism is in line with the history of humanity, the first acts of terrorism are often identified with the Jewish Sicarias operating in Palestine before Christ (Karaağaç, 2019: 231), and the Order of Assassins of Hassan-i Sabbah's are shown as the first organized terrorist movement. However, the word "terrorism" entered into the literature is based on its use to describe the period of violence after the French Revolution (Tilly, 2004: 8). Terrorism refers to the threat of violence used to fulfill political and ideological demands, and terrorism indicates that terrorist acts are carried out in a continuous, systematic and organized manner. Therefore, while terrorism draws attention to the action, terrorism draws attention to strategy.

'Terrorism is the systematic implementation or threat of murder or extermination to intimidate individuals, groups, society or governments to ensure that certain political demands are met (Wilkinson, 1977: 49). Terrorism is a strategy of violence that is planned, calculated, and implemented systematically to establish sovereignty or create power in the region where there is a lack of authority (Hoffman, 2006: 23).

The most sensitive statement about terrorism is that a terrorist for one state can be a freedom fighter for another state (Laqueur, 2007: 22). The lack of a common definition of terrorism and the use of terrorism as a tool to weaken another state creates the terrorist-freedom fighter duality. The preference of terrorism as a tool by the states is the main challenge of combating terrorism. Because terrorist organizations continue their existence if they have external support. In this study, samples of the selected cases as Turkey, the PKK terrorist organization, requires a brief historical and ideological to be addressed.

2 Terrorism and the PKK's Activities in Turkey

The Republic of Turkey since its establishment has been faced with divisive and destructive acts of terrorism, especially ethnic and religious motifs. But it has been the longest and most destructive separatist activities of the terrorist organization PKK terror wave that Turkey experienced. It is known that more than forty thousand people lost their lives in PKK attacks (Portzer, 2020: 93). PKK is considered among the top 25 terrorist organizations in the world in terms of terrorist attacks and the number of people killed as a result of these attacks (Mandala, 2017: 364).

The PKK was established on 26–27 November 1978 in the village of Fis (visiting) in the Lice district of Diyarbakır, under the leadership of Abdullah Öcalan (Özcan, 1999: 42). On August 15, 1984, it simultaneously carried out the first armed terrorist acts in Eruh and Şemdinli districts (Ersever, 1994: 101–102).

PKK is a terrorist organization established under the conditions of the Cold War, adopting Marxist-Leninist ideology, applying Mao's rural guerrilla method in terrorist acts and shaped around Öcalan's one-man authoritarianism (Demir, 2008: 68). The target of the PKK; Turkey, Iraq, the Kurdish presence in Iran, and Syria are brought together to establish an independent Kurdistan. PKK has received assistance from foreign countries periodically since its establishment to achieve this goal. For example; Greece, Iran, Iraq and Syria PKK; supported the military, education, logistics and shelter (Rubin and Rubin, 2008: 74). Iran, Iraq and Syria of supporting the PKK, despite the organization's goals are based on what they see as Turkey's eroding the aim of regional competitors.

PKK terrorist actions since the 1980s has been more frequent in Turkey's eastern and southeastern regions, increased power capacity up to 1992 (Polis Akademisi Başkanlığı, 2017: 13). The Turkish Armed Forces (Alan, 2020: 200), which made its weight dominant with the strategy of field domination since that date, succeeded in breaking the power and resistance of the PKK terrorist organization and ensured the expulsion of Abdullah Öcalan, who resided in Syria since 1979. Abdullah Ocalan, with a special intelligence operation in Kenya on 15 February 1999 was arrested and brought to Turkey (Marcus, 2009: 359–372).

The PKK, which entered the period of confusion following the capture of Öcalan, declared a ceasefire for 5 years without making any claims (Cronin, 2009: 20–21). In May 2002, the European Union included the PKK on the list of terrorist organizations. Since the PKK predicted this decision in advance, it was dissolved in April under the name Kurdistan Freedom and Democracy Congress (Kurdish: KADEK- Kongreya Azadî û Demokrasiya Kurdistanê), and Öcalan was brought back to it (Mango, 2005: 68). KADEK structuring was terminated on November 11, 2003, and The People's Congress (KONGRA-GEL) was established. On April 2, 2004, the European Union declared that its ban decision for the PKK also applies to KADEK and KONGRA-GEL (Mango, 2005: 72). PKK, trying to ensure its legitimacy against the international public with the change of name, has not been able to get the return it wants from the strategy it has pursued and declared the establishment of Kurdistan Communities Union (Kurdish: KCK-Koma Civakên Kurdistan) as a new upper structure (Sezer, 2012: 47).

In 2013, a political solution environment was tried to be created using state policy that military power should be negotiated for peace by producing rhetoric about the inadequacy of the fight against terrorism. This new initiative, called "Solution Process", was consulted with Abdullah Öcalan (Köse, 2017: 17). For the Solution Process to proceed, 3 main objectives have been determined:

1. Gradual withdrawal from the territory of Turkey of PKK elements,
2. The fulfillment of the commitment by the democratic government of Turkey
3. To adapt the PKK elements to civil and political life after disarmament (DPI, 2013: 11).

However, the solution process ended as a failed process because both parties could not advance to the main goals (Çiçek and Coşkun, 2016: 19), and the main reason for this process to fail was the elections of June 7, 2015.

3 Local Politics – Terror Relationship

In the elections of 7 June 2015, PDP's 79% vote in Sur, where the Kurdish population predominates, 91% in Cizre, 89% in Silopi, 92% in Nusaybin gave birth to the idea that the public would support them in the PKK (Ural, 2018: 19), and subsequently the PKK tried to achieve its self-management goal by adopting the city guerrilla method in its new city-centered terrorist strategy. The PKK's understanding of city terrorism, known as the Trench Wars, is an extremely important example in terms of showing that local government and terrorist phenomenon can be watched in an intricate relationship.

The PKK called for self-management to municipalities with DRP (Democratic Regions Party) with organic ties among them, and the terrorist organization's activities have deepened in cities other than the countryside (Duran, 2018). Şırnak Municipality on August 10, 2015 and KCK on August 12, in 4 provinces and 15 districts (Silopi, Cizre, Nusaybin, Yüksekova, Varto, Bulanık, Edremit, Ipekyolu, Sur, Silvan, Lice, Dogubayazıt, Hizan, Gulsuyu, Gazi) declared that declared self-government (Duran, 2019).

By establishing hegemony over some local political units chosen by democratic methods to meet the local needs of the society, the PKK has created an illegal system by transferring the municipal resources to it (Güler and Yılmaz, 2019: 138).

PKK has used the resources of DRP municipalities extensively during and after the trench wars with activities such as logistic support, recruiting the organization and propaganda. Concrete findings have been obtained that municipalities proclaiming self-government are recruited directly with the PKK and that is the primary reference in job applications (Duran, 2018).

With the call for self-government, the PKK worked in coordination with local political units and carried terrorist acts to city centers, forcing the citizens of the region to migrate, turning their residences into positions. Besides, they dug ditches on the streets and streets with municipal vehicles and set up barricades and equipped the district centers with handmade explosives and

Fig. 1.2.1: Terrorist Organization Propaganda in Municipal Vehicles (Ministry of the Interior, 2017: 24)

bombs. Therefore, by disrupting the public's access to basic services (Güler and Yılmaz, 2019: 134), it terrorized the local government approach.

According to the report prepared by the Ministry of Internal Affairs and it can be seen in Figure 1.2.1., the vehicles of the municipality were used in bombing attacks in the Trench Wars strategy carried out by the local administrations, and barricades were dug in the streets between the municipal construction machines and trenches. Tenders made by municipalities were given to PKK members or sympathizers, and the organization was cut from the salaries of municipal employees. The citizens in the region opposed to the PKK were tried to punish the innocent people by not providing municipal services (Ministry of the Interior, 2017: 9).

The taxes collected directly by the local governments and the financial budget sent by the central government were largely used for the terrorist organization. These allowances were used in the employment of PKK-related personnel and financing terrorism, and individuals seeking membership from a terrorist organization were hired in the municipality and subcontractors working with the municipality (Ministry of the Interior, 2017: 43).

As can be seen from the financing images in Fig. 1.2.2, the local political units provided financially stamped and sealed financial aid from the local budget to People's Defence Forces (Kurdish: HPG-Hezen Parastina Gel), the

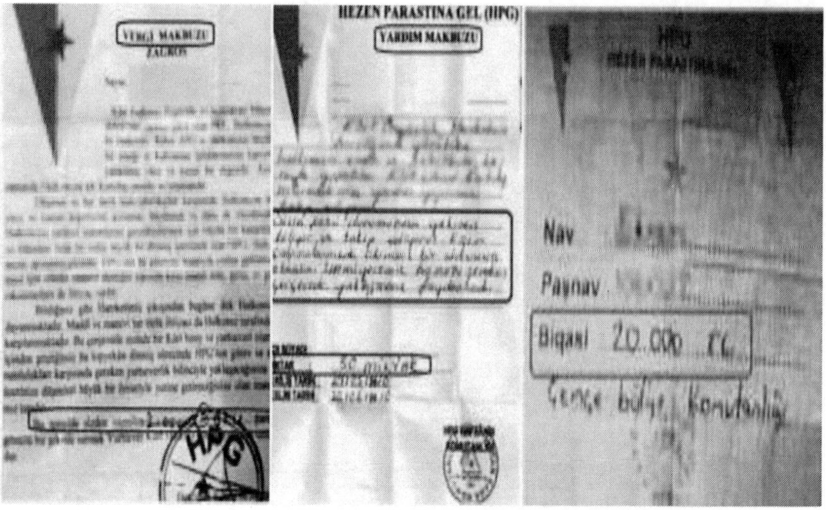

Fig. 1.2.2: Tribute that PKK Collected by Local Political Units (Alptekin and İlhan, 2018: 29)

military flank of the PKK. The receipt of the PKK was legitimized under the Kars-Kağızman structuring.

The ambulance and funeral vehicles of the municipality were used to kidnap and hide terrorists, and treatment opportunities were provided for injured terrorists with ambulances (Ministry of the Interior, 2017: 45). The fact that the vehicle, which opened fire in the police in Van in June 2016, and which the terrorists were in, belongs to the Municipality of Van. Also it was revealed that ammunition was carried to the organization by municipal vehicles in many provinces, especially in Hakkâri, Mardin and Iğdır (Duran, 2018).

Local politics units affiliated with the PKK attend commemoration activities for PKK militants and teach PKK anthems to the masses, positive discrimination against terrorist relatives in recruitment, and acts of terrorist names on the streets (Alptekin, 2019) show the extent of local governments' terrorist relationship and potential targets within the scope of autonomy as it can be seen in Figure 1.2.3.

As a result, it was revealed that as of 2014, mayors elected from the Democratic Regions Party, which is the extension of PDP in the Eastern and Southeastern Anatolia regions, provided great support to the PKK in terms of finance and logistics, and also prevented the operations carried out by the security forces against the PKK (Miş, 2019).

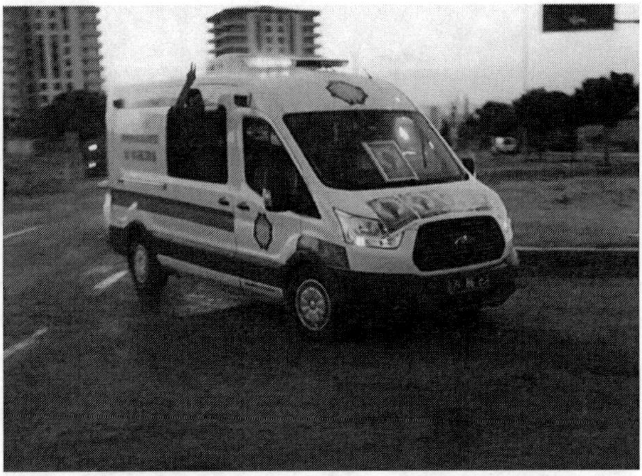

Fig. 1.2.3: Terrorist Organization Propaganda in Municipal Funeral Vehicles (Ministry of the Interior, 2017: 45)

4 The Effect of Local Politics-Terrorism Relations on Local Government and Regional Development

In Turkey, it is reserved for the general municipal budget of between 10% and 20% of staff costs. However, when the municipalities that announced the self-government announcement were examined, it was seen that the ratio of personnel expenses to the budget reached 75%, therefore it was revealed that the local service budget was spent as salaries for PKK members (Erdoğan, 2019: 253). Social aids to be transferred to the people in need through local politics were made to the members of the organization and their relatives. The people of the region; a road, drinking water, sewage, etc. It has been determined that the appropriations allocated to meet their needs are used for the financing of the terrorist organization (Ministry of Interior, 2019: 6). Therefore, appropriations and tools reserved for local politics were not used for the benefit of the people and local service was not carried out.

The emergence of the terrorist organization being supported by municipalities in terms of financing, human resources and equipment (Güler and Yılmaz, 2018: 1803) has prompted the central authority to take several public order measures against the manipulated local politics.

With the allegation of supporting terrorism, 94 local political administrators were removed from their posts and a 'trustee' was appointed from their central

Fig. 1.2.4: PKK Barricades Created by Municipal Facilities (Ministry of the Interior, 2017: 24)

administration. It is stated that the municipalities that have been found to cooperate with terrorism directly or indirectly support terrorist activities in their regions by using their financial powers and service tools (Keleş and Özgül, 2017: 308).

As a result of the trustees' appointments, the following actions carried out by the terrorist organization PKK over the municipalities with DRP were blocked:

- Transfer of salaries, cash benefits and tender commissions to the terrorist organization within the scope of mandatory donations from employees,
- Publication activities that make organization propaganda through youth and cultural centers, and publications of articles, posters and materials supporting the terrorist organization,
- Supporting the local political units' tools, zoning, excavation, road closure arrangements and residential uprisings,
- The attempts to establish authority, such as the blessing of PKK militants who lost their lives in terrorist activities with condolence activities and monumental tombs, and the effort to establish judicial institutions similar to state institutions (Alptekin and İlhan, 2018: 55).

As a result of the appointment of trustees, the understanding of local politics, which moved away from its existential purpose and target, and which was

Fig. 1.2.5: District of Cizre Before and After the Trustee (En Son Haber, 2018)

under the direction of the terrorist organization, was pulled to its legal ground and the resources of the local region were converted back into service. Thus, the possibilities and opportunities of local politics started to be transferred to the public within the framework of the local government approach. Prepared for the war environment by the local politics and terrorist organization, and in this context, ditches opened in the streets with municipal vehicles, the images belonging to the local people in Cizre reflect the damage caused by local politics and terrorist cooperation and show how the region can develop after the appointment of the trustee as it can be seen in Figure 1.2.5.

Conclusion

The basis of the understanding of local politics, which is a result of democracy, is based on the fulfillment of services such as infrastructure, zoning, transportation, water distribution, fire brigade, police duties and education. In some cases, the legal personality, budget and autonomy of local politics create a center of attraction to illegal formations and constitute the causes of terrorist organizations' targets to take over the local government. 1984, the first act of terrorism by acting on Turkey's division of the PKK's 2015 elections after his call on democratic autonomy and self-government to declare the DRP's city council and mayor, was a poor example of local political relations with terrorist organizations.

With the vehicles and construction machines belonging to local political units, ditches were opened on the streets and barricades were established, and the PKK's strategy for urban terrorism was supported by the local government. Not only about terrorist acts but also transferring the taxes and budgets of the local government to the organization as financing, using the funeral and ambulance service tools to the supporters of the organization, determining the recruitment process in the municipalities, providing social assistance to the relatives of the organization, providing written resources in the cultural houses including the propaganda of the organization; local politics have also been in close contact with the terrorist organization in applications such as giving the names of PKK terrorists to the streets, not meeting the basic needs of citizens in the anti-PKK region.

As a result, the central authority dismissed local politicians who had a relationship with the terrorist organization and appointed local supervisors to local politics to bring local politics still in line with its existential purpose and disrupted services were trying to be eliminated through new appointments.

References

Akdoğan, Y. (2008). Yerel Siyaset-Kavramlar [Local Politics-Concepts]. *Local Politics Symposium*, İstanbul: Okutan Publications, 9–14.

Alan, E. (2020). *Terör-PKK: 40 Yıllık İhanet* [Terror-PKK: 40 Years of Betrayal]. İstanbul: Bilgi Publisher.

Alkan, H. and Çiftçioğlu, H. (2007). Yerel Siyasette Belediye Meclisi ve Siyasi Parti Örgütleri: Göksun Örneği [Municipal Assembly and Political Party Organizations in Local Politics: The Case of Göksun]. *Kocaeli University Journal of Social Sciences Institutes*, (14): 1–27.

Alptekin, H. (2019). Kayyum ile Terör Arasında HDP Belediyeciliği [HDP Municipal Office Between Trustees and Terror]. *SETA*, 31.08.2019, https://www.setav.org/kayyum-ile-teror-arasinda-hdp-belediyeciligi/, (Access 22.05.2020).

Alptekin, H. and İlhan, B. (2018). *Kayyum Atanan Belediyelerin PKK Terörü ile Mücadeledeki Rolü* [The Role of Municipalities Appointed as Trustees in Combating PKK Terrorism], İstanbul: SETA Publications.

Cronin, A. K. (2009). *How Terrorism Ends: Understanding the Decline and Demise of Terrorist Campaigns*. New Jersey: Princeton University Press.

Çelik, V., Çelik, F. and Usta, S. (2008). Yerel Demokrasi ve Yerel Özerklik İlişkisi [Relationship of Local Democracy and Local Autonomy]. *Niğde University Faculty of Economics and Administrative Sciences Journal*, 1(2): 87–104.

Çiçek, C. and Coşkun, V. (2016). *Dolmabahçe'den Günümüze Çözüm Süreci: Başarısızlığı Anlamak ve Yeni Bir Yol Bulmak* [Solution Process from

Dolmabahçe to Today: Understanding Failure and Finding a New Way], Ankara: Barış Vakfı Publishers.

Demir, C. K. (2008). Öğrenen Örgütler ve Terör Örgütleri Bağlamında PKK [The PKK in the Context of Terrorist Organizations and Learning Organizations]. *International Relations*, 5(19): 57–88.

DPI. (2013). *Turkey's Kurdish Conflict: An Assessment of the Current Process*, London: Democratic Progress Institute.

Duran, A. E. (2019). Türkiye'yi Sarsan Beş Ay: 7 Haziran-1 Kasım 2015 [Five Months That Shook Turkey: June 7-November 1, 2015], *Deutsche Welle Turkish*, 28.08.2019, https://www.dw.com/tr/t%C3%BCrkiyeyi-sarsan-be%C5%9F-ay-7-haziran-1-kas%C4%B1m-2015/a-50204527 (Access 25.05.2020).

Duran, H. (2018). Kayyum Belediyelerinin Geleceği [The Future of Trustee Municipalities]. *Criterion Magazine*, 3(29), https://kriterdergi.com/dosya-ak-parti-ve-yerel-yonetimler/kayyum-belediyelerinin-gelecegi (Access 21.05.2020).

En Son Haber, (2018). Cizre'nin Tercihi HDP [Cizre's Choice HDP], 25.06.2018, https://www.ensonhaber.com/gundem/cizrenin-tercihi-hdp (Access 26.05.2020).

Erdoğan, O. (2019). Belediyelere Kayyum Atanması Uygulaması Üzerine Bir Değerlendirme [An Evaluation on Appointment of Trustees to Municipalities]. *Turkish Administrative Journal*, 91(488): 245–264.

Ersever, A. C. (1994). *Kürtler, PKK ve Abdullah Öcalan* [Kurds, PKK and Abdullah Ocalan], Ankara: Ocak Publishers.

Ertan, K. A. (2018). Küreselleşme, Yerel Yönetimler ve Kentli Hakları [Globalization, Local Governments and Urban Rights]. A. Mengi and D. İşçioğlu (Eds.). *Küreselleşme Sürecinde Yerel Hizmet Yerel Siyaset* [Local Service Local Politics in the Globalization Process] in, Ankara: Ankara University Publications, 23–43.

Güler, T. and Yılmaz, A. (2018). Local Governments in the Context of Local Democracy-Security: The Practice of Appointing Trustees in Turkey. *Electronic Journal of Social Sciences*, 17(68): 1801–1816.

Güler, T. and Yılmaz, A. (2019). Bir Terörle Mücadele Stratejisi Olarak Belediyelerde Kayyum Uygulaması [Application of Trustees in Municipalities as an Anti-Terrorism Strategy]. *Celal Bayar University Journal of Social Sciences*, 17(4): 129–141.

Hoffman, B. (2006). *Inside Terrorism*, New York: Columbia University Press.

Karaağaç, Y. (2019). Terörizmle Mücadele Yöntemleri: İngiltere ve Kolombiya Örneği [Methods of Combating Terrorism: The Case of UK and Colombia]. *Eurasian Journal of Researches in Social and Economics*, 6(1): 231–242.

Keleş, R. and Özgül, C. G. (2017). Belediye Organlarına "Kayyım" Atamaları Üzerine Bir Değerlendirme [An Evaluation on "Trustees" Appointments to Municipal Bodies]. *Journal of Ankara University Faculty of Political Science*, 72(2): 299–313.

Köse, T. (2017). Çözüm Sürecinin Yükseliş ve Düşüşü [The Rise and Fall of the Solution Process], *Turkish Journal of Middle Eastern Studies*, 4(1): 13–40.

Kuçuradi, İ. (2002). İnsan Haklarından Devlet Kavramına [From Human Rights to the Concept of State]. C. Güzel (Ed.), *Silinen Yüzler Karşısında Terör* [Terror Against Erased Faces] in, Ankara: Ayraç Publisher, 332–344.

Laqueur, W. (2007). Terrorism: A Brief History. *Foreign Policy Agenda*. 12(5): 20–23.

Mandala, M. (2017). Terrorist Assassinations: A Criminological Perspective, G. LaFree ve J. D. Freilich (Ed.). *The Handbook of the Criminology of Terrorism* in, West Sussex: Wiley Blackwell, 353–369.

Mango, A. (2005). *Türkiye'nin Terörle Savaşı*. (Çev. O. Azizoğlu), [Turkey's War on Terror], İstanbul: Doğan Book.

Marcus, A. (2009). *Kan ve İnanç: PKK ve Kürt Hareketi*, (Translate. A. Alkan), [Blood and Faith: PKK and the Kurdish Movement], İstanbul: İletişim Publishers.

Miş, N. (2019). Kayyumdan Önce Bazı Belediyeler PKK'ya Hizmet Eden Birimler Haline Gelmişti [Before the Trustee, Some Municipalities Became Units Serving the PKK], *SETA*, 13.03.2019, https://www.setav.org/kayyumdan-once-bazi-belediyeler-pkkya-hizmet-eden-birimler-haline-gelmisti/ (Access 24.05.2020).

Ndreu, A. (2016). The Definition and Importance of Local Governance, *Social and Natural Sciences Journal*, 10(1): 5–8.

Özcan, N. A. (1999). *PKK (Kürdistan İşçi Partisi) Tarihi, İdeolojisi ve Yöntemi* [PKK (Kurdistan Workers' Party) History, Ideology and Method]. Ankara: ASAM.

Portzer, J. M. M. (2020). The People's Protection Units' Branding Problem: Syrian Kurds and Potential Destabilization in Northeastern Syria. *Military Review*, May-June, 100(3): 92–103.

Republic of Turkey Ministry of Internal Affairs (2017). Appointments to Municipalities Due to Terror. *Republic of Turkey Ministry of Interior*, Mart 2017, https://www.icisleri.gov.tr/kurumlar/icisleri.gov.tr/IcSite/diab/duyurular/Belediyeler.pdf (Access 23.05.2020).

Republic of Turkey Ministry of Internal Affairs (2019). *Belediyelerdeki Kayyum Sistemi ve Mevcut Durum Raporu* [Trusteeship System in Municipalities and Current Situation Report], https://www.icisleri.gov.tr/kurumlar/icisleri.gov.

tr/IcSite/illeridaresi/Yayinlar/KayyumRaporu/kayyum_nihai_rapor.pdf (Access 25.05.2020).

Republic of Turkey Police Academy Directorate (2017). *Terör Çalıştayı Raporu* [Terror Workshop Report]. Ankara: International Terrorism and Security Research Center.

Rubin, B. and Rubin, J. C. (2008). *Chronologies of Modern Terrorism.* New York: M. E. Sharpe.

Semercioğlu, H. (2016). Uluslararası Terörizmde Küresel İşbirliği: Bir Ütopya [Global Cooperation on International Terrorism: A Utopia]. *Hacettepe University Journal of Economics and Administrative Sciences,* 34(2): 97–114.

Sezer, T. (2012). The Discourse of the PKK/KCK: From the Manifest Through KCK Agreement, *International Journal of Security and Terrorism*, 3(1): 41–65.

Taşkın, Y. (2017). Siyaset Nedir? [What is Politics?]. Y. Taşkın (Ed.) *Siyaset: Kavramlar, Kurumlar, Süreçler* [Politics: Concepts, Institutions, Processes] in, 22–48, İstanbul: İletişim Publishers.

Tilly, C. (2004). Terror, Terrorism, Terrorists. *Sociological Theory*, 22(1): 5–13.

Ural, İ. (2018). *PKK'nın Şehir Savaşı ve PYD/YPG Tarihi* [The PKK's City War and the PYD/YPG History]. İstanbul: İleri Publishers.

Wilkinson, P. (1977). *Terrorism and the Liberal State*, London: The Macmillan Press.

Yayla, A. (2019). *Siyaset Bilimi* [Political Science]. Ankara: Adres Publishers.

Prof. Dr. Filiz Balta Peltekoğlu and Dr. Zuhal Akbayır

1.3 The Perception of Istanbul's Chromatic Identity through Urban Furniture: A Study on College of Communication Students

Abstract: Color, as a component of urban identity, illustrates the cultural ties of a city and highlights its distinctive qualities, shaping the image. The colors of city furniture are, therefore, a significant component in terms of the identity of a city. The research, in which we processed the survey results of the college of communication students, Marmara Unversity, has revealed that color is a component of the urban identity; there is a correlation between urban furniture and this urban identity; although participants have certain awareness of the colors of urban furniture, they do not have a common sense of color regarding the city of Istanbul.

Keywords: Urban identity, City color, Urban furniture, Urban planning, Visual identity.

Introduction

As a sign of visual identity of countries and cities, color is essential for illustrating visual characteristics of a city, and reveals its historical background as well as cultural ties, symbolizing "sui-generis" aspects thereof. A solid, favorable, and sustainable city image with globally competitive power, which produces an economic value for a city, can only be created if the city has a strong identity. Indeed, as Molavi (2015) stated, the lack of color palette of buildings in cities leads to a growing debate about the identity and aesthetics of the city in terms of this deficiency.

According to Tornay (1978), color as a sign of visual identity is not only a cosmetic gloss but also a characteristic of the essence of that thing (Zıllıoğlu, 1996). Thus, color, a component of a city and urban identity, is indispensable in terms of connotations to be attributed to the city.

Zybaczynski (2014) describes permanent colors as the natural texture of a city related to the geography and climate (e.g., soil, rock, vegetation, water, and daylight); semi-permanent colors as street colors, buildings and urban furniture, while temporary colors as billboards, lightings, store windows, and traffic signs. In this sense, we suggest that semi-permanent and variable color preferences can be specified considering the texture of the city.

Colors have various qualities in terms of connotations, symbols, preferences, and their connection with the essence (Taft, 1998, Madden et al., 2000; Schlossat et al., 2018). Moreover, the fact that color has a complex quality with regard to connotations, symbols and preferences is a common opinion among researches (Zybaczynski, 2014). According to Kauppinen-Räisänen (2014), "colors have the capacity to communicate." Colors affect emotions and thoughts culturally, politically, and socially. For instance, a color may represent an ideology and passion, as well as excitement. The election of urban furniture colors thus requires a particular study supported by various disciplines.

Certain studies (Xiao-peng and Xiao-ping, 2011) focus on the historical development of city colors and examine them in the sense of their connotation of the city's historical and cultural make-up, while some others (Qunyuan and Yanhua, 2011) deal with the systematic urban color management. In the literature, besides the researches that examine color preferences and fragmentation of cities in terms of urban planning (Zhang and Li, 2013), we also witness several studies exploring the relationship between the communication, security culture, and color of cities (Zhen-fu, 2006). Furthermore, certain studies identify the color as an effective factor in preserving the local identity of a city (Zybaczynski, 2014). In the context of Public Relations activities, color is the way a city defines its urban identity; it reveals who and what the city is and therefore constitutes an essential component of the city image. From this perspective, color as a reminder of a city cannot be disregarded since it is an essential component of visual identity indicators, such as urban furniture, city design and landscaping, and the logo and symbols thereof. As an important component of visual identity, color should be part of local governance communication strategies. Color becomes even more crucial in the sense of its relationship with the identity and image of a city if this city is a metropolis that straddles two continents, which has a rich historical background of thousands of years, bringing together many civilizations.

1 Color in City Identity and the Street Furniture of Istanbul

Colors become a symbol that leads to specific emotional experiences in individuals and then grow into a source of interest and reminiscence. This process determines the symbolization of colors based on individual and social life, and the role they play in societal communication (Zıllıoğlu, 1996).

According to Hynes, color, as a component of visual identity, has persuasive power at the subconscious level (Hynes, 2008). While colors stimulate emotional responses (Hynes, 2008, Kauppinen-Räisänen, 2014), they also (i) play a role in conveying information, and creating a permanent identity as well as symbolic value, (ii) become a part of the visual identity of the city, (iii) provide information thereabout, (iv) contribute to the formation, representation and preservation of city identity and culture.

Lynch (1960) states that one of the essential factors in terms of city image is color; Liu (2012) however approaches from a different angle and suggests that countries employ colors to define their identity[1]. According to Mehta (2007), streets are not only an essential part of public space but also significant civic symbols of these spaces.

In the past, the use of colors and local materials with a traditional notion provided a more local quality (Zybaczynski, 2014), whereas today, the globalization has made manufactured products marketed or be accessible all over the world. Thus, urban furniture produced in fashion colors with cutting edge technology has been easily distributed all around the world. These developments driven by technological innovations and globalization, on the one hand, expand the color scale, offering numerous color and design options, on the other hand, make it challenging to preserve the unique identities of the cities.

The fact that fashion trends and anthropogenic preferences prevail in urban designs makes the selection of city furniture and public transportation colors of a metropolis with a long historical background like Istanbul that brings together many diverse cultures even more critical.

2 The Research on Perception of Istanbul's Chromatic Identity and Urban Furniture

The purpose of the research is to reveal the perception of the Istanbul residents regarding the relationship between color, urban furniture, and urban identity. Therefore, the research is aimed at understanding whether: (i) Istanbul residents perceive color as a component of urban identity, (ii) there is a common color perception symbolizing urban identity in Istanbul, (iii) the Istanbul residents associate urban furniture with urban identity, and (iv) they have awareness of the colors of urban furniture in Istanbul.

1 To illustrate, China is identified by its red and ink color (Liu, 2012); Dutch by orange (Lakens, 2011); Australia by golden and green; India by white and blue, while Canada by red and white (Minahan, 2010).

Hypotheses:

H1. Color is perceived as a component of urban identity in Istanbul.
H2. Istanbul residents have a common sense of color regarding the city.
H3. Istanbul residents believe there is a relationship between urban furniture and urban identity.
H4. Istanbul residents have an awareness of the colors of urban furniture.

2.1 Methods

In the research, the survey method was used as data collection methodology. A face-to-face survey was conducted in May 2019. On the margin of the survey, a total of 14 question (including but not limited to demographic ones) was developed.

The research sample consisted of 274 undergraduates of the Faculty of Communication University of Marmara, Istanbul. Before the questionnaire was applied to the sample mass of the research, a sample of 27 people selected by convenience sampling was pre-tested. Research questions were posed to the undergraduates face-to-face, using questionnaire forms. Data were analyzed through the statistical package SPSS Version 18.0 set at a 95% confidence level. According to the personal information of the participants, the frequency, mean and the level of agreement with the expressions were calculated, and the Chi-Square Test was used to determine the relationship between categorical variables.

2.2 Limitations of the Study

Since the questionnaire contained conceptual questions about communication discipline, the research was limited to the undergraduates living in Istanbul and receiving communication education. To ensure the robustness of the statistic, we drew the sample of the study from a population who were the undergraduates in Faculty of Communication at Marmara University, because they had gotten their education in three different districts of Istanbul (Kadıköy, Bahçelievler, and Beşiktaş) that are different from each other in terms of location and character. Another limitation of the research is that it addresses only the color component among the visual identification indicators.

2.3 Participants

65 % of the participants were female, and 35 % thereof was male. 1.1% of the participants were minor (under the age of 18). 82.8% of the participants were between 18 and 24 years old; 13.1%, 25 and 29; 1.1%, 30 and 34; 1.1%, 35 to 39,

while 0.7% were over 40 years old. The distribution of the participants in terms of their level of education reveals that 28.1% thereof was freshman; 15.7%, sophomore; 26.3%, 3rd grade; 26.3%, 4th grade; 3.6%, 5th grade and over. The distribution of their residence duration demonstrates that 36.5% of them have been living in Istanbul for 1 to 5 years; 9.1% for 5 to 10 years; 4.4% for 10 to 15 years; 6.9% for 15 to 20 years; and 43.1% for 20 years and more. The distribution of the participants according to the regions they live in Istanbul shows that 38% of them have been residing in the 1st Region, 37.2% of them, in the 2nd Region, and 24.8%, in the 3rd Region[2].

3 Results

In this part of the study, the findings of the analysis of the data obtained from the research are explained in the tables presented below.

The participants were asked the question that reads as "Do you think colors are significant as a component (a visual indicator) of urban identity?" 95.3% of the participants stated that they see colors as a component of urban identity,

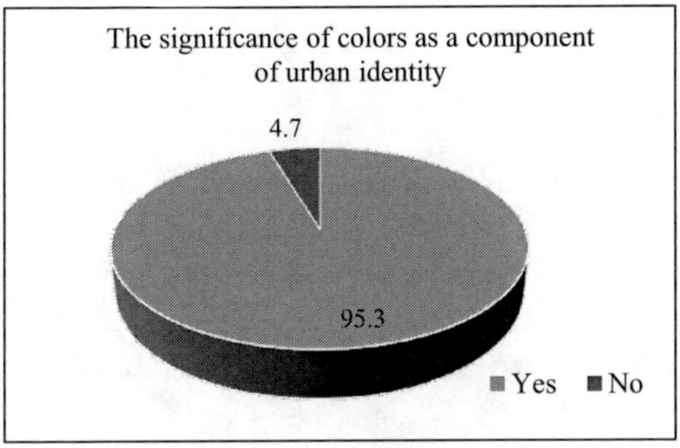

Fig. 1.3.1: The Significance of Colors as a Component of Urban Identity.
Source: Authors

2 Istanbul Districts in the 1st Region: Adalar, Ataşehir, Beykoz, Çekmeköy, Kadıköy, Kartal, Maltepe, Pendik, Sancaktepe, Sultanbeyli, Şile, Tuzla, Ümraniye and Üsküdar.
Istanbul Districts in the 2nd Region: Bayrampaşa, Beşiktaş, Beyoğlu, Esenler, Eyüp, Fatih, Gaziosmanpaşa, Kağıthane, Sarıyer, Sultangazi, Şişli, and Zeytinburnu.
Istanbul Districts in the 3rd Region: Arnavutköy, Avcılar, Bağcılar, Bahçelievler, Bakırköy, Başakşehir, Beylikdüzü, Büyükçekmece, Çatalca, Esenyurt, Göngören, Küçükçekmece, and Silivri.

while 4.7% stated that they do not The significance of colors as a component of urban identity shown in Fig. 1.3.1.

The question of "What color do you think symbolizes Istanbul?" was posed to the participants, and 35.7% of them replied, "blue"; 24.9% thereof, "turquoise"; and 16.7%, "gray." Colors that are believed to symbolize Istanbul are given in Tab. 1.3.1.

Tab. 1.3.1: Colors that are Believed to Symbolize Istanbul.
Source: Authors

	N	%
Red	29	10.8
Yellow	7	2.6
Turquoise	67	24.9
Purple	23	8.6
Green	2	0.7
Blue	96	35.7
Gray	45	16.7
Total	269	100.0

The participants responded to the question of "Where do you come across the color that symbolizes Istanbul?", for which multiple markings were allowed, as "in public transport" by 14.1%, "in architectural structures" by 12.5%, and "in waste containers" by 9.5%. Distribution of Places/Objects Attributed to the Color Believed to Symbolize Istanbul are given in Tab. 1.3.2.

Tab. 1.3.2: The Distribution of Places/Objects Attributed to the Color Believed to Symbolize Istanbul. Source: Authors

	N	%
Street lights	22	3.6
Bus stops	55	9.0
Waste containers	58	9.5
Memorials	29	4.7
Telephone booths	34	5.6
Traffic lights	31	5.1
Street signs	57	9.3
Kiosks	33	5.4
Fountains	20	3.3
Fireplugs	9	1.5
Green space designs/landscape	56	9.2
Sitting benches in parks and streets	44	7.2
Public transportation vehicles	86	14.1
Architectural structures	78	12.5
Total	612	100.0

Due to multiple responses, the quantity of places/objects exceeds the total number of the participants

The question of "What elements do you think urban furniture consist of? ", for which multiple markings were allowed, were posed to the participants, and 13.9% of them replied, "architectural buildings"; 10.9% thereof, "green space designs/landscaping"; and 10.7%, "street lights." (Tab. 1.3.3)

Tab. 1.3.3: The Distribution of the Responses on the Elements that Make-Up Istanbul's Urban Furniture. Source: Authors

	N	%
Street lights	111	10,7
Bus stops	86	8,3
Waste containers	57	5,5
Memorials	89	8,5
Telephone booths	54	5,2
Traffic lights	44	4,2
Street signs	52	5,0
Kiosks	27	2,6
Fountains	79	7,6
Fireplugs	17	1,6
Green space designs/landscape	114	10,9
Sitting benches in parks and streets	99	9,5
Public transportation vehicles	68	6,5
Architectural structures	145	13,9
Total	1042	100,0

Due to multiple responses, the quantity of places/objects exceeds the total number of the participants

The participants responded to the question of "Do you think that the color, which is the symbol of urban identity, should be preferred in urban furniture?" as "Yes" by 95.3%, and "No" by 4.7%. Distribution of the responses on whether the color as a symbol of urban identity should be used in urban furniture shown in Fig. 1.3.2.

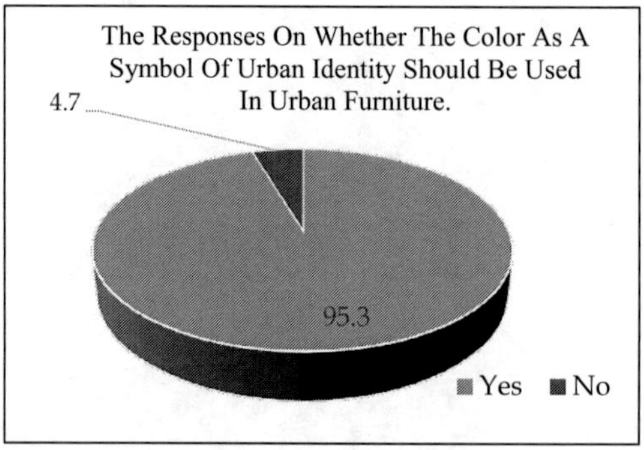

Fig. 1.3.2: The Distribution of the Responses on whether the Color as a Symbol of Urban Identity should be used in Urban Furniture. Source: Authors

The participants whose answer was "Yes" were posed the question of "Where should the color, which is the symbol of urban identity, be applied to?", and 11.7% of them replied, "bus stops"; 10.4% thereof, "street signs"; and 10.2%, "telephone booths." The data obtained are given in Tab. 1.3.4.

Tab. 1.3.4: The Distribution of the Responses on the Urban Furnitures which should have the Color Symbolizing Urban Identity. Source: Authors

	Sayı	**Yüzde(%)**
Street lights	78	8,5
Bus stops	108	11,7
Waste containers	84	9,1
Memorials	38	4,1
Telephone booths	94	10,2
Traffic lights	35	3,8
Street signs	96	10,4
Kiosks	66	7,2
Banks	48	5,2
Floor coverings	48	5,2
Fountains	28	3,0
Fireplugs	39	4,2
Green space designs/landscape	48	5,2
Sitting benches in parks and streets	46	5,0
Public transportation vehicles	40	4,3
Architectural structures	27	2,9
Total	923	100,0

Due to multiple responses, the quantity of places/objects exceeds the total number of the participants

The participants responded to the question of "What is the color that springs to your mind first when you think about buses (Public Transport) of Istanbul?" as "yellow" by 35.2%, "blue" by 16.5%, "purple" by 15.4% (Tab. 1.3.5).

Tab. 1.3.5: The Distribution of the Participants' Preferences Regarding the Bus (Public Transport) Color of Istanbul. Source: Authors

	N	%
Gray	27	9.9
Achromatic	4	1.5
Red	22	8.1
Yellow	96	35.2
Turquoise	29	10.6
Purple	42	15.4
Green	8	2.8
Blue	45	16.5
Total	273	100.0

The participants responded to the question of "What is the color that springs to your mind first when you think about the bus stops of Istanbul?" as "gray" by 41.6%, "achromatic" by 29.9%, "green" by 11.7%. The distribution of the participants' preferences regarding the color of bus stops of Istanbul are given in Tab. 1.3.6.

Tab. 1.3.6: The Distribution of the Participants' Preferences Regarding the Color of Bus Stops of Istanbul. Source: Authors

	N	%
Gray	114	41.6
Achromatic	82	29.9
Red	7	2.6
Yellow	16	5.8
Turquoise	6	2.2
Purple	1	0.4
Green	32	11.7
Blue	16	5.8
Total	274	100.0

The participants responded to the question of "What is the color that springs to your mind first when you think about the telephone booths of Istanbul?" as "blue" by 60.2%, "gray" by 16.4%, "achromatic" by 7.7%. The distribution of the participants' preferences regarding the color of telephone booths of Istanbul are given in Tab. 1.3.7

Tab. 1.3.7: The Distribution of the Participants' Preferences Regarding the Color of Telephone Booths of Istanbul. Source: Authors

	N	%
Gray	45	16.4
Achromatic	21	7.7
Red	15	5.5
Turquoise	17	6.2
Green	10	3.6
Blue	165	60.2
Total	273	100.0

The chi-square analysis was performed to test the relationship between the variable of "the participants' residence duration in Istanbul," and "color preferences that symbolize Istanbul", "places/objects where these colors are noticed," as well as "perceiving colors as a component of urban identity." However, the testing showed that the relationship between these variables was not statistically significant at the 95% confidence level (The p-value of the Chi-Square Test for the relationship between the participants' residence duration in Istanbul and color preferences that symbolize Istanbul is 0.078 (i.e., $p > 0.05$, meaning the variables are independent); that of the test for the relationship between the participants' residence duration in Istanbul and places/objects where these colors are noticed is 0.158 (i.e., $p > 0.05$, meaning the variables are independent); and that of the test for the relationship between residence duration in Istanbul and perceiving colors as a component of urban identity is 0.840(i.e., $p > 0.05$, meaning the variables are independent).

The chi-square analysis of the relationship between the color preferences that symbolize Istanbul and the urban furniture where these colors are noticed has shown that the relationship between the variables was statistically significant at a 95% confidence level (X^2=313,730; sd. = 84; p=0.000 <0.05). Regarding in which city furniture the first three colors that are thought to symbolize Istanbul are noticed, the participants, who believe that the color symbolizing Istanbul is blue, stated with the highest percent of 17.22 that they noticed this color in public transportation vehicles; the participants, who believe that the color symbolizing Istanbul is turquoise stated with the highest percent of 19.67 that they noticed this color in public transportation vehicles; and the participants, who believe that the color symbolizing Istanbul is gray stated with the highest percent of 17.21 that they noticed this color in waste containers. The data are given in Tab. 1.3.8.

Tab. 1.3.8: The Chi-Square Test Results for the Relationship between the Color Preferences that Symbolize Istanbul and the Places/Objects where These Colors Are Noticed. Source: Authors

The places/objects where these colors are noticed		What color do you think symbolizes Istanbul?						
		Red	Yellow	Turquoise	Purple	Green	Blue	Gray
Street lights	N	9	3	2	1	0	3	4
	%	11.25	15.79	1.64	1.82	0.00	1.44	3.28
Bus stops	N	2	0	10	4	2	25	12
	%	2.50	0.00	8.20	7.27	40.00	11.96	9.84
Waste containers	N	2	1	10	3	2	19	21
	%	2.50	5.26	8.20	5.45	40.00	9.09	17.21
Memorials	N	1	2	8	4	0	4	10
	%	1.25	10.53	6.56	7.27	0.00	1.91	8.20
Telephone booths	N	1	0	9	0	0	22	2
	%	1.25	0.00	7.38	0.00	0.00	10.53	1.64
Traffic lights	N	16	0	0	0	0	6	9
	%	20.00	0.00	0.00	0.00	0.00	2.87	7.38
Street signs	N	13	3	11	2	0	22	6
	%	16.25	15.79	9.02	3.64	0.00	10.53	4.92
Kiosks	N	11	0	5	3	0	12	2
	%	13.75	0.00	4.10	5.45	0.00	5.74	1.64
Fountains	N	3	0	3	2	0	7	5
	%	3.75	0.00	2.46	3.64	0.00	3.35	4.10
Fireplugs	N	4	0	3	1	0	0	1
	%	5.00	0.00	2.46	1.82	0.00	0.00	0.82
Green space designs/landscape	N	0	1	14	13	1	14	13
	%	0.00	5.26	11.48	23.64	20.00	6.70	10.66
Sitting benches in parks and streets	N	3	1	12	4	0	12	12
	%	3.75	5.26	9.84	7.27	0.00	5.74	9.84
Public transportation vehicles	N	7	3	24	11	0	36	5
	%	8.75	15.79	19.67	20.00	0.00	17.22	4.10
Architectural structures	N	8	5	11	7	0	27	20
	%	10.00	26.32	9.02	12.73	0.00	12.92	16.39
Total	N	80	19	122	55	5	209	122
	%	100.00	100.00	100.00	100.00	100.00	100.00	100.00

X^2=313,730; sd=84; p=0,000*

#Percentage is calculated based on column values. *p<0.05

#Due to multiple responses, the n value may exceed the total number of the sample.

In the study, the chi-square analysis was performed to test the relationship between the color preferences that symbolize Istanbul and the places/objects where the colors, which is a symbol of urban identity should be applied to; however, the testing showed that the relationship between these variables was not statistically significant at the 95% confidence level (p=0.062 >0.05). Furthermore, chi-square analysis was also conducted to test the relationship between the significance of colors as a component of urban identity and the belief that the color, which is the symbol of said identity, should be used in urban furniture, and the testing again showed that the relationship between these variables was not statistically significant at the 95% confidence level (p=0.058 >0.05).

4 Discussion

Participants in the study represent all three regions of Istanbul in terms of their residence locations (38% of the participants live in the 1st Region, 37.2% thereof in the 2nd Region, and 24.8% in the 3rd Region).

The data, which indicates that 95.3% of the participants perceive that colors are components of urban identity and that 4.7% thereof perceive otherwise, has confirmed the H1. Hypothesis of "Color is perceived as a component of urban identity in Istanbul."

Although a majority of 95.3% of the respondents perceived colors as a component of urban identity, they did not have a common sense of a single color for the city of Istanbul. The distribution of the answers given to the question of "What color do you think symbolizes Istanbul?" was "blue" with the percent of 35.7, "turquoise" with the percent of 24.9, and "gray" with the percent of 16.7. Considering the proportional distribution of the responses, we conclude that the participants do not have a common sense of color with regard to the city of Istanbul. Based on these data, the H2. Hypothesis of "Istanbul residents have a common sense of color regarding the city" has not been confirmed. Why the city was mostly associated with blue and turquoise may stem from the fact that (i) since Istanbul is a sea-city, it connotes "blue" as a natural texture, (ii) the logo of Istanbul Metropolitan Municipality is dark blue, and (iii) turquoise, a traditional color of Ottoman period, has been popular again throughout the country for the last 15 years.

Again, 95.3% of respondents believed that the color that is a symbol of urban identity should be applied to urban furniture. Moreover, the results of the chi-square analysis regarding in which city furniture the first three colors that are thought to symbolize Istanbul are noticed have revealed that participants responding in blue and turquoise stated (with the highest percent of 17.22, and 19.67, respectively) that they noticed these colors in public transportation vehicles; while the participants responding in gray stated (with the highest percent of 17.21) that they noticed this color in waste containers. Thus, the H3. Hypothesis of "Istanbul residents believe there is a relationship between urban furniture and urban identity" appears to have been confirmed.

However, "Istanbul's buses" were defined by the respondents as "yellow" (35.2%), "blue" (16.5%) and "purple" (15.4%)[3]. Considering the current bus colors, we may conclude that the participants of the study were aware of these colors. Istanbul's bus stops are generally defined as in Gray by 41.6%, and in achromatic by 29.9%. These data and the fact that IETT (Istanbul Electric Tramway and Tunnel Establishments) has replaced the metal-sheeted green bus stops with achromatic ones with gray elements (IETT, 2020) suggest that there is an awareness about the colors of the bus stops in Istanbul residents. The fact that regarding the question about telephone boots in Istanbul, 60.2% of the respondents answered "blue" means that this color (corresponds to and thereby) represents the color of the current telephone booths of Istanbul. In the light of these data and the above assessment on the colors of buses, bus stops and telephone booths, which are the city furniture of Istanbul, H4. Hypothesis of "Istanbul residents have an awareness of the colors of urban furniture" has been confirmed.

Conclusion

Presence of a common sense of color with regard to a city and public awareness of the colors of its urban furniture create a favorable condition to properly reflect the urban identity and image. To this end, research aiming to explore the relationship between urban furniture and color has been performed in Istanbul. Based on the findings of the survey on the communication students, the study has concluded that color is a component of urban identity and that there is a relationship between urban furniture and urban identity. The results of the study have also demonstrated that although participants have awareness about the colors of urban furniture and transportation vehicles, they do not have a common sense of color, which represents the visual identity of Istanbul.

The results are far from confirming that the natural texture and cultural structure of the city are primarily considered in determining the colors of urban

3 According to 2019 data (Transporter, 2019), municipal buses in Istanbul are yellow (3030 buses) and purple (985), while public (contracted) buses are blue (2.154).

furniture renovated in Istanbul, especially for the last ten years. Today, the colors and designs of urban furniture in Istanbul mostly reflect fashion trends instead. However, Istanbul, a meeting point for many civilizations and a capital of numerous religions and sects, in terms of contributing in regional growth, should have a design and colors that reflect the qualities of this historical and cultural heritage. For the landscaping activities in Istanbul and the election of street furniture, which are intended to ease the life, designs and colors that duly reflect the real identity of the city should thus be preferred, and accordingly city-mapping should not be disregarded. Only in this way can a common perception of the colors of Istanbul be created and can the permanence of an image that corresponds to its identity be ensured. In conclusion, the city of Istanbul needs scientific methods and approaches to color plan and color-mapping as a part of local governance communication strategies.

References

Hynes, N. (2009). Colour and Meaning in Corporate Logos: An Empirical Study, Journal of Brand Management, 16(8), 545–555.

İETT, (2020). Retrieved from https://www.iett.istanbul/tr/main/pages/otobus-duraklari/87, Date of Access: 13-01-2020.

Kauppinen-Räisänen, H. (2014). Strategic Use of Colour in brand Packaging, Packaging Technology and Science, 27(8), 663–676.

Lakens, D. (2011). Orange as a Perceptual Representation of the Dutch Nation: Effects on Perceived National Identification and Color Evaluation, European Journal of Social Psychology, 41(7), 924–929.

Liu, H. U. (2012). Analysis of the Role of China's National Colors in Modern Graphic Art Design, Packaging Engineering, 24, Retrieved from http://en.cnki.com.cn/Article_en/CJFDTotal- BZGC201224039.htm, Date of Access: 10-02-2020

Lynch, K. (1960). The Image of the City, MIT Press, Cambridge.

Madden, T. J., Hewett, K., Roth, M. S. (2000). Managing Images in Different Cultures: A Cross National Study of Color Meanings and Preferences, Journal of International Marketing, 8(4), 90–107.

Mehta, V. (2007). Lively Streets. Determining Environmental Characteristics to Support Social Behavior, Journal of Planning Education and Research, 27(2), 165–187.

Minahan, J. B. (2010). The Complete Guide to National Symbols and Emblems, ABC-CLIO, California.

Molavi, M. (2015). Preserving City Color Plan, Surveying Iranian Submontane Cities, Urbanism. Architecture. Constructions, 6(2), 7–18.

Qunyuan, C., Yanhua, D. (2011). City Color Planning and Management in Changsha [J]. Planners, (1) 18, Retrieved from http://en.cnki.com.cn/Article_en/CJFDTotal- GHSI201101018.htm, Date of Access: 15-02-2020.

Schloss, K. B., Lessard, L., Walmsley, C. S., Foley, K. (2018). Color Inference in Visual Communication: The Meaning of Colors In Recycling, Cognitive Research: Principles and Implications, 3(1), 1–17.

Taft, C. (1997). Color Meaning and Context: Comparisons of Semantic Ratings of Colors on Samples and Objects. Color Res. Appl. 22, 40–50.

Taşımacılar, (2019). Retrieved from http://www.tasimacilar.com/istanbul-toplu-tasima-araclari-verileri-20725h.htm, Date of Access: 15-02-2020.

Tornay, S. (1978). De la Perception Des Couleurs À L'aperception Symbolique Du Monde. Image (s) et Culture (s). Paris, Eds. Du Seuil, 29(1), 119–140.

Xiao-peng, J., Xiao-ping, H. (2011). City Color Control of Xi'an Old Districts, Urban Problems, 2, Retrieved from http://en.cnki.com.cn/Article_en/CJFDTotal-CSWT201102010.htm, Date of Access: 10-02-2020.

Zhang, S., Li, J. (2013). Visual·City's Color Design Management. International Conference on Education Technology and Management Science, 2013, 347–349.

Zhen-fu, L. (2006). Color Psychology and City Communication Safety Culture [J]. Safety and Environmental Engineering, 4, Retrieved from http://en.cnki.com.cn/Article_en/CJFDTotal- KTAQ200604017.htm, Date of Access: 10-02-2020.

Zıllıoğlu, M. (1996). What is Communication? [in Turkish], İletişim Nedir?, Cem Pub, İstanbul, Turkey.

Zybaczynski, V. M. (2014). Colour-Important Factor in Preserving the Local Identity, Urbanism. Architecture. Constructions, 5(4), 87–92.

Assoc. Prof. Ouidad Yousfi and Assoc. Prof. Nadia Loukil

1.4 Why Should Firms Achieve Strategic CSR?

Abstract: The current chapter shows that strategic corporate social responsibility (hereafter CSR) drives more pioneering socially responsible initiatives than responsive CSR based on "imitative" activities introduced to meet stakeholders' basic expectations. We conclude that strategic CSR leads to more sustainable financial performance as well as more socially and environmentally responsible innovation. We show that more diversity in top management positions could be a necessary requirement to shape more strategic CSR strategies. We present a critical survey of the literature structured in the following. First, we discuss the main features of CSR strategies and how they have evolved in the last years. Second, we shed light on the puzzled CSR-financial performance association. Then, we focus on the tools provided by strategic CSR to foster innovation potential of businesses and why we should rethink CSR to drive more sustainable innovations. Finally, the chapter discusses how hiring more diverse profiles in top positions could help to get out of the narrow CSR thinking and to go beyond stakeholders' expectations and reports' standards this could provide valuable opportunities to widen the innovation range in businesses through the implementation of more social, organizational and marketing innovations as well as the introduction of new products and processes.

Keywords: CSR performance, Strategic CSR, Innovation, Diversity.

1 Introduction

In the last years, many policy and market-makers have introduced programs to increase the firms' involvement in socially responsible activities. For instance, the French government has provided many incentives to increase CSR investments and transparency, like for example the New Economic Regulations (NER law, 2001)[1], the Grenelle Environment Forum (2007 and 2010)[2], the Energy Transition Act (2015)[3] and the France's Due Diligence Law (2017)[4]. The main aim of these programs is to provide incentives to the firms, particularly listed ones, to get involved in more socially responsible activities. In fact, for

---

1 https://www.eurofound.europa.eu/publications/article/2001/new-economic-regulations-law-adopted

2 http://www.oecd.org/gov/regulatory-policy/FRA-Grenelle-Environment-Forum.pdf

3 https://www.gouvernement.fr/en/energy-transition

4 https://www.legifrance.gouv.fr/affichTexte.do?cidTexte=JORFTEXT000034290626&categorieLien=id

many years, the decision-making process has been drawn on the challenge of how to increase short-term returns, most often at the expense of long-term and sustainable development. Focusing solely on increasing shareholders' wealth is not any more the guarantee for the business' survival and legitimacy. Firms have to adopt a more inclusive holders' philosophy and to be concerned about the identification of their stakeholders and their needs. They have to increase the social performance as well as the financial one. Indeed, socially responsible projects could provide an alternative way to increase the firms' resources and connections, the effectiveness of their management, and to achieve a sustainable development (Carvalho et al., 2018).

The survey of the literature on corporate governance and CSR shows that there are two main CSR approaches: strategic CSR and responsive CSR. In the following, we present the development of CSR strategies and their specific features. Then, we address how they could benefit to businesses, and help to overcome the current challenges. The last part of this chapter discusses the moderating role of top managers, specifically the influence of their cognitive and demographic traits, on achieving more socially and environmentally responsible businesses.

2 CSR Strategies

Recent studies show the presence of two forms of CSR strategies: strategic CSR and responsive CSR (see among others Vishwanathan et al., 2020; Bocquet et al. 2017). In fact, CSR strategies have matured: firms were first developing CSR activities that are closely related to the scope of their main activities to meet reporting standards and basic expectations of stakeholders. Then they have started to initiate more pioneering and strategic CSR projects based on an active and dynamic interaction with multiple stakeholders' groups. These strategies have led to the implementation of a more comprehensive and inclusive CSR thinking. These initiatives go beyond basic stakeholders' requests (Bocquet et al., 2017).

The survey of CSR literature shows that despite the booming number of studies on strategic CSR, it is not yet clearly established how to define strategic CSR strategies in comparison with responsive ones. More specifically, very rare academic papers have tried to distinguish between responsive and strategic strategies of CSR. In the following, we discuss the different CSR approaches in the last years and how they led to the definition of this dichotomous approach of CSR.

2.1 Responsive CSR

2.1.1 The Defensive CSR

The first age of CSR is based on "defensive" initiatives: they are undertaken when they are profitable. Accordingly, managers are prone to prefer CSR activities protecting financial results, specifically short-term returns, at the expense of more sustainable and less profitable socially and environmentally responsible activities. Consequently, it cannot provide a good understanding of different expectations which increase agency conflicts. Also, as it is focused on actions enhancing the corporate reputation, it could be "poor a vector" of innovation (Bertrand et al., 2020). Despite the involvement in CSR activities, many large corporates have collapsed during the financial crisis. Green models have been promoting to enhance their market image, have been green-washing models initiated to gain customers and suppliers legitimacy. Their practices have contributed to the quick spread of the crisis (Miller, 2009). The consequences of subprime crisis have policy- and market-makers, and managers to think of their role on promoting more sustainable system through responsible governance and management. Enron scandal is definitely a juncture in CSR literature that serves to the introduction of the second age of CSR (Owen, 2005).

2.1.2 The Charitable CSR

In the second CSR age, CSR strategies become more associated to charitable actions: this is the philanthropic age of CSR. Investors have to raise their money in projects serving communities' interests (Carnegie, 1889). In addition to increasing shareholders' wealth, CSR investments are undertaken to empower the community through an equal distribution of wealth: they are considered the "Gospel of Wealth" that drives growth. The association of philanthropy and investments could initiate strong partnerships between universities and non-profit organizations which increase creativity and carry innovative opportunities (Bereskin and Hsu, 2016). However, this association must be consistent with the main activities of the business to avoid wasting money and non-profitable activities. Accordingly, the undertaken CSR projects have to be profitable as much as conventional activities and to generate significant cash-flows. In fact, these two conditions seem to be prominent when it comes to choosing the appropriate ones, which reduces the scope of "compliant" CSR activities. Consequently, the implemented CSR activities failed drastically to solve real social and environmental issues. According to Burke and Logsdon (1996), binding this philanthropic condition is one of the dimensions of strategic CSR, namely the "specificity" dimension. However, in the philanthropic CSR, the specificity dimension is generic, and not strategically involved in the CSR policy of the business. Furthermore, Porter and Kramer (2006) underlined that each firm has to deal with social and environmental issues, specific to its industry. Accordingly, CSR actions must be consistent and entirely incorporated with the global business strategy. Philanthropic CSR failed to create dynamic effects able to influence the business strategy, specifically its everyday operations, competitiveness and growth. However, very recently, De Silva and Wright (2019) pointed out that the charity aspect in CSR activities could be a necessary requirement to open innovation, particularly due to the strong connections it is able to establish between profit and non-profit structures.

2.1.3 The Promotional CSR

Relying on stakeholders to build a brand image conveys more dynamic exchanges in CSR projects: this is the age of social marketing. It comes also from the need of stakeholders to see businesses taking socially responsible initiatives transforming the real world (Lefebvre, 2012). Then, optimal CSR strategy has to align the interests of shareholders and stakeholders by enhancing the stakeholders' perception of the business. Thus if stakeholders are highlighting environmental issues related to the business activities, the firm is supposed to take advantage of these opportunities to gain the stakeholders trust. This approach is definitely meant to reduce reputational risk through increasing visibility (Singh and Dhir, 2019). Unlike charitable CSR, promotional CSR and its marketing dimension have been strategically integrated in CSR policies. Singh and Dhir (2019) notice, however, that customers find that many real social issues with low visibility are marginalized at the expense of less significant social issues with greater visibility. They suspect CSR marketing to manipulate stakeholders as there is a huge gap between how CSR shows off and how it is practiced. CSR marketing leads to the development of CSR as an advertising tool and greenwashing (Esper and Barin Cruz, 2019). Many large corporates have been involved in CSR scandals such as Volkswagen test cheating, Siemens bribe scandal, BAE corruption scandal, and General Motors defective ignition switches. Finally, firms that do not apply CSR strategically are applying it in a responsive way: defensive, charitable and promotional CSR approaches are responsive and were not able to integrate CSR as a hardcore of the business global strategy.

2.2 Strategic CSR

The consecutive ethical scandals leads to the development of a more integrated CSR strategy: a more strategic CSR (Brenkert, 2019). The strategic dimension of CSR seems to be a promising and relevant field for further research (McWilliams and Siegel, 2011). However, the lack of consideration of the strategic aspects of CSR, and the scarcity of theoretical research on the determinants of strategic CSR led several scholars to call for identifying the determinants of strategic CSR. Burke and Logsdon (1996) argue that CSR is strategic "when it yields substantial business-related benefits to the firm, in particular by supporting core business activities and thus contributing to the firm's effectiveness in accomplishing its mission". Then, the concept was developed to cover actions put into practice to achieve sustainable competitive advantages. Strategic CSR is, therefore, a set of activities that are simultaneously good for the company and the society, thus improving company's performance and creating social and economic performances (Porter and Kramer, 2006).

Recently, studies have become more specific regarding the definition of strategic CSR. Athanasopoulou and Selsky (2016) define strategic CSR as a continuous process that takes into account its effect, and helps the company to pursue its business goals while considering the stakeholders' engagement. It related CSR to the corporate core business, auditing, setting of social targets, reporting, and implementation of social management systems (Visser, 2010). Ruggiero and Cupertino (2018) emphasize that CSR is strategic when it increasingly goes beyond the needs of a company's stakeholders. They also argue that the assumption of a strategic perspective implies not only the definition of the business' future direction and objectives but also an understanding of the amount and apportionment of available resources. Sufficient resources allow the firm to develop strategies suitable for pursuing opportunities coherent with its current and prospective environment and capacities. Thus, resources have to be strategically invested and allocated in order to enhance CSR performance. Lately, Vishwanathan et al. (2020) described the non-strategic side of CSR as a blind spot to CSR researchers. Indeed, investigations' focus has been oriented to the strategic CSR. They have identified specific areas of strategic CSR: (1) reputation enhancement, (2) stakeholder reciprocation, (3) risk mitigation, and (4) innovation capacity.

From a theoretical perception, a company is whether strategic or responsive, while in reality, it can develop responsive CSR strategies in some areas and strategic CSR in other areas. It is clear that Vishwanathan et al. (2020)'s approach encompasses promotional, charitable and promotional aspects of CSR. At this stage, we should point out there is no sole definition of the strategic CSR which makes the CSR understanding more blurred.

3 Strategic CSR and Financial Performance

Many studies have focused on building arguments on how corporate responsibility may influence corporate financial performance. From a resource-based view, the firm may perform better than its competitors when it relies, over time, on specific resources such as human, physical and organizational assets: this is the hardcore of the stakeholder theory (Freeman, 1984) Building better relations with employees, customers, suppliers and communities could increase financial performance. In fact, financial outcomes are driven by tangible as well as intangible assets which could be valuable sources of competitive advantages (Hart, 1995; Hillman and Keim, 2001). Raising money in socially responsible activities is likely to enhance the firm's reputation among customers, suppliers, employees, regulators (Brammer and Pavelin, 2006). It could also decrease agency conflicts between managers and the firm's stakeholder: reducing agency conflicts leads to a better financial performance. For many years, traditional economic theory considers corporate engagement on CSR activities as an economic disadvantage (Friedman, 1970; Jensen and Meckling, 1976). Indeed, "the social responsibility of business is to increase its profits" (Friedman, 1970, p. 1). In other words, managers must focus on the purpose of maximizing shareholders' return even when they are raising money on CSR projects: CSR returns are not supposed to increase their personal reputation (Barnea and Rubin, 2010). Indeed, corporate social activity is considered as agency costs that could deteriorate corporate profits (Krüger, 2015).

Jensen (2001) argues that firms cannot achieve value maximization without satisfying the interests of its stakeholders: this is the enlightened stakeholder theory. "This strategic CSR is simply a profit-maximization strategy motivated by self-interest and not by a conception of corporate social responsibility" (Baron, 2001, p. 9). Indeed, Porter and Kramer (2006) argue that firms investing strategically with respect to social interests will have a competitive advantage, which leads to enhance firm value. In the same vein, Reinhardt et al. (2008) state that, in most cases, firms make the decision to invest in social activities based on the criterion of profitability like other traditional investments. From another angle of view, Baron (2008) point out that CSR investments could be productive ones. In fact, consumers are more attracted by socially profitable firms and some investors prefer raising their money on CSR activities even when they display lower returns in short term. Accordingly, more responsible firms could have higher value due to their reputational premium (Besley and Ghatak, 2007).

Nelling and Webb (2009) reject the causality in CSR-financial performance association. Their findings provide evidence that strong stock market performance leads to greater firm investment in CSR activities when these activities are dedicated to enhancing employees' relations but the CSR activities do not influence financial performance. In contrast, Hillman and Keim (2001)' findings confirm the existence of a virtuous circle.

The relationship between CSR and financial performance may be nonlinear. The idea is to assess the trade-off between costs and benefits of CSR. Nollet et al. (2016) shows a U-shaped relationship between CSR performance and accounting performance indicators. Social performance could drive financial performance only when it reaches a certain level. Otherwise, any additional investment on CSR activities lowers financial performance. In hospitality sector, Franco et al. (2020) advance that stakeholders may appreciate firms performing well in CSR but they do not depreciate less socially profitable firms. They conclude that CSR costs could be covered by CSR benefits only when CSR strategy is successful. Their study provides evidence of U-shaped relationship.

4 Strategic CSR and Innovation

The innovation-CSR association has been examined extensively in last decade based on the intuition that innovation and CSR are the both corporate strategies with long-term perspectives (Katila and Shane, 2005). Indeed, Porter and Kramer (2006), argue that investments in CSR are a source of opportunities, innovation, and competitive advantages. In addition, corporate abilities that create long-term value through social responsible activities include innovation through the introduction of new technologies, operating methods, and management approaches (Porter and Kramer, 2011). Hence, the ability to focus on long-term value creation through a strategy based on economic and social values, improves cognitive flexibility and promotes creative ideas to solve problems (Grant and Berry, 2011). Cook et al. (2019) provide evidence that firms with higher CSR performance produce more patents and patent citations while Lefebvre, (2012) argue that social marketing could drive more marketing innovation. Also, innovation may be a smart device to solve environment issues and achieve corporate sustainability. In fact, innovation could create value and deal with the environment and society issues (Labatt, 1997; Pavelin and Porter, 2008). Hence, it is a hardcore of any sustainable strategy aiming to reduce environmental burdens or to reach ecologically specified sustainability targets (Rennings, 2000). According to the European Commission (2006), CSR may contribute to corporate sustainability development and increase corporate competitive potential by driving innovation. In the same vein, Nidumolu et al. (2009) argue that the CSR is considered a fundamental driver of innovation while Rexhepi et al. (2013) argue that corporate social activities and innovation are the core of business competencies. Innovative investments are necessary for firms' growth and survival (Kim et al., 2014). They may guarantee long-term profit since they focus on technology and on R&D and ensure sustainability to human, social, environmental, technical, and economic investments. Szutowski and Ratajczak (2016) show that the influence of innovation on strategic CSR practices depend on the type and intensity of innovation. They provide evidence also that the influence of CSR on innovation depend on CSR features, such as the type of reaction, degree of development, and field of activity.

5 Strategic CSR and Diversity

The strategic CSR-diversity association is supported by many theories. Under the upper echelons theory (Hambrick and Mason, 1984), diversity is likely to increase the business involvement in a more strategic CSR (Aggarwal et al., 2019; Tasheva and Hillman, 2018). From an agency perspective (Jensen and Meckling, 1976), the board effectiveness is closely related to its composition. According to Resource dependence theory (Pfeffer and Salancik, 1978), appointing more diverse profiles to boardrooms allows firms to get access to more diverse resources, in terms of experiences, skills and networks (Taljaard et al., 2015). All these resources are valuable when the firm have to meet expectations, and therefore for the development of a CSR strategy (Béji et al., 2020; Harjoto et al., 2015). Hereafter, we discuss the effects of different forms of diversity on CSR strategy.

5.1 Structural Diversity in Boards and CSR

Structural diversity refers to diversity of boards. In fact, boards display different features in terms of structure, size, separation between management and control functions as well as the percentage of independent members and committees. Indeed, in order to develop their CSR strategies, many firms have decided to establish specialized board committees, namely CSR committees CSRC (Peters and Romi, 2015; Rodrigue et al., 2013); CSRCs aim to guide the company towards more strategic CSR actions, through the implementation of

CSR initiatives, decreasing CSR risks and pursuing new opportunities (Hussain et al., 2018).

CSRCs could lead to best-integrated CSR models and to meet, therefore, the plurality of existing demands. They play a key role in the development of a strategic CSR policy and improving social performance. They also have to check the compliance with regulations and initiatives in order to decrease CSR risks (Peters and Romi, 2015). Not surprisingly, corporate governance literature shows that the presence and the composition of CSRC influence corporate outcomes (Klein, 1998). Diverse boards are prone to create diverse committees, which is valuable, specifically in CSRC, when it comes to the implementation of strategic CSR policies. The attributes of CSRC members could, therefore, matter in the definition of a CSR strategy and its implementation.

5.2 Demographic Diversity in Board

The profile of board members has changed in the last years, because of a social pressure: the boards are expected to appoint more diverse profiles in the image of the society they produce. Consequently, gender, foreign, and generational diversities have attracted an increasing interest. Many studies put forward that female directors are likely to increase CSR performance at different levels (Beji et al., 2020; Harjoto et al., 2015; Hafsi and Turgut 2013). In line with the social role theory (Eagly, 1987), women are prone to be altruistic and to care about relationships. From the upper echelons' theory perspective (Hambrick and Mason, 1984), women display specific cognitive features. They have different academic and professional backgrounds which give access to more resources and specific networks (the resource dependence theory, Pfeffer and Salancik, 1978). These resources are valuable when it comes to the implementation of CSR projects (Boulouta, 2013).

Appointing young and old members could influence social performance. When they mature, directors could become more sensitive to society's needs: they get involved in a giving-back to society process (Hafsi and Turgut, 2013). However, because of the changes in universities curricula, specifically on management and business programs, young directors could also be sensitive to CSR issues. In the last years, universities have introduced specific programs on CSR and offer degrees dedicated to the management of sustainable development. For instance, Post et al. (2011) provide evidence that young members are sensitive to environmental and ethical issues.

Another interesting feature of diversity in boards, is the presence of foreign members. The international expertise, broader and diversified networks, awareness of environmental and social issues and willingness to use new technologies are value-enhancing in terms of social performance (Beji et al., 2020; Tihanyi et al., 2005). Non-local directors bring their cultural values and new connections to the business, specifically on environmental projects (Beji et al., 2020; Hafsi and Turgut, 2013).

Appointing members who have different educational backgrounds is also a source of cognitive diversity that could be valuable for social performance and strategic CSR (Rupley et al., 2012). Many studies show that post-graduated directors are positively associated with the firm's success (Geletkanycz and Black, 2001; Hambrick and Mason, 1984). In terms of CSR, they are likely to be more sensitive to environmental issues (Shahgholian, 2017).

Finally, directors sitting in other boards could get inspired by what is conducted in other firms specifically in terms of social responsible investments. Accordingly, they could drive the firm to prefer more strategic CSR projects (Beji et al., 2020). For instance, busy directors are familiar with board practices in different businesses. They have, therefore, more information and could provide more perspectives, specifically in the implementation of new CSR initiatives (Beji et al., 2020). On the same vein, many studies put forward a positive association between multiple directorships and the involvement in proactive environmental strategies (De Villiers et al., 2011).

Conclusion

The current chapter reviews the literature on CSR, specifically the different CSR approaches. We show that for many years, CSR strategies have been developed to respond to stakeholders 'expectations and comply with reporting standards: they have been responsive strategies. They encompass defensive, charitable and promotional CSR strategies and are meant to enhance the market image and the firm reputation to gain legitimacy in the eyes of basic stakeholders such as customers, suppliers and policymakers. Lately, many firms have get involved in CSR strategies based on original and pioneering actions to foster interactions between the firm and stakeholders, going beyond CSR regulations and standards: strategic CSR. It needs the mobilization of specific resources and capabilities driving superior social performance. The CSR literature does not establish yet criterion to identify responsive and strategic CSR strategies. Furthermore, many firms could raise money in responsive CSR activities as well as strategic CSR activities: this dichotomous approach of CSR strategies provides a biased view of the firm's involvement in CSR. To implement more strategic CSR policies, the survey of corporate governance literature shows that more diverse boards could drive better social performance than less diverse ones: diversity of boards and diversity in boards could be an advantage for the decision-making process, specifically in terms of socially responsible activities. This heterogeneity can increase exchanges and business' connections, offer new perspectives, and influence the board's functioning. Diverse boards are prone to implement more strategic CSR strategies. Consequently, it increases both financial and social performances. We also shed light on the key role of CSR committees on CSR performance and the implementation of strategic CSR policies and how they could decrease CSR risks.

References

Aggarwal, R., Jindal, V., & Seth, R. (2019). Board diversity and firm performance: the role of business group affiliation. International Business Review, 28, 1–17.

Athanasopoulou, A., & Selsky, J. W. (2016). The social context in CSR research: a contextualist approach with critical applications. In *Research Handbook on Corporate Social Responsibility in Context*. Massaschusetts: USA, Edward Elgar Publishing.

Barnea, A., & Rubin, A. (2010). Corporate social responsibility as a conflict between shareholders. Journal of Business Ethics, 97, 71–86.

Baron, D. (2001). Private politics, corporate social responsibility, and integrated strategy. Journal of Economics & Management Strategy, 10(1), 7–45.

Baron, D. (2008). Managerial contracting and corporate social responsibility. Journal of Public Economics, 92(1–2), 268–288.

Beji, R., Yousfi, O., Loukil, N., & Omri, A. (2020). Board diversity and corporate social responsibility: empirical evidence from France. Journal of Business Ethics, 2020: 1–23. DOI: 10.1007/s10551-020-04522-4.

Bereskin, F. L., & Hsu, P. H. (2016). Corporate philanthropy and innovation: the case of the pharmaceutical industry. Journal of Applied Corporate Finance, 28(2), 80–86.

Bertrand, D., Le Bas, C., Mathieu, A., & Chapuis, S. M. (2020). Types of innovation and firm societal commitment intensity: analytical and empirical insights. Innovations, 62(2), 221–247.

Besley, T., & Ghatak, M. (2007). Retailing public goods: the economics of social responsibility. Journal of Public Economics, 91(9), 1645–1663.

Bocquet, R., Le Bas, C., Mothe, C., & Poussing, N. (2017). CSR, innovation, and firm performance in sluggish growth contexts: a firm-level empirical analysis. Journal of Business Ethics, 146(1), 241–254.

Boulouta, I. (2013). Hidden connections: the link between board gender diversity and corporate social performance. Journal of Business Ethics, 113(2), 185–197.

Brammer, S., & Pavelin, S. (2006). Corporate reputation and social performance: the importance of fit. Journal of Management Studies, 43, 435–455.

Brenkert, G. G. (2019). Mind the gap! The challenges and limits of (Global) business ethics. Journal of Business Ethics, 155(4), 917–930.

Burke, L., & Logsdon, J. M. (1996). How corporate social responsibility pays off. Long range planning, 29(4), 495–502.

Carnegie, A. (1889). 'Wealth'/'Gospel of wealth'. North American Review, 148(391), 653–664.

Carvalho, F., Santos, G., & Gonçalves, J. (2018). The disclosure of information on Sustainable Development on the corporate website of the certified Portuguese organizations. International Journal for Quality Research, 12(1), 253–276.

Cook, K. A., Romi, A. M., Sánchez, D., & Sánchez, J. M. (2019). The influence of corporate social responsibility on investment efficiency and innovation. Journal of Business Finance & Accounting, 46(3–4), 494–537.

De Silva, M., & Wright, M. (2019). Entrepreneurial co-creation: societal impact through open innovation. R&D Management, 49(3), 318–342.

De Villiers, C., Naiker, V., & Van Staden, C. J. (2011). The effect of board characteristics on firm environmental performance. Journal of Management, 37(6), 1636–1663.

Eagly, A. H. (1987). Sex Differences in Social Behaviour: A Social-Role Interpretation, Hillsdale. NJ: Erlbaum. DOI: 10.2307/2073813.

Esper, S., & Barin Cruz, L. (2019, July). Controversies around CSR and SD: The Role of Stakeholders in the Spiral of Hypocrisy. In *Academy of Management Proceedings* (Vol. 2019, No. 1, p. 12170). Briarcliff Manor, NY 10510: Academy of Management.

European Commission. (2006). Green Paper. A European Strategy for Sustainable, Competitive and Secure Energy. Brussels, Belgium.

Franco, S., Caroli, M. G., Cappa, F., Del Chiappa, G. (2020). Are you good enough? CSR, quality management and corporate financial performance in the hospitality industry. International Journal of Hospitality Management, 88, 102395.

Freeman, E. (1984). Strategic Management: A Stakeholder Approach, Pitman, Boston, MA.

Friedman, M. (1970). The social responsibility of business is to increase its profits. New York Times Magazine, 32 (13), 122–126.

Geletkanycz, M. A., & Black, S. S. (2001). Bound by the past? Experience-based effects on commitment to the strategic status quo. Journal of Management, 27(1), 3–21.

Grant, A. M., & Berry, J. W. (2011). The necessity of others is the mother of invention: intrinsic and prosocial motivations, perspective taking, and creativity. Academy of Management Journal, 54(1), 73–96.

Hafsi, T., & Turgut, G. (2013). Boardroom diversity and its effect on social performance: conceptualization and empirical evidence. Journal of Business Ethics, 103, 385–402.

Hambrick, D. C., & Mason, P. A. (1984). Upper echelons: the organization as a reflection of its top managers. Academy of Management Review, 9, 193–206.

Harjoto, M., Laksmana, I., & Lee, R. (2015). Board diversity and corporate social responsibility. Journal of Business Ethics, 132, 641–660.

Hart, S. (1995). A natural resource-based view of the firm. Academy of Management Review, 20, 986–1014.

Hillman, A., & Keim, G. (2001). Shareholder value, stakeholder management, and social issues: what's the bottom line? Strategic Management Journal, 22, 125–139.

Hussain, N., Rigoni, U., & Cavezzali, E. (2018). Does it pay to be sustainable? Looking inside the black box of the relationship between sustainability performance and financial performance. Corporate Social Responsibility and Environmental Management, 25, 1198–1211

Jensen, M. C. (2001).Value maximization, stakeholder theory, and the corporate objective function. Journal of Applied Corporate Finance, 14(3), 8–21.

Jensen, M. C., & Meckling, W. (1976). Theory of the firm: managerial behavior, agency costs and ownership structure. Journal of Financial Economics, 3, 305–360.

Katila, R., & Shane, S. (2005). When does lack of resources make new firms innovative? Academy of Management Journal, 48(5), 814–829.

Kim, Y., Brodhag, C., & Mebratu, D. (2014). Corporate social responsibility driven innovation. Innovation: The European Journal of Social Science Research, 27(2), 175–196.

Klein, A. (1998). Firm performance and board committee structure. The Journal of Law and Economics, 41, 275–304.

Krüger, P. (2015). Corporate goodness and shareholder wealth. Journal of financial Economics, 115(2), 304–329.

Labatt, S. (1997). Corporate response to environmental issues: packaging. Growth and Change, 28(1), 67–92.

Lefebvre, R. C. (2012). Transformative social marketing: co-creating the social marketing discipline and brand. Journal of Social Marketing, 2(2), 118–129.

McWilliams, A., & Siegel, D. (2001). Corporate social responsibility: a theory of the firm perspective. Academy of Management Review, 26(1), 117–127.

Miller, R. T. (2009). Morals in a market bubble. University of Dayton Law Review, 35(1), 113–137.

Nelling, E., & Webb, E. (2009). Corporate social responsibility and financial performance: the "virtuous circle" revisited. Review of Quantitative Finance and Accounting, 32(2), 197–209.

Nidumolu, R., Prahalad, C., & Rangaswami, M. (2009). Why sustainability is now the key driver of innovation. Harvard Business Review. Retrieved from https://hbr.org/2009/09/why-sustainability-is-now-the-key-driverof-innovation.

Nollet, J., Filis G., & Mitrokostas, E. (2016). Corporate social responsibility and financial performance: a non-linear and disaggregated approach. Economic Modelling, 52(B), 400–407.

Owen, D. (2005). CSR after Enron: A role for the academic accounting profession? European Accounting Review, 14(2), 395–404.

Pavelin, S., & Porter, L. A. (2008). The corporate social performance content of innovation in the UK. Journal of Business Ethics, 80(4), 711–725.

Peters, F., & Romi, M. (2015). The association between sustainability governance characteristics and the assurance of corporate sustainability reports. Auditing: A Journal of Practice and Theory, 34, 163–198.

Pfeffer, J., & Salancik, G. R. (1978). The External Control of Organisations: A Resource Dependence Perspective, New York, NY: Harper and Rob Publishers.

Porter, M. E., & Kramer, M. R. (2006). Strategy and society: the link between competitive advantage and corporate social responsibility. Harvard Business Review, 84(12), 78–92.

Porter, M. E., & Kramer, M. R. (2011). Creating a shared value. Harvard Business Review, 89(1 2), 62–77.

Post, C., Rahman, N., & Rubow, E. (2011). Green governance: boards of directors' composition and environmental corporate social responsibility. Business and Society, 50, 189–223.

Reinhardt, F. L., Stavins, R. N., & Vietor, R. H. (2008). Corporate social responsibility through an economic lens. Review of Environmental Economics and Policy, 2(2), 219–239.

Rennings, K. (2000). Redefining innovation–eco-innovation research and the contribution from ecological economics. Ecological Economics, 32(2), 319–332.

Rexhepi, G., Kurtishi, S., & Bexheti, G. (2013). Corporate social responsibility (CSR) and innovation the drivers of business growth? Procedia-Social and Behavioral Sciences, 75, 532–541.

Rodrigue, M., Magnan, M., & Boulianne, E. (2013). Stakeholders' influence on environmental strategy and performance indicators: a managerial perspective. Management Accounting Research, 24, 301–316.

Ruggiero, P., & Cupertino, S. (2018). CSR strategic approach, financial resources and corporate social performance: The mediating effect of innovation. Sustainability, 10(10), 3611.

Rupley, K. H., Brown, D., & Marshall, R. S. (2012). Governance, media and the quality of environmental disclosure. Journal of Accounting and Public Policy, 31(6), 610–640.

Shahgholian, A. (2017). The effect of board roles on firm environmental governance. In *2017 Academy of Management Meeting Proceeding.* https://doi.org/10.5465/AMBPP.2017.13070abstract, Retrieved from: https://journals.aom.org/doi/abs/10.5465/AMBPP.2017.13070abstract, Accessed date: 20.10.2020

Singh, S., & Dhir, S. (2019). Structured review using TCCM and bibliometric analysis of international cause-related marketing, social marketing, and innovation of the firm. International Review on Public and Nonprofit Marketing, 16(2–4), 335–347.

Taljaard, C. C, Ward, M. J., & Muller, C. J. (2015). Board diversity and financial performance: A graphical time-series approach. South African Journal of Economic and Management Sciences, 18, 425–447.

Tasheva, S. N., & Hillman, A. (2018). Integrating diversity at different levels: multi-level human capital, social capital, and demographic diversity and their implications for team effectiveness. Academy of Management Review, 44, 746–765.

Tihanyi, L. D., Griffith, A., & Russel, C. J. (2005). The effect of cultural distance on entry mode choice, international diversification, and MNE performance: A meta-analysis. Journal of International Business Studies, 36, 270–283.

Vishwanathan, P., van Oosterhout, H., Heugens, P. P., Duran, P., & van Essen, M. (2020). Strategic CSR: a concept building meta-analysis. Journal of Management studies, 57(2), 314–350.

Visser, W. (2010). The age of responsibility CSR 2.0 and the new DNA of business. Journal of Business Systems, Governance and Ethics, 5(3), 7–22.

Part 2 Regional Development

Assoc. Prof. Fatih Ayhan and Elias Esteban Silva Lecuna

2.1 Conceptual View of Economic Development

"Poverty has no causes. Only prosperity has causes. Analogically, heat is a result of active processes; it has causes. But cold is not the result of any processes; it is only the absence of heat. Just so, the great cold of poverty and economic stagnation is merely the absence of economic development".

Jane Jacobs (1969). "The Economy of Cities".

Abstract: Economic development is a concept that a country should realize to reach a high human development level. In the literature there are several theories to explain the proper ways to sustainable development. All these development theories, beyond doubt, try to find a model or indices to diminish the inequalities, achieve the sustainable growth, provide higher living standards for the people and protect the environment. This chapter reviews some of the most prominent theories of the economic development. In this context the aim of this chapter is to examine and compare these theories to enlighten the policymakers.

Keywords: Regional development, Poverty, Economic development.

1 Introduction

Human development is defined as the process in which a society, based on economic development, comprehensively improves the living conditions of its members. In this sense, human development means not only that individuals have sufficient resources to cover their basic needs, but also that they have access to health and education systems, adequate levels of personal security, full political and cultural liberties, the ability to cultivate their interests and develop their productive and creative potential, among other things.

Economic development is characterized by its heterogeneity and non-uniqueness of criteria around of a set of various approaches. Throughout the evolution of development economics, numerous and distinct theories have emerged. These theories all come together in different currents of thought and ideologies. And due to important historical moments they were defined with the intention of overcoming obstacles in search of progress. At the present time, the search for development is an everyday issue, but with a more humanistic approach.

Within this framework, in this study firstly, Development versus Economic Growth, with their definitions and differences are conceptualized. Second, the Importance of Development and Modern Development Theories with their socioeconomic dimensions and importance are discussed. Third, a summary of some of the most important development theories is presented, considering the innovations and different perspectives that modern development theories have brought to the concept of development. Following this presentation, the measurement of Development of economic development between countries and their differences according to the main indicators is briefly explained. In addition, up-to-date development indicators and statistics on the countries with the most advanced level of development and the countries with the lowest development level are presented. Next, the terms of Regional Development and their importance for society are described. Finally, the conclusions and final remarks are presented.

2 Development versus Economic Growth

It is important to understand the difference between economic growth and economic development as they advise both government and policy makers on the policies and measures to be taken to improve their performance and that of the country.

Economic growth corresponds to the increase in the value of final goods and services, or the value of the income produced by an economy. When the indicators of economic growth (saving, investment, increased energy consumption, production of goods and services, a favorable trade balance, as well as the increase in calorie consumption per capita, among others) improve, it is a positive sign for the region or the country. This is because theoretically it is an indication that a rise in the living standards of the population is taking place. The economic growth is measured by percentages of increase in the real Gross Domestic Product (GDP).

When a society experiences economic growth, the quality and qualification of human capital increases and progress is made progressively towards industrial development and diversified production. Capital, education and technological advances are some of the causes of economic growth.

The growth of the economy is measured through the Gross Domestic Product (GDP), that is, with the annual increase in GDP in a nation. The countries focus their efforts and advances on economic growth to reach their economic solvency. On the other hand, Economic Development is the ability of a country or region to create wealth in order to promote or maintain the economic and social well-being of its people.

A combination of indicators is used to measure the economic development of a country, including the Gross Domestic Product per capita, life expectancy, education, and other indicators related to economic prosperity and quality of life. All these indices are included in the Human Development Index (HDI) prepared by the United Nations Development Program (UNDP), created to determine how countries help their citizens develop as human beings.

A high growth rate is often mistakenly associated with a high level of development. Both definitions are totally different even though a tight and unbalanced relationship exists between them. That's evident in economies with unstable state models and considerable institutional weakness where high growth rates do not correspond to acceptable levels of development.

There are well defined differences between both terms. It can be said that economic growth means a change in the value of goods and services bringing quantitative changes in the economy over time, while economic development implies changes in the socioeconomic structure of the country related to the Human Development Index (HDI) which mark qualitative and quantitative changes in the economy.

Also, economic growth is measured through Gross Domestic Product (GDP), GDP per capita, gross national product (GNP), and net national product (PNN) while economic development is measured through the human development index (HDI), gender index (GDI), human poverty index (HPS), literacy rate, infant mortality, socioeconomic development, inequalities, etc.

When comparing the performance of two countries, economic growth is used as a parameter, while economic development is only used to measure the progress of developing countries or nations.

3 Importance of Development and Modern Development Theories

The concept of development has several implications in the economy, finances, society and environment. In this respect it promotes a change in the way goods are produced and distributed, productive efficiency, technological advances, economic growth, increase in the levels of investment, savings, income distribution, infrastructure, employment, education, freedom, sustainable development, quality of life, among others.

Development is a comprehensive concept that includes not only the economic aspect, but social and environmental. This transformation of structures within a society (economic and social) should be reached through a better distribution of income and wealth and a participatory democracy in order to constantly improve the development planning. All these supported by the required sustainable economic growth.

When researching on the theories of economic development, you will find a wide variety of theories, which are considered to have been designed throughout the history of capitalism. For the economic development theories, economic growth becomes only an element of development, where it is evaluated economically, humanly and environmentally, from a more comprehensive perspective.

Modernization, dependency, world systems and globalization are generally considered to be the most important economic development theories. Therefore these four theories are presented as follows:

3.1 Modernization Theory

The main assumptions of modernization theory are fundamentally based on the theory of economic development of Rostow (1961). The theory assumes that for less advanced societies in social, economic and cultural matters, that is, less developed ones, become equal to those developed, they must pass in an accelerated way, consciously and by the will of their rulers (which implies social planning) through an equal transition of stages of development as the stages experienced by the most evolved or developed countries socially, economically and culturally.

According to Rostow's theory of economic development, there are five stages for a particular society: the traditional society; precondition for takeoff; the take-off process; the path to maturity; and a society of high mass consumption.

The concept of modernization refers to a sheaf of cumulative processes that are mutually reinforcing: capital formation and resource mobilization; to the development of the productive forces and the increase of labor productivity; to implementation of centralized political powers and the development of identities national; to the dissemination of the rights of political participation; and to the secularization of values and norms; etc.

Modernization processes involve the calculation and control of social processes and that correspond to the development of instrumental rationality, which is contrasts with the concept of normative rationality that corresponds to the modernity oriented to moral autonomy and political self-determination. Not less important among these predictions was the expectation that demographic factors would respond to modernization and fertility rates would decline. It also states that modern societies are more productive, children are better educated, and the needy receive more benefits.

Modernization is a defined as a long, progressive, irreversible, homogenizing and desirable process. It's a change based more on evolution than on a revolutionary leap. It will take generations and even centuries to culminate, and its impact will only be felt through time but in the end it is irreversible.

During the 1960s and the 1970s, it was widely criticized in connection with demonstrating that development is not necessarily unidirectional, showing only one development model (of United States and Europe), and above all because it induces the loss of traditional values.

3.2 Dependency Theory

Economic dependence is a situation in which the production and wealth of some countries is conditioned by the development and conjunctural conditions of other countries to which they are subjected. The "center-periphery" model describes the relationship between the self-sufficient and prosperous central economy and the peripheral, isolated, weak and uncompetitive economies. Faced with the classic idea that international trade benefits all participants, these models argue that only the central economies benefit.

Raul Prebish proposed the economic model called 'Center-Periphery', which describes the relationship between the central and peripheral economies. It presents the former as a self-sufficient and prosperous economy, and the peripheral economies as isolated from each other, weak and not very competitive (Sprout, 1992).

It reacts to the idea that international trade benefits all participating countries and argues that only central economies are benefited. Initially they addressed the Latin American environment although later they were generalized by neo-Marxist economomists. The dependency theory is based on a Marxist view of the world, where globalization is seen in terms of the spread of market capitalism, and the exploitation of cheap labor and resources. All these in exchange for obsolete technologies.

Prebisch (1984) explained how the economic structure based on center-periphery relations produces structural unemployment, imbalance in the trade balance, deterioration in the terms of trade, difficulties in the balance of payments, devaluations and shortage of foreign exchange.

3.3 The World System Theory

Following the theory outlined by Wallerstein (1974), a world-system is a type of social system, (currently the only one existing on a planetary level) based on the existence of a single world division of labor and, at the same time, from multiple cultural systems (which could be equated to civilizations, countries ...). Thus, the concept of the world system, understanding it as a whole, constitutes a "unit of analysis" to understand current international relations. And depending on whether or not the world-system has a common political system for its organization, current political geography distinguishes between world-empires and world-economies

The market is the axis of a single world system induced by globalization processes under the principles of economic liberalism that elevates the liberties of the individual until he achieves his isolation. World systems theory focuses on the study of the social system and its interrelations with the advance of world capitalism as determining forces between different countries, including small ones.

International capital markets shape a new supranational factual power that surpasses the sovereignty of states and controls and imposes a discipline of economic policy that on several occasions causes crisis. Globalized production processes are standardized to integrate into a single global system, subjecting the "logic of geography to the logic of production" in a "space-time compression". The standardization and homogenization of norms is an unavoidable step to deepen globalization processes. The world system proposes the separation of the political and cultural superstructures connected by an international division of labor.

The inequality that exists between the national states that make up the world system is the reason why the most advanced ones appropriate the surpluses of the least advanced. The World-system refers to the interregional and transnational division of labor, which divides the world into Core countries, Semi-periphery countries, and the Periphery countries.

3.4 The Globalization Theory

The theory of globalization emphasizes the development of information and communication technologies. These technologies have transformed the way of doing business and in the lifestyle of the world's population. The Interaction takes place between countries is carried out by the use of very new technologies. Connecting people through these technological advances has as a consequence great structural modifications in the economies and societies of the countries through the creation of different platforms to carry out economic transactions, taking advantage of the "virtual money mechanisms" and unifying the exchange patterns around the world.

Through the process of globalization, one of the essential assumptions is that more and more nations are relying on integrated conditions of communication, the international financial and trading system. Thus, a scenario of greater intercommunication between centers tends to be generated world power and its commercial transactions (Reyes, 2001).

Therefore, Globalization is based on the fact that there is a greater degree of integration within and between societies that directly affects the economic and social changes that are taking place. In addition to technological, financial and political relationships, there are significant elements that emerge thanks to economic communication between countries through institutions, governments, companies and people around the world.

The theory of globalization assumes three fundamental points. The first, establishes that cultural factors in societies. The second assumption establishes that countries are not a priority as units of analysis in the framework of present world conditions, because international relations and global communications make it less significant. And third, thanks to technological advances, a greater number of social sectors will be able to connect with each other and with other groups worldwide.

4 The Measurement of Development

Human development is defined as the process in which a society, based on economic development, comprehensively improves the living conditions of its members. In this sense, human development means not only that individuals have sufficient resources to cover their basic needs, but also that they have access to health and education systems, adequate levels of personal security, full political and cultural liberties, the ability to cultivate their interests and develop their productive and creative potential, among other things.

HDR is an annual report, which is published by the Human Development Report Office of the UNDP. It was first released in 1990. The annual Human Development Report, provides measurement tools, innovative analysis, and policy proposals. The Reports mainly establish five parameters related to Human Development; vulnerability and human development, the state of human development, the position of vulnerable people in a vulnerable world, building resilience and fostering progress. The term vulnerability must be combated, so that all people have the same opportunities and in this way make the principle of universality effective. All of these parameters are presented in a series of analysis and tables related to the five composite human development indices and their components:

- The HDI (Human development index),
- The IHDI (Inequality-adjusted HDI),
- The GII (Gender inequality index)
- The MPI (Multidimensional Poverty Index)
- The GDI (Gender development index), which compares the HDI calculated separately for women and men.

To calculate the HDI it is necessary to take several measures into account such as life expectancy, education, and wealth. For this purpose the UNDP gathers all the date from different UN programs to develop the indicator. Some of the sources consulted are UNESCO, ICF, UNICEF, OECD, UNDESA, THE WORLD BANK and the IMF among others. After all the information has been collected for each country, first dimension indices are calculated and then the HDI is determined. Each country can get a score according to each dimension index as follows:

Health: life expectancy in years, 20 years (minimum) and 85 years (maximum).
Education: expected years of schooling, 0 years (min) and 18 (max); average years of schooling 0 years (min) and 15 (max).
Income: Gross Domestic Product per capita (2011 PPP $) 100 (min) and 75,000 (max).

If a country is found to have the maximum value in everything, its HDI is 1. This means that it has a very high level of development. Otherwise, if a country is found to have minimums in everything, its HDI will be 0. And it means that it has a low development level. The categories given to a country based on its score are shown in the Tab. 2.1.1.

Tab. 2.1.1: The Categorization of the Countries according to HHI Levels. Source: UNDP

HDI Value (x)	Classification of Development
≥ 0,8	Very High Human Development
0,7 $yx < 0,8$	High Human Development
0,55 $x < 0,7$	Medium Human Development
$x < 0,55$	Low Human Development

Tab. 2.1.2: The Countries with the Highest Human Development Indices. Source: UNDP Report, 2019

Rank	**Country**	**Human development index**	**Life expectancy at birth**	**Expected years of schooling (years)**	**Mean years of schooling (years)**	**Gross national income (GNI) per capita (PPP $)**
1	**Norway**	**0.954**	82.3	18.1	12.6	68,059
2	Switzerland	0.946	83.6	16.2	13.4	59,375
3	Ireland	0.942	82.1	18.8	12.5	55,660
4	Germany	0.939	81.2	17.1	14.1	46,946

Tab. 2.1.3: The Countries with the Lowest Human Development Indices. Source: UNDP Report, 2019

Rank	**Country**	**Human development index**	**Life expectancy at birth**	**Expected years of schooling (years)**	**Mean years of schooling (years)**	**Gross national income (GNI) per capita (PPP $)**
177	Eritrea	0.434	65.9	5	3.9	1,708
178	Burkina Faso	0.434	61.2	8.9	1.6	1,705
179	Sierra Leone	0.438	54.3	10.2	3.6	1,381
180	**Mozambique**	**0.446**	60.2	9.7	3.5	1,154

Currently and according to the UNDP report from 2019, the country with the highest Human Development Index is Norway, with a score of 0.954 as it is seen in Tab. 2.1.2, while the country with the lowest score is Mozambique, with a score of 0.446 as it is seen in Tab. 2.1.3.

The HDI has served a lot, especially in raising awareness that not only wealth determines how developed a country is. On the contrary, it shows the existence of countries with great wealth and very low human development.

Nevertheless, the HDI is just an indicator and cannot encompass the entire reality that constitutes a society. In this regard, the HDI leaves out variables that may reflect a delicate situation in a country. Without going too far, we can visualize as an example, a country with an HDI equal to 1. If this country suffers an abrupt drop in its GDP and its population begins to starve, life expectancy would decrease slowly and would not be meaningful but in time. Thus, the HDI is an indicator of how a society develops in the long term.

Another problem that can affect the human development index is unreliable or imprecise data sources, as the case of certain institutions from totalitarian regimes. And finally there is the criticized conception of education, establishing the idea that the more years of schooling, the better the education that people receive.

In any case the HDI constitutes a valuable tool for the Governments and policy maker to have a better perspective when leading their countries on the road to achieve development and to reduce the inequalities in their societies.

5 The Terms of Regional Development and Its Importance for Society

The theory of regional development is based on the same bases as the theory of national development. Both theories attempt to explain the long-term evelopment of a group of people living together within a given territory.

Regional development arises especially to create an environment that favor the adaptation of groups with difficulties to adapt to the new rules of the economic game, through new modes of organization and production that integrate social, environmental and cultural concerns together with the economic considerations, since local development is a strategy whose actors they are the beneficiaries themselves (Segrelles Serrano, 2015). The regional theory has as starting point the Growth pole. It consists in affirming that the growth phenomenon is almost never generalized, but rather is situated within a limited number of cores in which each supplementary activity tends to improve the conditions for growth multiplication.

It is therefore, a process of economic growth and change structural that leads to an improvement in the standard of living of the local population. Three fundamental aspects can be identified: The first one, with an economic nature, where local entrepreneurs use their resources to organize local productive factors with sufficient productivity levels to be competitive in the markets. The second one is socio-cultural, in which values and institutions underpin the process of development. And the third one a political-administrative dimension, where the policies territorial areas allow creating a favorable local economic environment, protecting it from external interference and promote local development.

6 Conclusion

It is undeniable that changes in States can and should be explained from the trends that are present from every development theory. However, the general tendencies of the capitalist mode of production or of the development theories are not expressed in the same way in the different modalities as capital is reproduced, nor under the class struggles in different economic-social formations, which the study demands States and particular economic-social formations.

Although it is not so inexorable that the process translates a backward economy to a "developed" state, it is also likely that the process itself will generate forces that lead to stagnation before such a happy state arises. The experience of underdeveloped countries does not seem to contradict this perspective.

The UNDP postulates that the wealth of a nation constitutes it its people are rescued in the creation of the Human Development Index measure (HDI). The HDI is a composite index of the health index, education index and the income index (and income growth is a partial and erroneous measure of the development of countries). But it has an important factor in opposition: Inequalities.

Measuring inequality of is quite difficult for several reasons. First, opportunities are not observable, as is the case with consumption or income that can be directly estimated. It is a set of options that individuals have to develop their objectives that are not always exercised. Second, the normative nature of equal opportunities gives rise to numerous approaches when measuring this type of inequality and, although there is consensus regarding the basic principles that measures of inequality of opportunity must comply with the rapid development of this field of research, in recent years has led to the use of measures that are not consistent with these principles. Third and lastly, the measurement can be carried out using different methodologies through which different results are obtained whose comparability is not guaranteed.

In any case, all these development theories, with their models and indices are a great and recent effort to push the countries into a better future, where the inequalities are diminished, the economic growth is sustainable, people live in optimum conditions and the environment is fully protected. It looks like impossible and altruistic vision, but Governments and policy makers should plan and achieve it for the generations to come.

References

Jacobs J. (1969). "The Economy of Cities". Knopf Doubleday Publishing Group, July 20, 2016.

Prebisch, R. (1984). Five Stages in My Thinking on Development, Retrieved from http://www.rrojasdatabank.info/pioneers7.pdf (Date of Access: 01.10.2020).

Reyes, G. E. (2001). Teoria de la Globalizacion: Bases Fundamentales, Revista Tendencias, 2(1): 43–53.

Rostow, W. W. (1961). The Stages of Economic Growth: A Non-Communist Manifesto, Cambridge, MA, Cambridge University Press, 1961.

Segrelles Serrano, J. A. (2015). Conceptos Básicos Sobre Desarrollo Local Y Sostenibilidad. Geografía Y Desarrollo Local, Retrieved from https://rua.ua.es/dspace/bitstream/10045/48107/1/Tema_1_DLS.pdf (Date of Access: 02.10.2020).

Sprout, R. V. A. (1992). The Ideas of Prebisch, CEPAK Review, No:46, Retrieved from https://repositorio.cepal.org/bitstream/handle/11362/10395/461771921_en.pdf?sequence=1&isAllowed=y (Date of Access: 01.10.2020).

UNDP (2019). Human Development Report 2019, Retrieved from http://hdr.undp.org/sites/default/files/hdr2019.pdf (Date of Access: 28.09.2020).

United Nations Development Programme (UNDP), Human Development Reports (HDR), Retrieved from http://hdr.undp.org/en/composite/HDI (Date of Access: 02.10.2020).

Wallerstein, I. (1974). The Modern World-System: Capitalist Agriculture and the Origins of the European World-Economy in the Sixteenth Century. (Studies in Social Discontinuity) New York: Academic Press. 1974. Pp. xiv, 410.

Dr. Omca Altın

2.2 The Impact of the EU Regional Policy Developed within the Scope of Lisbon Strategy and Europe 2020 Goals on Overcoming Interregional Differences

Abstract: The European Union, which is a unique form of integration in the world, has made significant economic contributions to the continent. However, developmental differences among the regions within the Union appear as an important problem in the European Union. Especially the dimensions of this problem have increased with the expansion waves of the Union. Hence, the European Union, which includes many different structures, aims to support the development of these regions by creating a strong regional policy for the efficient functioning of the economy, monetary union and common market. By this way, it aims to reduce the existing differences between the regions with the contributions it will provide to the underdeveloped countries and regions in the Union. The European Union tries to facilitate the adaptation of not only the countries and regions within the Union, but also the candidate and potential candidate countries and regions with regional policy. In this chapter, the European Union Regional Policy developed within the scope of the Lisbon Strategy and Europe 2020 targets set forth as a result of global developments, and the effectiveness of the European Union Regional Policy in eliminating interregional differences in the European Union has been tried to be evaluated. In this chapter, literature scanning method was used and current articles, books and European Union reports were examined. As a result of the study, although successful attempts have been made by the European Union with the European Union Regional Policy established within the scope of both the Lisbon Strategy and Europe 2020 targets in order to eliminate regional differences, increase regional competition and ensure regional development; interregional differences continue to be a problem that does not lose their validity in the European Union. Therefore, the European Union should make more effort on this issue and develop different kind of policies to eliminate interregional differences.

Keywords: European Union, EU Regional Policy, Lisbon Strategy, Europe 2020 goals, Interregional differences.

Introduction

Interregional developmental differences in the EU are described as an important problem that can adversely affect both economic and political stability.

Especially, the dimensions of these differences have increased with the enlargement process of the Union. Therefore, the EU Regional Policy was created in order to eliminate interregional development differences which are one of the most important obstacles to European integration, and it has been developed with various regulations in the historical process.

Since 2000, the EU has entered into an important economic and social structuring process. Especially in the face of the new world order brought about by the progressive development of technology and globalization, the EU felt the need to strengthen both its economic and social structure and increase its competitiveness. Therefore, with the Lisbon Strategy EU aimed to make its region's economy to be the most competitive, dynamic and knowledge-oriented one in the international arena until 2010. Especially, by emphasizing the importance of regional policy frequently, regional policy has been an indispensable element of the EU's competitive position. Therefore, the 2007–2013 EU Regional Policy has been revised according to the priority issues within the scope of the Lisbon Strategy targets. However, by the end of 2010, it was observed that the targets set within the scope of the Lisbon Strategy could not be achieved, especially due to the lack of coordination between the member countries and the global economic crisis. For this reason, the attempts of the regional policy of 2007–2013, which were shaped within the scope of the Lisbon Strategy, have not been effective in eliminating the differences between the regions in terms of ensuring income harmony between regions, increasing the competitive structure and employment rate of the regions, realizing both economic and social integration and increasing interregional cooperation,

Following the failure of the Lisbon Strategy, Europe 2020 Strategy was developed by the European Commission, taking into account the serious debt crises faced by the EU peripheral countries as a result of the spread of the crisis of 2008 to Europe in 2010. Within the scope of this Strategy, it is aimed to turn the EU into an economy that focuses on information and innovation, uses its resources appropriately, protects the environment, is competitive and at the same time increases employment opportunities and ensures both social and regional harmony. The importance of regional policy has been emphasized in the Europe 2020 Strategy, and the 2014–2020 EU Regional Policy has been revised according to the Europe 2020 Strategy targets. Some arrangements were made in the EU Regional Policy for the period 2014–2020 and the EU Regional Policy for the period 2007–2013, which were shaped within the scope of the Europe 2020 goals. However, the EU Regional Policy for the period 2014–2020, which was restructured within the scope of the Europe 2020 Strategy, failed to meet the solution expectations regarding interregional development differences. In short, regional development differences continue to be a problem in the EU.

1 The Concept of Territory in the European Union and Current Regional Differences

The region, described as "regio: surrounding area" in Latin, is a concept that has many kinds of meanings. (Sülün, 2005). The region, which is a level used functionally by both the public and private sectors in European countries, is expressed as units with political, economic and administrative characteristics. However, the same regional level cannot be used for all purposes.

For this reason, it should not be forgotten that many factors are effective while defining regions. (Colins and Copperthwaite, 1990: 23). While the factors like geographical, cultural, historical and population factors play an important role in defining the regions, the economic factor appears as another important criterion in this definition. In particular, the evaluation of per capita income within the region reflects the economic situation. (Karluk, 2007: 362–363).

Especially the EU Regional Policy is an important factor in evaluating the level of economic development and welfare factors as important criteria in defining the region (Miric, 2010). Therefore, the fact that the economic development levels differ greatly between the EU member states and the regions within the EU member states has been an important factor in the EU's need for a regional policy. Especially, these differences have increased with the inclusion of new member countries in the EU (Rumford, 2000: 22). For this reason, the EU has created a regional policy in order to create a problem-free economic and social union and at the same time to operate the domestic market without any problems (Efe, Kemahlı & Demirci, 2018: 87). In this way, it aims to minimize the economic and social differences between EU member states by supporting regional development (Miric, 2010). In addition to these, the regional policy established by the EU not only supports regional development but also tries to create a link at the EU level by minimizing the existing development gap between regions (Miric, 2010).

At the same time, factors such as the distribution of natural resources, the distance to domestic and foreign markets, the labor force and the structure of the consumer sector play an important role in determining the development differences between the regions in the EU (Candan, 2001: 36). Especially when we look at the regions with lower levels of development, it is seen that the economies of these regions are mostly based on agriculture, and these regions have low income, high unemployment and a weak infrastructure. The fact that some regions are rich in natural resources that support their economic development, having suitable settlement and transportation facilities, having a good climate and capital equipment make these regions very advantageous compared to other regions (Candan, 2001: 36)

The fact that resources are not evenly distributed in the EU has caused many regions to fall behind. Especially the underdeveloped regions within the EU occupy more space in terms of surface area and although the population living in these regions is more crowded compared to other regions, they are the regions with the lowest contribution to the EU national income. Central countries, on the other hand, occupy the least amount of space and contribute the most to the EU national income. The largest area belongs to underdeveloped and developing countries (Baldwin, 2009: 243).

Therefore, the EU has put the Nomenclature of Territorial Units for Statistics (NUTS) system in order to eliminate these existing differences between the member states and the regions within the EU member states. With the NUTS system, the EU is categorized at the regional level, obtaining, processing and harmonizing regional data, analyzing the regions in socio-economic terms and providing accurate information and data at the regional level in order to implement the regional policy. It is more accurate to compare the data at the regional level, as it is difficult to compare EU member countries with low population such as Malta and Luxembourg with countries with a huge population such as Germany (Efe, Kemahlı, & Demirci, 2018: 90).

With NUTS, the EU classifies regions according to population, economic and social structure (Atmaca and Sağır, 2017: 71). Funds are also distributed according to the NUTS system. Therefore, the NUTS system is extremely important in order to benefit from the financial support provided by the EU, to reduce regional differences, to implement a much more effective regional policy, to determine a strategy, and to realize development projects (Efe, Kemahlı and Demirci, 2018: 91).

With the NUTS system, the EU has tried to reduce the central government and develop local governments. Thus, abandoning the traditional top-down management model of all EU member states. It is aimed that they prefer a bottom-up management model with a modern management policy (Uzay, 2005: 131).

2 EU Regional Policy for the Period 2007–2013 Developed within the Scope of Lisbon Strategy and Its Impact on Overcoming the Interregional Differences

The Lisbon Strategy was prepared by the European Commission as a measure against the problems arising from globalization and at the Lisbon Summit held in March 2000, making the EU the most competitive and knowledge-oriented economy in the world in 2010 and sustainability with more and better job opportunities. It is a document considered as a strategy to achieve economic growth and achieve a wider social cohesion. (Karluk, 2007: 366; Yazıcı, 2018: 436–442).

It has been inevitable for the EU to adapt to the ever-developing information and communication technologies and the new world order that has occurred as a result of globalization. Especially, the rapid increase in competition made it necessary for the EU to reach the level of technologically advanced countries such as the USA and Japan and at the same time to maintain its competitive strength in the international arena by transitioning to a knowledge-based economy against countries such as India, China and South Korea, whose economies are growing gradually. (Akses, 2014: 19). Therefore, by focusing on the knowledge-based economy and competitiveness with the EU Lisbon Strategy, it has determined many targets to increase European competitiveness (Borras, 2009: 97) Thus, the EU tries to close its gap with countries such as the USA and Japan, which are Europe's main global competitors (Bruijn and Langendıjk, 2005: 1153). However, in the Lisbon Strategy, when transitioning to a knowledge-based economy, preventing unemployment caused by this situation has also been an important issue. Within the scope of the Lisbon Strategy, emphasis has also been placed on making social security more modern, creating a strong social cohesion and making efforts to prevent social exclusion (Akses, 2014: 21–22).

The EU which tries to find solutions to the problems arising with globalization with a competitive and at the same time knowledge-oriented economic society (Yazıcı, 2018: 436), has made regional policy an indispensable element of the competitive situation of the EU, especially by stating the importance of regional policy. Therefore, the EU aimed to increase the living standards and quality of the underdeveloped regions within its body on the one hand, and to enable the regional boundaries to compete in the world market and to include strong regional economies in the global production network (European Union, 2009: 6; Yazıcı, 2018: 438).

In this context, the 2007–2013 period EU Regional Policy has been shaped according to the priority issues within the scope of the Lisbon Strategy targets. In this period, it was aimed to ensure income harmony between regions, to increase the competitive structure and employment rate of the regions, to achieve a much more harmonious integration in both social and economic fields and to increase cooperation between regions. In this period, since harmonization and cooperation constitute the basic elements of the EU Regional Policy, the regional policy was also expressed as cohesion policy (Ergüder and

Kocagül, 2008: 68; Kara and Taş, 2013: 111). Therefore, it is foreseen that the EU's cohesion policy will be harmonized with the goals of the Lisbon Strategy by encouraging competition, growth and employment (Wamser, Nam and Schoenberg, 2013: 37).

The EU Regional Policy objectives for the 2007–2013 period have been collected under 3 headings. The first of these goals, the convergence target, was created with the aim of reducing interregional development disparities, and in this context, supporting innovative and knowledge-oriented society understanding in regions with the least development level, adapting to the changes that occur both economically and socially, making the environment better quality and increasing efficiency in administrative terms (Ergüder and Kocagül, 2008: 56). It is envisaged to support competition, regional attractiveness and employment in regions that are outside the target of regional competitiveness and employment, which is the second objective, and convergence from the EU Regional Policy targets. (European Commission, 2006: 2) The third goal, the European regional cooperation goal, aimed to ensure the strong integration of the EU regions in all aspects. In this direction, it has been tried to eliminate obstacles and contribute to the balanced and sustainable development of EU regions with the sharing of experiences and cross-border cooperation (Commission of The European Communities, 2005: 10). Therefore, cooperation within the scope of the goal focuses on international, cross-border and interregional cooperation and completes the other two objectives of the EU Regional Policy for the period 2007–2013 with its applications (European Union, 2007: 20).

On the other hand, the European Neighborhood and Partnership Tool has been used to support cooperation with regions outside the EU. The European Neighborhood and Partnership Tool has been developed especially for non-EU countries such as Switzerland and Norway which are located within Europe. At the same time, The Instrument for Pre-accession Assistance (IPA) was created in order to bring the development levels of the candidate and potential candidate countries to EU standards before they became a member of the EU (Ergüder and Kocagül, 2008: 65; Cihangir, 2011: 23).

In the Fifth Economic and Social Cohesion Progress Report entitled Growing Regions, Growing Europe in 2008, regions were analyzed in three categories as convergence zones, transition zones, and regional competitiveness and employment zones, each of which has different socio-economic characteristics (European Union, 2008: 8).

Especially in the report, while the sectoral distributions of regional economies focusing on EU growth sectors are analyzed, three growth sectors at the regional level are focused on. The first one is financial and business services, the second is trade, transportation and communication, and the third is construction. In this context, as shown in Tab. 2.2.1, these three sectors accounted for 40% of the employment in the convergence regions in 2005 and 50% of the employment in other regions. Therefore, these three sectors are less important in the convergence regions than in other regions. According to 2005 data, it is seen that the agricultural sector constitutes approximately 15% of employment in convergence regions, 5% in transition regions, and 2% in regional competitiveness and employment regions. Therefore, it is seen that the agricultural sector is a very important sector for the convergence regions in terms of employment. Considering the construction sector according to 2005 data, while the construction sector constitutes 10% of the employment in the transition regions, this rate is 7% in the harmony regions and 6% in the regional competitiveness and employment regions. Therefore, transition regions are the region with the highest employment rate in the construction sector compared to other regions. Again, within the scope of 2005 data, it was seen that the region with the highest share of employment in finance and business services is regional competition and employment regions. While the finance and business services sector constitutes 16% of employment in regional competition and employment regions, this rate is seen as 11% in transition regions and 8% in convergence regions. When we look at the trade, transportation and communication sector, which is another sector, it is seen that in 2005, the trade, transportation and communication sector constituted 29% of employment in transition regions, 25% in regional competition and employment regions, and 23% in convergence regions. Therefore, the most advantageous region in this sector is transition zones (European Union, 2008: 8–12).

According to the report, it was emphasized that the sectors such as construction, finance and business services, trade, transportation and communication services for growth in Europe have great contributions in ensuring harmony, but as can be understood from the data, the sectoral distributions differ between regions. Although these three growth sectors in particular play a major role in job creation in convergence zones, they were not sufficient to determine a significant employment decline in agriculture. In short, it has been observed that the economic structure between the three regions differed and the convergence regions underwent an important economic restructuring (European Union, 2008: 10).

In the Economic, Social and Regional Cohesion Progress Report titled Urban and Regional Dimension of the Crisis published by the European Commission in 2013, it was stated that the 2008 crisis had a widespread effect on both developed and less developed regions within the EU. The crisis has ended a long

Tab. 2.2.1: Employment Rates in Six Sectors (%), 2005

Share in 2005 in %	**EMPLOYMENT**			
	CONV	**TRANSITION**	**RCE**	**EU27**
Agriculture, hunting and fishing	15.5	5.2	2.7	6.4
Total industry, including energy	21.4	15.1	17.0	18.1
Construction	7.5	10.4	6.6	7.1
Trade, transport& communication	23.3	29.2	25.9	25.4
Financial and business services	8.5	11.1	16.9	14.2
Other services	23.9	29.0	30.8	28.8
Total	100.0	100.0	100.0	100.0
Share of EU27	**27.5**	**6.1**	**66.4**	**100.0**

Kaynak: European Union, 2008, https://ec.europa.eu/regional_policy/sources/docoffic/official/reports/interim5/com_2008_371_en.pdf.

period of declining regional inequalities in GDP per capita and unemployment. As shown in Fig. 2.2.1, regional differences in per capita GDP decreased every year between 2000 and 2008, while these decreases stopped in 2009 and even started to increase in 2010 and 2011. Likewise, it has been observed that regional unemployment rates converged from 2001 to 2007, but increased every year from 2007 until 2012 (European Commission, 2013a: 13). Therefore, with the effect of the 2008 crisis, it is seen that there is a serious decrease in GDP and interregional adjustment in unemployment. This increasing difference between the regions shows that the regional policy of 2007–2013, in other words, the main objective of the cohesion policy, interregional harmony and cooperation, has been undermined.

On the other hand, more than 6800 projects have been supported within the scope of the cross-border program until 2013 at the point of ensuring international, cross-border and interregional cooperation, which are the European regional cooperation objectives of the EU Regional Policy for the 2007–2013 period. In particular, these projects mostly cover the creation and expansion of economic clusters, the establishment of centers of excellence, cooperation networks between higher education, education and research centers, and cross-border cooperation for businesses and business initiatives. At the same time, until 1300, projects were carried out on subjects like joint management of

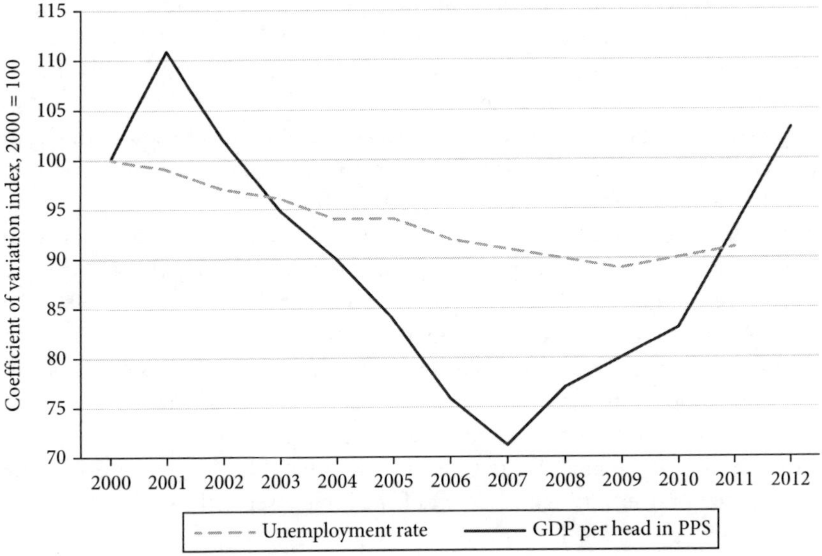

Fig. 2.2.1: Regional Convergence and Crisis. Source: European Commission, 2013a, https://ec.europa.eu/regional_policy/sources/docoffic/official/reports/interim8/interim8_en.pdf.122

natural resources, climate changes, renewable energy, etc. within the scope of these projects, 3500 jobs were created, 487 km of roads were rebuilt, and more than 500,000 people participated in educational activities. However, despite all these developments, most of the projects could not have noticeable effects on the development and integration of the regions (European Commission, 2016: 40–41).

As can be seen, although many attempts were made to eliminate interregional differences with the EU Regional Policy for the period 2007–2013, which was shaped within the scope of the Lisbon Strategy objectives, it was observed that the interregional differences continued.

3 European Regional Policy for 2014–2020 Developed within the Scope of the EU 2020 Goals and Its Impact on Overcoming the Interregional Gaps

With the Lisbon Strategy, the EU has undertaken a very important project that will strengthen its economy and increase its competitiveness in the global arena (European Commission, 2010); however, the multidimensional goals and implementation plans determined by the Lisbon Strategy made this project quite complicated, and serious uncertainties occurred in the distribution of tasks between the EU and member countries at the point of implementation of the measures taken. Therefore, these weak cooperation and conflicting priorities in the reform process were the factors that caused the Lisbon Strategy not to achieve the expected results (Akses, 2014: 24).

On the other hand, as a result of the terrorist attacks of September 11, 2001, rising prices, environmental pollution, and the sudden drop in the stock market indexes of technology-related companies as a result of the "Dot.com bubble" in the USA, investments made in companies operating in the field of information and communication technologies gradually decreased. As a result of this, global developments such as the negative effects of the economies of the USA and the EU from this situation and the decrease in investments in the field of research and development due to economic difficulties have also been other factors that prevent the achievement of the targets set within the scope of the Lisbon Strategy (Kok, 2004).

Another situation preventing the achievement of the targets determined within the scope of the Lisbon Strategy was the financial crisis that emerged in the USA in 2008 and affected the EU (Akses, 2014: 1). Especially the EU's goal of creating an economic structure that can provide better and more job opportunities and social reconciliation and sustainable economic growth has not reached its goal (Akses, 2014: 25). At the same time, this crisis prevented the Lisbon Strategy from achieving its goals regarding employment (European Commission, 2010).

As a result of the enlargement waves in the EU since the adoption of the Lisbon Strategy, which is among the targets of a comprehensive social cohesion in addition to the global financial crisis, the number of members in the EU has increased and economic and social differences within the Union have grown even more (Akses, 2014: 28).

Therefore, following the complicated and challenging implementation of the Lisbon Strategy, as an alternative to the further development of the European integration area in the next decade (Terem, Cajka and Rysova, 2015: 154), the European Commission prepared the Europe 2020 Strategy in 2010 as a continuation of the Lisbon Strategy. The Europe 2020 Strategy tries to increase the competitiveness of Europe in the world economy just like the Lisbon Strategy (Erixon, 2010: 29). With this Strategy, the European Commission aims to make the EU an information and innovation-oriented economy with smart growth until 2020; to establish the foundations of an economy based on sustainable growth and competitive and sustainable use of available resources; with inclusive growth, it aims to harmonize the EU both socially and regionally and to transform it into an economy with high employment rate (Antonescu, 2014: 1094). As it can be understood from here, Europe 2020 Strategy aims to strengthen and develop the economies of all member countries based on knowledge, which is the main factor that determines economic competitiveness in the international arena (Stec and Grzebyk, 2018: 120).

In the Europe 2020 Strategy, it was emphasized that especially the regional policy will contribute to growth and development, and the support given for regional development will accelerate the research, innovation, education and future development of the EU member countries. (European Commission, 2013b: 16). Thus, by reforming the EU Regional Policy by the European Commission in 2011, the legal framework of the EU Regional Policy for the period 2014–2020 was determined in line with the objectives of the Europe 2020 Strategy. In other words, the EU 2020 Strategy has formed the basis of the EU Regional Policy for the period 2014–2020 (European Union, 2011: 1; Efe, Kemahlı and Demirci, 2018: 105).

Within this framework, regions are divided into three as underdeveloped regions, transition regions and developed regions in order to allocate funds for regional development in accordance with GDP. Underdeveloped regions consist of regions whose GDP is less than 75% of the EU average. Supporting the regions in this scope is the priority of the EU Regional Policy. Transition regions include all regions with a GDP between 75% and 90%. Regions with a GDP per capita above 90% of the EU average are also considered as developed regions. The global competition between knowledge-oriented economies in developed regions and problems involving all EU countries such as low-carbon economies are being emphasized (European Union, 2011: 5).

According to the evaluations made regarding the point reached in the seventh Economic, Social and Regional Cohesion Report titled My Region, My Europe, Our Future published by the European Commission, the employment rate of the group between the ages of 20 and 64 increased 1% in 2016 compared to 2008, but it is observed that this rate is below the 75% target set in the Europe 2020 Strategy. On the other hand, the unemployment rate across the EU has dropped from 10.9% in 2013 to 8.6% in 2016 and 7.7% in 2017, although this seems to be a good development, these rates are 7% in 2008 above the unemployment rate. In some countries, this rate is lower than in 2008, while in others it is at least 5% higher. In the report, it is stated that regional differences in unemployment rates did not shrink until 2016, but did not show any expansion. However, according to the report, people under the age of 25 still face

Tab. 2.2.2: Europe 2020 Regional Achievement Indices (EU Targets), 2010–2015

	2010	2015	Change
Less Developed Regions	36	46	10.0
Transition Regions	55	56	3
			0.6
More Developed Regions	76	80	4.5

Source: European Commission, 2017, https://op.europa.eu/en/publication-detail/-/publication/014d75b6-aefa-11e7-837e-01aa75ed71a1.

job problems. Therefore, although some progress has been made towards the European 2020 targets, the targets are still not fully achieved (European Commission, 2017: xii, xiv).

It was also stated in the report that innovation is concentrated in a limited number of regions. Especially in the Northwest Member States, good interregional connections, highly skilled workforce, quality business environments have enabled neighboring regions to benefit from their proximity to the regions of interest. It is stated that innovation is weak in the eastern and southern member states. Regions close to the innovation center cannot benefit from proximity (European Commission, 2017: 34).

When the regions are looked at in Tab. 2.2.2, it is seen that especially the underdeveloped regions achieved a significant success in reaching Europe 2020 targets, as their score increased from 36 in 2010 to 46 in 2015. While the transition regions showed a marginal increase showing the impact of the crisis, the score increased from 76 to 80 in the more developed regions. However, despite the developments, these rates show that there are serious differences between the regions and that these rates are insufficient to reach the Europe 2020 targets (European Commission, 2017: 80–82).

Results and Conclusions

Regional differences in the EU are seen as one of the most important threats endangering the economic and political process. For this reason, reducing interregional differences is among the priority issues of the EU. Especially with the enlargements experienced, the differences between regions have increased even more. Therefore, as a result of the gradual growth of interregional differences, the EU Regional Policy was created in order to eliminate interregional differences and this policy was developed with the arrangements made in the historical process.

For the EU, which has recently followed a policy focused on growth and increasing its competitiveness in the global arena, eliminating interregional differences is a very difficult process. Especially with the EU Regional Policy for the period 2007–2013 developed within the scope of the Lisbon Strategy and the EU Regional Policy for the period 2014–2020 developed within the scope of the Europe 2020 targets, successful steps were taken to eliminate interregional disparities, and an increase in interregional competition in the EU with the funds provided within the scope of regional policy interregional differences are still a problem in the EU.

Therefore, the EU should develop long-term policies and be in more cooperation in the implementation phase in order to achieve the goals within the scope of regional policy, in other words, to reduce interregional disparities. For the EU, the efficient functioning of the economy, monetary union and common market is only possible with a strong regional policy.

References

Akses, S. (2014). Avrupa 2020 Stratejisi (Europe 2020 Strategy). (Publication Number: 269). İstanbul: Economic Development Foundation.

Antonescu, D. (2014). Regional Development Policy ın Context of Europe 2020 Strategy, Procedia Economics and Finance, 15: 1091–1097.

Atmaca, Y. and Sağır, H. (2017). Avrupa Birliği Bölgesel Politikası ve Türkiye: Kalkınma Ajansları Bağlamında Bir Analiz (European Union Regional Policy and Turkey: An Analysis in the Contex of Development Agencies), Artvin Çoruh University International Journal of Social Science, 3(2): 67–88.

Baldwin, R. and Wyplosz, C. (2009). The Economics of European Integration. London: McGraw Hill.

Borras, S. (2009). The Politics of the Lisbon Strategy: The Changing Role of the Commission. West European Politics, 32(1): 97–118.

Bruijn, D. P. and Langendijk, A. (2005). Regional Innovation System in the Lisbon Strategy, European Planning Studies, 13(8): 1153–1172.

Candan, T. (2011). Avrupa Birliği Politikaları (European Union Policies). Ankara: İmaj Publishing.

Cihangir, D. (2011). Sorularla AB Politikaları ve Türkiye Serisi (EU Policies in Questions and Turkey Series), Economic Development Foundation, Number. 8, Publication Number. 247, https://oldweb.ikv.org.tr/images/upload/data/files/bolgesel.pdf, Date of Access: 07.04.2020.

Efe, H., Kemahlı, F. and Demirci, E. (2018). Avrupa Birliği'nde Bölgelerarası Gelişmişlik Farklarının Azaltılması Sorunu ve Birliğin Bölgesel Politikası (The Issue of Development Disparities Among Regions in the European Union and Its Regional Policy), Akdeniz Faculty of Economics and Administrative Sciences Journal, 38: 85–123.

Ergüder, C. and Kocagül, A. D. (2008). Avrupa Birliği'nde Bölgesel Politika'nın Gelişimi ve Yapısal Fonlar (Development of Regional Policy in the European Union and Structured Funds). Ankara: The Economic Policy Research Foundation of Turkey.

Erixon, F. (2010). The Europe 2020 Strategy: Time for Europe To Think Again, European View, 9: 29–37.

European Commission. (2006). Regional Policy, Retrieved from http://ec.europa.eu/regioanl_policy. Date of Access: 03.03.2020.

European Commission. (2010). Commission Staff Working Document: Lisbon Strategy Evaluation Document, Retrieved fromhttps://ec.europa.eu/transparency/ regdoc/rep/2/2010/EN/SEC-2010-114-F1-EN-MAIN-PART-1.PDF. Date of Access: 09.03.2020.

European Commission. (2013a). The Urban and Regional Dimension of the Crisis: Eighth Progress Report on Economic, Social and Territorial Cohesion, Retrieved, from https://ec.europa.eu/regional_policy/sources/docoffic/official/reports/interim8/interim8_en.pdf. Date of Access: 14.04.2020.

European Commission. (2013b). Eurostat Regional Year Book, Retrieved, from https://ec.europa.eu/eurostat/documents/3217494/5784301/KS-HA-13-001-EN.PDF. Date of Access: 08.03.2020.

European Commission. (2016). Commıssıon Staff Workıng Document: Ex Post Evaluation of the ERDF and Cohesion Fund 2007–2013, Retrieved from https://ec.europa.eu/regional_policy/en/information/publications/evaluations/2016/commission-staff-working-document-ex-post-evaluation-of-the-erdf-and-cohesion-fund-2007-13. Date of Access: 15.03.2020.

European Commission. (2017). My Region, My Europe, Our Future: Seventh Report on Economic, Social and Territorial Cohesion, Retrieved, from https://op.europa.eu/en/publication-detail/-/publication/014d75b6-aefa-11e7-837e-01aa75ed71a1. Date of Access: 17.04.2020.

European Union. (2007). Cohesion Policy 2007-13: Commentaries and Official Texts, Retrieved fromhttps://ec.europa.eu/regional_policy/sources/docoffic/official/regulation/pdf/2007/publications /guide2007_en.pdf. Date of Access: 06.03.2020.

European Union. (2008). Growing Regions, Growing Europe: Fifth Progress Report on Economic and Social Cohesion, Retrieved from https://

ec.europa.eu/regional_policy/sources/docoffic/official/reports/interim5/com_2008_371_en.pdf. Date of Access: 08.03.2020.

European Union. (2009). European Regional Policy, An Inspiration for Countries Outside the EU?: Applying the Principles, Sharing the Lessons, Exchanging Experience, Retrieved from https://ec.europa.eu/regional_policy/sources/docgener/presenta/international/external_en.pdf, Date of Access: 11.04.2020.

European Union. (2011). Cohesion Policy 2014–2020: Investing in Growth and Jobs, Retrieved from https://ec.europa.eu/regional_policy/sources/docoffic/official/regulation/pdf/2014/ proposals/regulation2014_leaflet.pdf. Date of Access: 03.04.2020.

Kara, A. M. and Taş, S. (2013). Avrupa Birliği'nde Bölgesel Dengesizlikler ve Bu Dengesizlikleri Gidermeye Yönelik Ekonomik Politikaların Analizi (Regional Imbalances in European Union and the Analysis of Economic Policies to Decrease the Imbalances). Marmara Journal of European Studies, 21(1): 111–137.

Karluk, R. (2007). Avrupa Birliği ve Türkiye (European Union and Turkey). İstanbul: Beta Publishing.

Kok, W. (2004). Facing the Challenge: the Lisbon Strategy for Growth and Employment. Belgium: The High Level Group.

Mellors, C. and Nigel, C. (1990). Regional Policy. London: Routledge in Association with the University of Bradford and Spicers Centre for Europe Ltd.

Miric, O. (2010). The Regional Policy of the European Union as an Engine of Economic Development, Retrieved from http://arhiva.emins.org/uploads/useruploads/knjige/10-regional-policy-eu.pdf. Date of Access: 11.04.2020.

Rumford, C. (2000). European Cohesion?: Contradictions in EU Integration. United Kingdom: Palgrave Macmillan.

Stec, M. and Grzebyk, M. (2018). The Implementation of the Strategy Europe 2020 Objectives in European Union Countries: The Concept Analysis and Statical Evaluation, Springer Qual Quant, 52: 119–133.

Sülün, D. (2005). Avrupa Birliği Bölgesel Politikasının Esasları (Principles of the European Union Regional Policy). İzmir: İzmir Chamber of Commerce Publishing.

Terem, P., Cajka, P. and Rysova, L. (2015). Europe 2020 Strategy: Evaluation, Implementation and Prognoses for the Slovak Republic, Economic and Sociology, 8(2): 154–171.

Uzay, N. (2005). Bölgesel Gelişmişlik Farklılıklarının Giderilmesi ve Bölgesel Kalkınma Ajansları (Elimination of Regional Development Differences and Regional Development Agencies). Ankara: Seçkin Publishing.

Wamser, G., Nam, W. C. and Schoenberg, A. (2013). The Lisbon Agenda and Innovation-Oriented Cohesion Policy: A New Challenge for Economic Integration Among the EU Regions, 28(1): 37–58.

Yazıcı, G. İ. (2018). Lizbon Stratejisi ve Avrupa 2020 Hedeflerinde Bölgesel Kalkınma ve Sosyal Politikalar (Regional Development and Social Policies in Lisbon Strategy and Europe 2020 Targets). International Journal of Management Academy, 1(3): 436–451.

Dr. Selin Pelek and Dr. Olivier Gajac

2.3 Solidarity Economics in Turkey: Its Ecosystem and Relations with Public Authorities

Abstract: The emergence of solidarity economy initiatives in Turkey calls us more generally to question the relationship between the actors of social entrepreneurship and the public authorities, and more particularly, the way that they evolve in an unfavorable ecosystem. If history reminds us that the actors of social entrepreneurship in Turkey have suffered from recurrent political instability, and that they have more or less deviated from the legal essence of their vocation, we would like to better understand recent solidarity economy initiatives and their socio-economic and socio-political dimensions. We rely on the field research carried out between September 2017 and September 2019 in several sectors (short food circuit, alternative education, self-construction, and social assistance to refugees). These data allow us to claim that solidarity economy initiatives are taking up issues in order to meet expectations, aspirations and more justice compared to society market and state structures. Secondly, for most of them, it emerges that they also do not renounce the principles of the rule of law by promoting the functioning of participatory democracy. Nevertheless, while they contribute to real civic governance, their instrumentalization by the public authorities should not be ruled out.

Keywords: Solidarity economy, Public authorities, Self-organization.

Introduction

This chapter explores the recent rise of solidarity economy initiatives in Turkey. First of all, contemporary forms of social entrepreneurship have a long history which dates back to the late Ottoman period. We begin with a brief summary of this history. The issue concerning civil society actors and their interactions with public authorities is highly complicated by reason of the fact that civil society is a relatively unclear notion itself and difficult to understand. In this regard, François Rangeon emphasizes that the notion of civil society finds its full meaning in a genealogical approach that history makes it possible to better understand over time and in its context (Rangeon, 1986: 10–11).

Associated with a process of individualization and amplified through their experiences related to unique events in contemporary Turkey, these new solidarity economy initiatives reflect a form of emancipation and/or "desertion" leading people to reconsider themselves (Sue, 2016: 25). In this chapter, we aim at examining specifically their relationships with the public authorities in the context of the various purposes that they serve. We focus on an analysis of the emancipatory potential of solidarity economy initiatives in a neoliberal context, and a political re-hierarchization of the territory (Massicard, 2014: 8). We discuss the fragility and precariousness of their economic model and explain the institutional constraints and/or the choice of actors to rely on self-organization and their involvement in cooperative networks. In addition, we seek to understand the ecosystem of these new solidarity economy initiatives which seems reluctant to establish partnership relations with public authorities. We argue that the history of social entrepreneurship in Turkey has been relatively marked by recurrent political instability, and sometimes this entrepreneurship would be instrumentalized for ideological, political and economic purposes. Lastly, we claim that the process of the emergence of new solidarity economy initiatives outside of the public power and the market takes shape in a context of political contestation and social movements to meet expectations, unfulfilled aspirations and to achieve more justice. This is a new associative fact that makes to emerge diverse forms of commitment, especially in terms of mutual aid (or reciprocity) and solidarity towards the most fragile populations such as refugees.

The literature on civil society and social entrepreneurship (namely, cooperatives, foundations and associations) in Turkey is relatively abundant. A number of studies focus on the foundations (*vakıfs*) of the Ottoman Empire and highlight their role in establishing public services (Peri, 1992: 168–167; Singer, 2005: 484; Veinstein, 2010: 87–88). Another group of works examines the nationalization process of these former organizations inherited from the Ottoman Empire (Bilici, 1992: 18) and the development of civil society organizations in line with the modern values of the 1923 Republic of Turkey. In general, they tend to demonstrate the strong control of the state and the instrumentalization of these civil society actors for political and economic purposes (İnan, 2004). The growth of civil society on the political agenda, however, was evident in the 1980s, and strengthened in the following decade due to two major events occurred in Turkey: the Second United Nations Conference on Human Settlements (Habitat II) held in Istanbul in 1996, Habitat II which mobilized civil society organizations, and the 1999 earthquake, which marked a surge of solidarity for the victims (Bikmen and Meydanoğlu, 2006: 14). We can also identify the Islamic movement of the 1970s and its philanthropic organizational capacity in the 1980s and 1990s. Through community-based civil society organizations such as foundations or associations, Islamic movement have survived in the turbulent political contexts associated with the coups d'états in 1971 and 1980 (Bilici, 1992: 18). This philanthropic organizational structure dealing with the social problems, enabled Islamic parties to be legitimized on the local political scene (Massicard, 2009). Besides, Dorronsoro (2005) highlights the emergence of social mobilizations in the 1990s and 2000s, and the different repertoires of collective actions challenging public policies. In this vein, in the 2010's, a literature appears on the theme of counter-public spaces, such as urbanization, ecology, consumption and housing (Gajac, 2018; Gajac and Akyıldız, 2020; Gajac and Pelek, 2019) but also on new generations of cooperatives (Gönenç and Rehber, 2007) and women's cooperatives (Çınar, 2020).

1 Civil Society Organizations and Public Authorities: A Conceptual Framework

For many scholars, the concept of civil society is relatively ambiguous (Otayek, 2002: 193–194; Pirotte, 2007; Rangeon, 1986: 9). The history of the word – in its Western conception – would not be comprehensible in isolation, as it takes on its full meaning in the shifts and transformations of the issues in which it is inserted (Rangeon, 1986: 10). As such, this concept would only have its equivalent in the depth of its scientific genealogy (Otayek, 2002: 194). In fact, civil society can often be seen as being in opposition to the state or as a place where the public and the private interact. Originally, civil society in Aristotle's thought referred to the community of citizens, i.e., the state, whereas today civil society is in opposition to the state (Rangeon, 1986).

Thus, in the West, the history of civil society could be linked to the process of individualization. From philosophers to contemporary thinkers, it would be the expression of an opposition to the state of nature, the state, bourgeois society and authoritarian regimes. For instance, its return in the 1970s is correlated with the anti-authoritarian problems of Eastern European countries (Otayek, 2002: 194).

In Turkey, the relationship between civil society and public authorities seems to have been marked by an ideological "back-to-back" or "backyard" relationship in the contemporary period, in which civil society organizations have always been perceived as a threat to order by the public authorities (Kaboğlu, 1990: 3). Indeed, freedom of association in Turkey would suffer from political instability due to the recurrent political-ideological quarrel between moderns and conservatives, which according to Ergun Özbudun is the most important dividing line in Turkey's modern politics (2014: 155). This fact leads us to analyze the current period in order to better understand the role of solidarity economy initiatives in Turkey. According to the findings of field research, the majority of solidarity economy initiatives are legally recognized but do not really find an echo with the public authorities. Besides, they produce positive results in terms of the consolidation of social links, the valorization or reactivation of local resources, as well as the economic and sustainable development (Gajac and Pelek, 2019). In this study, we try to understand their socio-economic and socio-political dimensions, that is to say, the process of emergence of new solidarity economy initiatives, their manner in terms of consolidation, and their relations with public authorities via a field study.

For this purpose, we used different qualitative survey methods over the period from September 2017 to September 2019. First, we conducted 25 semi-structured interviews from September 2017 to September 2018 across Turkey in different cities (Istanbul, Izmir, Ankara, Gaziantep, Eskisehir, Kocaeli) and one village (Sirince). These civil society actors are involved in various sectors such as short food circuit, alternative education, self-construction, collective catering and aid to refugees. In the second step, we employed the social intervention method during two working days in December 2018 by re-solicitation of the first solidarity economy initiatives met in the field and by inviting new initiatives from several cities and villages (Istanbul, İzmir, Artvin, Hatay, Düzce). A total of twenty-three actors took part in these two days, and discussed their experience on the basis of an established activity framework. The characteristic of these days was to develop a transversal analysis between actors involved in solidarity economy initiatives and actors from different sectors of intervention.

In the third step, we conducted a series of interviews, between February 2019 and September 2019, with two solidarity initiatives already met (Hatay, Artvin) and new seven initiatives in other cities (Adana, Mersin, Tunceli, Çanakkale, Istanbul). During this last stage, we focused on the relationship with the public authorities. For all the approaches, we preferred a content analysis of the interviews and exchanges of the social intervention method. The analysis of this large field work has been presented in the 7th CIRIEC International Research Conference on Social Economy in June 2019. This chapter is based on this field work and should be considered a synthetized version of the communique presented in the CIRIEC conference[1]. Even though, the field work covers several sectors, in this chapter we focus on four of them (short food circuit, alternative

1 For the French version of this communique, please see: http://www.ciriec.uliege.be/repec/WP20-02.pdf

education, self-construction, and social assistance to refugees) and exclude popular university, culture, collective catering and women's initiatives for the sake of brevity. We have preferred to identify the participants with reference to their field of activity without calling them by their individual names. These initiatives are formally organized as cooperatives and associations. Therefore, we would like to revise the history of them with a particular focus on their relations with public authorities.

2 Cooperatives and Associations: Two Contemporary Actors Inherited from the Ottoman Empire

As the intermediaries between society and the state, associations and cooperatives have been playing an essential role in terms of redistribution of the resources and the social welfare. In this part of the study, we aim at looking the evolution of these two elements in a brief historical perspective beginning from the Ottoman Empire to present.

The history of cooperatives in Turkey begins with "Community Funds" (Memleket Sandıkları) founded by Mithat Pasha in 1863 (Kocturk, 2006). This funding system was based on the direct collaboration between state and peasants. The aim was to provide cheap credits to peasant by eliminating pawnbrokers. However, it was not until 1969, the modern democratic cooperatives were defined in a legal basis. 1961 constitution act put emphasis on cooperatives. Article 51 on the development of cooperatives was saved in 1982 constitution:

> "The state shall take measures in keeping with national and economic interests, to promote the development of cooperative, which shall be primarily designed to increase production and protect consumers" (Article 171).

Referring to 1961 constitution, a special law concerning cooperatives (Law No: 1163) came into force in 1969. In this legal framework, State is supposed to have responsibility to support cooperatives. According to the Law 1163, State should promote the development of the cooperatives without weakening the democratic structure and autonomy of them (Dogan and Yercan, 2016). Article 1 of the Law 1163 defines a cooperative as following:

> "A cooperative is defined as a body with variable members, variable capital and legal identity that is established by natural and public legal entities and private administrations, municipalities, villages, societies and associations in order to ensure and maintain certain economic interests and specifically the needs of their members

toward professional life and living standards by means of mutual assistance, solidarity and service as trustees to each other."

On the legal basis, the foundation of a cooperative is easier than the foundation of a company. Each member has a right to vote, hence the operation is intended to be democratic. Moreover, the tax burden of the cooperatives is quite mitigated. In the legal framework, they are exempted income tax and property tax given that the law considers them as a legal entity. The agricultural cooperatives are exempted from the value added tax and the transportation cooperatives are exempted from the corporate tax. In this regard, it could be argued that the tax burden of the cooperatives is smaller in Turkey compared to many European countries such as France or Germany. However, in Europe the cooperatives have a broader organizational power and collaboration with professional associations. These types of capacities are more limited for cooperatives in Turkey (Dogan and Yercan, 2016).

Three ministries are responsible for cooperatives: Ministry of environment and urbanization, ministry of agriculture and forestry and ministry of customs and trade. The later has prepared a comprehensive report on the cooperatives in Turkey in 2016. According to this report, the number of the cooperatives was 53259 as of 2016. They have approximately 7.5 million members in total. The participation rate to the cooperatives is about 9.5%. It should be noted that this percentage relatively low compared to European Union countries. In total, the participation rate to cooperatives in Europe is about 17%. This rate reaches to 85% in Finland. Therefore, one can suggest that the cooperative system in Turkey is far away from European standards and there is still room for its development.

The fields of activity of the cooperatives in Turkey are various. They operate in 30 economic fields including agriculture, construction, transportation, pharmacy, insurance, education, etc. According to directorate general of cooperatives, the numerous cooperatives are construction cooperatives, agricultural development cooperatives and motorized transporter cooperatives.

The associations are the most prominent component of NGOs in Turkey. According to governmental statistics, the number of active associations in Turkey is 116 686 as of 2018.[2] They vary in terms of types and topics. There are associations which are in service in professional, religious, educational, cultural, humanitarian relief, social assistance areas. In the field of social policy,

---

2 For the detailed statistics on associations in Turkey, see https://www.siviltoplum.gov.tr/dernek-sayilari

AKP government has placed emphasis on the Islamic associations within the context of "new welfare governance" (Bugra and Candas, 2011).

The political climate has significantly affected the historical evolution of the associations. The first associations with in-cash contributions had begun in the pre-Tanzimat reform era (Sezer, 2008). Although in the 1876 constitutional law there was not any provision on the liberty of founding an association, it was possible to create an association with the authorization of the sultan. The first Law of Associations dated to 1909. This law recognized the right to form an association, however this right was strictly under the control of the executive power (Sezer, 2008). After the second constitutional period in 1908, the constitutional change in 1909 firstly guaranteed the right of association and it was preserved in 1924 Constitution Act. However, the Treason Act on 24 April 1920 forbade to found an association who exploit religion for political gain. The new Law of Associations in 1938 No. 3512 authorized the government for the closure of the inappropriate associations. In 1946, with the change in law, the liberty to found an association was reinstated.

1961 and 1982 Constitutional Acts recognize the right to form an association, but during this period, some of them have been transformed into foundations so as not to be bothered by the State, such as Islamic associations (Bilici, 1993). However, the limitations on the practice has been criticized in terms of the implementation of the pluralistic democracy. Yet, in 2004 the actual Law of Associations No. 5253 went in effect and the provisions in accordance with the international conventions and the European Union criteria were accepted within the legal basis. However, there is still an ongoing debate about the pression exerted by the State on the right of association and freedom of expression of civil society as a whole, given that several civil society organizations have been closed from the Gezi Park movement of 2013 until recent years.

The issue of civil society actors in Turkey, whose projects of autonomy remained dependent on centralist policies, has taken a different direction as a result of the social movement in the Gezi Park in 2013. It seems obvious that, as a result of this social movement, many collective initiatives have emerged in Istanbul and throughout Turkey (Gajac and Akyıldız, 2020) addressing various social issues such as education, urban policies and major projects, the environment, social rights, academic freedom, women and consumption. In these new initiatives operating in various areas, citizens are committed to meeting expectations and have new aspirations for more justice that the State and the market do not satisfy. While some initiatives remain without status, others have adopted the status of enterprise, cooperative or association. These initiatives emanate, for the majority, of citizens, but they are still very much favored and controlled by the local authorities and the State in the case of women's cooperatives (Çınar, 2020) and NGOs for refugees (Danış, 2018; Nalbantoğlu, 2018).

3 New Forms of Solidarity-Based Economy Initiatives

If, as we have seen, citizens have grasped new social issues with regard to their aspirations and expectations, the resulting solidarity economy initiatives tend to highlight two features that characterize them in their relationship with public authorities. First of all, they aspire to operate on models of self-organization, which are based in their emergence phase on a principle of reciprocity, and in their consolidation phase, more on recourse to the market. Secondly, these non-monetary-market modes of self-organization will experience a process of differentiation, on the one hand, because of their plural form of commitment and multiple aims, and on the other hand, because of the limits of the ecosystem related to the field of activity in which they operate. In this sub-section, we would like to report the main outcomes of our interviews with the new solidarity initiatives according to their field.

3.1 Short Food Circuits

We observe new economic social movements in which solidarity economy initiatives adopt themselves to bring an external critique to the public authorities and the market in the field of short food circuit. There is a great diversity of forms in this field (consumer communities, producer cooperatives, urban gardens, and individual intermediaries, direct sales on the farm or via the web). They have been developed in many cities and tend to multiply as alternatives to traditional distribution channels based on intensive agriculture and agro-industrial actors. Mostly citizen-initiated, although some municipalities seem to be taking initiatives in this direction such as the creation of organic markets, their economic model of resource hybridization uses non-monetary and market resources.

Relying on both volunteer work and the sale of agricultural products, these initiatives seek to bring consumers closer to producers by eliminating the intermediaries. This type of citizen-market model aims to promote environmentally friendly agriculture, better prices for farmers and healthier food for consumers. These initiatives seek to establish a multilateral reciprocity, based on trust, which involves actors in the short food circuit (consumers and farmers) and ecologically sensitive civil society organizations. Since they have been set up outside the public authorities' sphere, they can preserve a form of self-management. On the other hand, the government seems to be anchored in a productive logic of agriculture, while local authorities seem to express some doubts about these initiatives due to the lack of agricultural product certification. However, local authorities tend more and more to get involved with farmers and village communities of female farmers in order to support small-scale farming, and to propose an alternative to agro-industrial agriculture, but also to enhance the value of their territory. In some cases, this interest of the local authorities has turned against the village communities of female farmers as they seek to emancipate themselves from patriarchal community. Some of these initiatives remain informal in order to avoid the administrative burdens which represent in a sense, a barrier for farmers wishing to commercialize their products.

3.2 Alternative Education

In a similar way, alternative education initiatives are part of a process of emancipation and desertion from public power and the market. The inadequacy of the public and private educational provision in terms of quality induces families to start creating innovative school models in which the educational project takes into account the development of children, their well-being and awareness of environmental and democratic issues. In their emergence phase, the economic model relies on non-monetary resources, i.e. the voluntary participation of families (as the members of the cooperative) in the running of the school and extra-curricular activities, but also of non-member volunteers. In fact, the model is based on peer reciprocity in order to meet the expectations of parents who wish to offer an educational model different from that proposed by the public authorities and the market. This economic model tends to be legitimized and consolidated with the use of market resources, i.e., paid schooling. This non-monetary and monetary market model also makes it possible to provide, at the margin, scholarships to families who would not have sufficient means to cover the school fees. They have experienced some reluctance to be legally recognized by the public administration. They also do not benefit from financial assistance from the public authorities, while the State supports private colleges, high schools and universities. In fact, they have sought recognition from the public authorities in order to be able to grant scholarships to families and reduce the cost of schooling. In the face of the public authorities' refusal, their economic model is precarious and fragile, even though they have demonstrated that they have the capacity to ensure the professionalization of teaching and technical staff. This professionalizing transition linked to a growing demand from families is not without tension between volunteer families and salaried employees.

3.3 Self-Construction

The recognition of public authority is much more conflictual in the field of construction. This initiative is first of all part of the register of modes of action of social movements. After the 1999 earthquake, abandoned residents initiated a cooperative to claim the right to live in their environment, they also objected to the government's failure to guarantee their right to housing, and refused to assume the financial cost themselves of moving individually. They hold a demonstration in 2003 in Ankara and sit-in protest in 2004. Faced with a form of indifference on the part of the public authorities, this cooperative then adopted a logic of movement in 2005 with legal proceedings against the Ministry. This logic of movement aims rather at "the modification of existing rights, or even more broadly of legal provisions in order to introduce into the local community people who are partially or totally excluded from it" (Haeringer, 2002, 38). This appeal by the cooperative received a favorable response from the administrative court in 2007, which obliged the State to make available to the cooperative building land at appropriate borrowing rates. Nevertheless, administrative reluctance persists, as the handover of the land by the Social Housing Organization (TOKI) and the Ministry of the Environment and Urbanization did not take effect until July 2012, five years after the administrative court's decision. This relationship with the public authorities will lead the members of the cooperative to adopt a model of self-organization for the construction of their own housing. This self-construction initiative is based essentially on peer reciprocity and the voluntary commitment of the members of the cooperative. At the same time, however, we observe the involvement of academics providing expertise and advice throughout the operation of this initiative, which also reflects the characteristics of multilateral reciprocity. This initiative has led both to internal criticism through demonstration and sitting and to external criticism through the adoption of a model of autonomous self-organization. By receiving the World Habitat Prize in 2017, after 18 years of resistance, this initiative has highlighted an alternative construction model in the face of public housing policies and private actors in the building sector.

3.4 Social Assistance to Refugees

In the face of the civil war in Syria and its open door policy, the Turkish government quickly perceived the limits of its policy of welcoming Syrian refugees, most of whom were located in camps close to the border area with Syria. This situation gave room for civil society organizations or local and national NGOs. Nevertheless, the government would remain reluctant until 2015 to allow international NGOs to intervene. As the work of Sare Nalbantoğlu shows, new NGOs would emerge alongside the existing civil society organizations in Turkey, which would broaden their scope of action on the refugee issue (Nalbantoğlu, 2018). While in the first few years these actors limited themselves to covering basic necessities, the continuation of the civil war and the massive influx of refugees raised questions about the action of all institutional actors, as Turkish government, NGOs or international organizations, in the perspective that Syrian refugees could remain in Turkey in the long term. Consequently, NGOs have turned to schemes for the social and professional integration of Syrians with the support of various countries (from the Middle East, the United States and European countries) (Nalbantoğlu, 2018). In addition to the fact that they will encounter some difficulties in obtaining permits for the implementation of training programs, many NGOs have relatively close links with the local municipalities that had taken the initiative to create them from the beginning of the refugee crisis. Generally speaking, the civic movement in favor of the Syrians and the subsequent inclusion of these NGOs in partnership relations with donors meant that these initiatives made use, in the emergence phase, of non-monetary resources coupled, in the consolidation phase, with non-market resources for the social and occupational integration of Syrian refugees into the labor market. In their emergence and consolidation phases, these solidarity initiatives are part of a logic of unequal assistance in the sense that refugees do not participate in decisions relating to the services offered to them. They are only the beneficiaries, with the exception of one association which has built its project by including the contribution of Syrians as main actors in the activities developed in a spirit of reciprocity with peers. While the majority of NGOs are rather instrumentalized by multiple institutional actors, few NGOs are able to reconcile participatory democracy and socio-economic integration. In this field, we see the instrumentalization of NGOs for the purposes of public power and the market, especially in employment programs.

Conclusion

The emergence of solidarity economy initiatives in Turkey would stand out from the history of social entrepreneurship by emanating from a citizen impulse. In this chapter, the four areas examined allow us to draw several observations from the perspective of the relationship between these solitary initiatives and the public authorities.

First of all, almost all of them rely, in their emergence phase, on a high degree of autonomy and a self-organization model, except for certain initiatives for refugees that are driven by municipalities. In this first phase, most of the solidarity initiatives (short food circuit, alternative education, self-construction and refugees) make an external criticism of the State and the market, and only one (self-construction) adopts a parallel internal criticism of the State in order to obtain recognition of the latter in terms of rights.

This criticism seems above all socio-economic rather than socio-political (except for self-construction), but their economic model, which is more autonomous and self-managing, emphasizing a much more horizontal rather than vertical functioning like the classic civil society organizations, is not without effect on the process of emancipation of individuals, as they are capable of creating a democratic citizen public space.

Secondly, in their consolidation phase, these solidarity initiatives develop various alterities to the market and the State. This differentiation would be based on the different aims and purposes of solidarity initiatives, but also on whether or not public power is recognized. In this way, two solidarity initiatives (short food circuit and self-construction), which are very attached to their autonomy, will strengthen their economic model through self-management and through multipartite reciprocity networks of actors at both the national and interurban levels. Conversely, alternative education, which has sought to establish a partnership relationship with the public authorities for the recognition of its solidarity-based economic model, has not obtained satisfaction and support from the State as is the case with private colleges, high schools and universities.

Finally, the majority of NGOs working on behalf of refugees, as a result of citizen impetus and the emergence of new NGOs and/or the orientation of existing NGO projects, have gradually been institutionalized for the purposes of the public authorities and the market. This instrumentalization seems to be effective for solidarity initiatives initiated by municipalities, but it has also been consolidated in the framework of the national reception policy and cooperation with international actors.

As a result, some actors tend to defend their principle of autonomy and democratic project, and others are forced by the ecosystem to maintain their self-organization model. This manifest lack of partnership relations, whether desired and/or constrained vis-à-vis the State, does not detract from their effect on local, social, cultural, economic and sustainable development. On the contrary, some of them demonstrate a capacity for social innovation, the reliability of their hybrid economic model, different from the market and the State, but also a strong potential for instilling civic or citizen governance.

What is at stake for these solidarity economy initiatives is the continuation of their internal democratic project and their capacity for coordination in order to strengthen their economic model. Full legitimacy with public authorities is also a crucial issue. The risk that they may fall into a form of political clientelism vis-à-vis local and public authorities or that they may be institutionalized for the purposes of the State and/or the market cannot be excluded, as the example of NGOs, whose operation is based much less on a principle of participatory democracy that is more beneficial to the Syrians, tends to prove. These results lead us to pursue and broaden our field of investigation in order to verify whether these solidarity economy initiatives would be a process in favor of civic or citizen governance and/or to identify other forms of governance.

References

Bikmen, F. and Meydanoğlu, Z. (2006), Civil Society in Turkey: An Era of Transition. Civicus civil society index country report for Turkey, Istanbul: TUSEV Publishing.

Bilici, F. (1992), « Acteurs de développement des relations entre la Turquie et le monde turc: les vakifs », dans CEMOTI, 14, 17–29.

Bilici, F. (1993), "Sociabilité et expression politique islamistes en Turquie. Les nouveaux vakifs." *Revue française de science politique*, 43(3), 412–434.

Bugra, A. and Candas, A. (2011), "Change and Continuity under an Eclectic Social Security Regime: The Case of Turkey", Middle Eastern Studies, 47(3), 515–528.

Çinar, K. (2020), *"Pour les femmes par les femmes". Une analyse des rapports entre les coopératives de femmes et les pouvoirs publics locaux à Istanbul*, unpublished manuscript, Galatasaray University, Department of Sociology.

Daniş, D. and Nazli, D. (2018), A Faithful Alliance between the Civil Society and the State: Actors and Mechanisms of Accommodating Syrian Refugees in Istanbul, International migration, 57(2), 143–157

Doğan, Z. A. and Yercan, M. (2016), Tu̇rkiye ve AB Ülkelerindeki Kooperatifçilik Mevzuatının Karşılaştırmalı Analizi [Comparative Analysis on Cooperative Legislation between Turkey and EU Countries], Turkish Journal Agricultural Economics, 22(2): 49–58.

Dorronsoro, G. (2005), La Turquie conteste. Mobilisations sociales et régimes sécuritaires, Paris: CNRS Éditions.

Draperi, J.-F. (2006), « L'État et les associations. Du face à face au coude à coude », in: Bureau M.-C. et al. (dir.), Défaillance et inventions de l'action sociale, Paris: éd.

Gajac, O. (2018), "Desertion (Forced) and Reconstruction of Another Society". In: A. E. Erbaş (eds.), Paradigms and Understanding Social Issues, London: IJOPEC Publication (IPOJEC Publication, 153–163.

Gajac, O. and Akyildiz, S. (2020), En cours de publication. Cinq ans après Gezi: de la contestation à l'émergence de formes plurielles d'engagement, Revue Confluences Méditerranée.

Gajac, O. and Pelek, S. (2019), Solidarity Economy Initiatives in Turkey: From Reciprocity to Local Development? Review of Applied Socio-Economic Research, 18(2), 30–42.

Gönenç, S. and Rehber, E. (2007), "The Restructuring of Agricultural Sales Cooperatives and New Generation Cooperatives, in, the Key Problems and Solutions of Cooperatives In Turkey, Ankara: Gazi University Cooperative Research and Application Center Directorate, 58–69.

Haeringer, J. (2002), « Identifier les logiques institutionnelles ». In: F. Traversaz, et J. Haeringer (Eds), Conduire le changement dans les associations d'action sociale et médico-sociale, Paris: Dunod, 19–53.

Inan, I. H. (2004), Tü̇rkiye'de Tarımsal Kooperatifçilik ve AB Modeli, Istanbul: İstanbul Ticaret Odası Publishing.

Kaboğlu, İ. Ö. (1990), De la liberte d'association en Turquie. Dicle Üniversitesi Hukuk Fakü̇ltesi Dergisi, 4(4), 3–43.

Koçtürk, O. M. (2006), Tü̇rkiye'de Kooperatiflerin Vergilendirilmesi. [Taxation on Cooperatives In Turkey] Journal of Celal Bayar Üniversity, 13(2), 119–136.

Massicard, E. (2009), « L'islamisme turc à l'épreuve du pouvoir municipal. Production d'espaces, pratiques de gouvernement et gestion des sociétés locales », Critique Internationale, 42(1), 21–38.

Massicard, E. (2014), "Une décennie de pouvoir AKP en Turquie : Vers Une Reconfiguration Des Modes De Gouvernement ?" *Les études du CERI,* 205.

Nalbantoğlu, S. (2018), *Rôle des organisations non gouvernementales à Istanbul sur l'insertion par l'activité économique des Syriens*, unpublished manuscript, Galatasaray University, Department of Sociology.

Otayek, R. (2002), « Vu d'Afrique. Société civile et démocratie. De l'utilité du regard décentré », Revue internationale de politique comparée, 2002, 2(9): 193–212. DOI 10.3917/ripc.092.0193.

Özbudun, E. (2014), "AKP at the Crossroads: Erdoğan's Majoritarian Drift", South European Society and Politics, 19(2), 155.

Peri, O. (1992), "Waqf and Ottoman Welfare Policy", Journal of the Economic and Social History of the Orient, 35(2), 167–186.

Pirotte, G. (2007), La notion de société civile, Paris: La Découverte.

Rangeon, F. (1986), « La société civile. Histoire d'un mot », dans CURAPP (eds.), La société civile: Presses Universitaires de France, 9–32.

Sezer, T. D. (2008), Dernek Kurma Özgürlüğünün İçeriği ve Gelişim Süreci Üzerine Karşılaştırmalı Bir İnceleme [Content of Freedom of Association and A Comparative Study on the Development: Process]. Journal of Dokuz Eylul Üniversity's Social Sciences Institute, 10(1), 1–58.

Singer, A. (2005), "Serving Up Charity: The Ottoman Public Kitchen", Journal of Interdisciplinary, 3, XXXV, 481–500.

Veinstein, G. (2010), « Trésor public et fortunes privées dans l'Empire ottoman (milieu xvie – début xixe siècles) », Cahiers de la Méditerranée, 80, 187–198.

Dr. Muhammet Arucu and Dr. Taner Kalaycı

2.4 Contribution of University-Industry Collaboration in Science, Technology and Innovation

Abstract: High technology, high-added value products, national innovation and patenting requirements for developing countries are key factors in sustainable growth in association with university-industry-state collaboration. Since collaboration is related to the transfer of information and technology, it is an extremely important field of study that helps companies to be more competitive for the world economies. In order to develop innovative solutions, research and development (R&D) centers and university-industry collaboration constitute strategic milestones for countries. These processes have become an indispensable element of R&D and innovation competition with university-industry-state collaboration today. Units such as technoparks, technology centers and R&D centers established in each country aim to create the most suitable environment for this collaboration. It encourages R&D investment activities to compete in collaboration with local governments and policy instruments innovation systems at the international level. This chapter presents new approaches to the effect of the proximity between research institutions and industry on international innovation, patenting and academic activities. We systematically examine collaborative research, co-patenting, academic research, and their knowledge transfer channels between science and industry sectors, practices and opportunities in evaluating the effects of information exchange on innovation in the university-industry-state collaboration. In this chapter, besides the influence of governments on regional R&D efficiency, the latest trends in the governance of public research related to the transfer of knowledge in science-technology-industry were used by using policy indicators around the world.

Keywords: R&D, Innovation, University-industry-state, Collaboration.

Introduction

Today, as knowledge plays an important role in the economic growth of countries, universities are described as the R&D institution of the innovation system which are becoming more and more important. Universities are considered not only as an educational institution to train qualified workforce with modern trainings, but also as an R&D center that will create valuable information and innovations for the society (Carla M. et al., 2018). Therefore, the R&D function of universities in recent years has been a key factor in fulfilling the role of innovation rather than the educational role. The R&D activities of universities tend not only to the economic factor at the individual level, but also to the depths of innovation at the regional level. In the innovation studies, universities show their role in technological innovations as they create many scientific revolution at the regional and national level. In particular, health, bio-engineering, electronics, telecommunications, software, etc. contributes to the innovation of science-based industries (Fritsch, & Slavtchev, 2007). Therefore, the society has high expectations from universities for innovative performance in creating its regional dynamics. (Üçler, & Karaçor, 2014).

In science and industry, the effects of knowledge transfer or collaboration on innovation emerge through various institutions and organizations among the fields of science and industry. These collaborative approaches include factors such as academic work, R&D activities, academic consultancy, intellectual property process, staff mobility (Becker & Dietz, 2004). Considering the differences of knowledge transfer among research disciplines in collaborative approaches, the impact of knowledge transfer in science-industry for achieving certain socio-economic goals on innovation is expected. The impact of science-industry interaction on innovation occurs, especially when the workforce and the flow of human capital from university to industry are captured in order to achieve positive outputs in university-industry collaboration (Özgüz and Mandal, 2013).

Collaborative activities between universities and companies for future planning in science and technology, and collaborative R&D centers are of great importance in increasing the export volume of countries. In addition, university-industry collaboration contributes to the development of innovative ideas of companies, as well as academic studies and national innovation globalization dimensions of education and training countries. In this study, by scanning the literature on university-industry collaboration, basic references in the innovation system and the opportunities offered by the collaborative studies are presented. This systematic literature review revealed that the industry is increasingly focused on collaboration with universities. The results include four clusters: (1) development capacity, knowledge and competitiveness in university-industry-state relations, (2) the effect of knowledge dissemination on university-industry relations in OECD, BRICS and LCD countries, (3) strategic alliances for industry and marketing innovation and key findings; and (4) recommendations for science, technology and innovation. These clusters contribute to a larger and more detailed understanding of the production flow, scientific practices and trends in the new and stimulating research area.

All countries believe that it will be an important factor to promote innovation strategies and policies, so that almost every country in the world can grow and compete with their economies. Innovation is considered not only as a necessary condition for increasing the competitiveness of an economy, but also as an indispensable condition. The link between innovation and the level of development of the economy should focus on the big difference between developed economies and some emerging economies and other emerging economies and emerging and least developed economies. This big difference is related to the basic qualifications, key features and funding sources for research and development (R&D) activities (Coldrick et al., 2005). In the category of developed countries, while state and public institutions have R&D bodies that they finance, most of them depend on the private sector or civil society organizationally, either administratively or financially. Government and public institutions are the main sponsors and funders of R&D, including work and results impacting on the economic structure, performance and competitiveness of the respective countries. R&D institutions affiliated or financed by the private sector are either non-existent or minimal.

1 University-Industry-State Collaboration in Development

While the only institution that produced information until the middle of the 20th century was universities, industry adopted traditional production and gave importance to mass production. Since traditional production lags behind in terms of competitiveness and production costs increase, it has prepared the ground for effective production-based on knowledge and technology. Universities inspired by Henry Etzkowitz's DNA model predicted that closer interaction with industry and state collaboration should be conducted (Etzkowitz, 2003). In this model, universities are the source of scientific development, industry is the user and marketer of new technology, and the state is undertaking the task of financing and organizing the research activities carried out in this interaction. This model, which is preferred by many countries today, enables advanced collaboration as a fiction (Koç and Mente, 2007). Schematic representation of the triple helix model proposed by Etzkowitz is given in Fig. 2.4.1.

Diverse methods and data sources should be exploited together to evaluate the effect of university-industry-state collaboration on innovation. Evaluating the patent, trademark, industrial design, geographical indications database of the World Intellectual Property Organization (WIPO), it can be observed that the applications of universities have a high potential to be effective

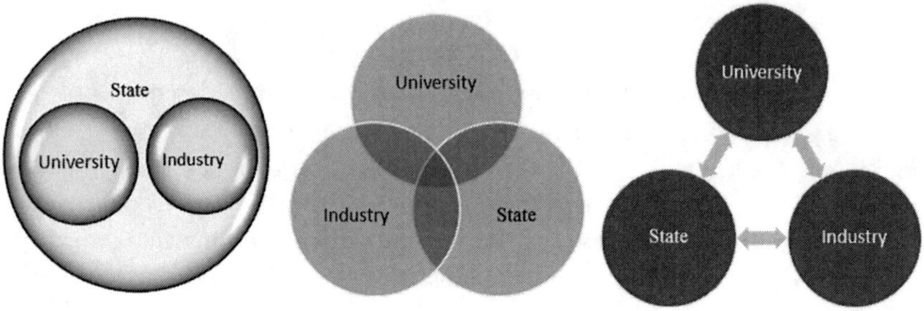

Fig. 2.4.1: University – Industry – Government Collaboration Schemes (Etzkowitz, 2003)

(WIPO-Cornell University, & INSEAD, 2017). Morever, the increase in the number of technology centers and offices in postgraduate exchange programs had also an influence on the increasing number of innovation in universities. In the innovation system, universities play an important role in developing scientific infrastructure and research ability, maintaining national excellence research centers, generating new ideas for development, developing interdisciplinary research and culture, and developing a scientific standard of the nation. (Karytinos & Ingham, 2015).

The logic of the establishment of technology centers in the world is to contribute to the development of technological innovations that contribute to economic growth, the problem of foreign dependency, firm establishment costs, competitive resistance in market conditions and innovative firm formations. In the 1950s, a technology center (technopark) was established under the leadership of a group that aimed to commercialize their studies at Stanford University resulting in the first foundation of the university-industry relationship. In the 1980s, the promotion of university-industry collaboration for R&D and innovation was accepted as an official public policy with the Bayh-Dole law adopted in the USA. Technoparks, which have gained speed all over the world since the 1980s, have been implemented as a policy that supports economic growth and development in industrialized countries such as China, Korea and India (Eyyuboğlu and Günay Aktaş, 2016). Technoparks, which have started to operate for national entrepreneurship and innovation within the framework of development policies in the world, have continued to be established in regions that have become industrialized and high in socio-economic development.

Various international reports and studies have shown the relationship between economic growth and development. One of the most important studies was The Global Innovation Index (GII), published by the World Intellectual Property Organization (WIPO) in 2019 (Index, 2019). It confirmed the correlation between innovation and the degree of development of an economy. Over the years, economically-developed countries and some of the developing countries have been at the forefront of the countries with the highest scores. However, even though the relationship between innovation and the degree and level of economic development has been clearly identified in GII or other similar periodic and regular global reports and studies related to innovation, there has been no clear scientific explanation to date.

According to the results summarized above, many sectors in the communities of the developed, developing and least developed economies need to be reconsidered, restructured and modernized, and an important and relevant example of them is education. At all levels, including higher education and research, its curriculum, educational materials and tools, well-trained and qualified instructors, facilities including laboratories and libraries, innovations including financial ones, an intellectual property office and a scientific institution in every university or equivalent institution, the advances can be transferred as encouraging research.

Innovation has become a central theme for most of the international meetings and conferences that have taken place in different parts of the world over the past few years, regardless of their subject matter. This is added to the emphasis of the concept of innovation, directly or indirectly, on the future action plans and visions of almost all countries. These related concepts include, but are not limited to, an innovative economy as well as an information-based economy and an information-based society as targets for future years. Innovation is perceived as an engine of economic growth in terms of helping both the qualitative transformation of the economy and the indispensable technology-based transformation, as well as ensuring the continuous and even increasing competitiveness of national economies.

2 Research Methodology

In this study, the development of the innovations of university-industry-state collaboration in developed, developing and least developed countries are examined. Innovation trends and results of these country groups have been prepared based on quantitative and qualitative methods. Data are taken from annual reports of the Global Innovation Index by Cornell University, INSEAD Institute and WIPO. In addition, extra data are also taken from OECD Database on Governance of Public Research Policy, BRICS information portal and The Least

Developed Countries (LDCs) Report to discuss the impact and importance of countries' collaboration in innovation. As existing data grows, data analysis is required to help developing public policies to have an innovation forecast and encourage the growth of innovation.

It has been observed that innovation is an important element for strategic change, growth, and better performance, and competitive advantage, economic development, creating value and achieving economic and social success in the globalized business world. Innovation is not only a matter of companies, but nations those target to increase their competitiveness in today's business world and to compete in the future must invest in innovation. This study also demonstrated that product, process, marketing and organizational factors should be taken into account as a result of collaborative agreements in science and technology with innovation investments.

2.1 University-Industry Collaboration in OECD Countries

Evaluating the impact of public research of countries on innovation, the various channels through the type of information transfer (Academic and collaborative research, patenting and licensing of university inventions, academic counseling, etc.) and their relative importance in relation to science have become a complex structure. In OECD countries, collaborative patents of higher education institutions and industry-state research centers, studies on information exchange channels are very important. Moreover, the impact of university-industry-state proximity on local innovation has accelerated the importance of student and researcher initiatives, industry and innovation studies. Academic spin-off activities have been another way of students and researchers to make a significant contribution to research activities. Information and communication technologies, especially in various disciplines, have been another important factor contributing to innovation for industry sectors. In addition to this, the geographical locations of countries have investigated the effects of university-industry-state collaboration on innovation, indicating a positive effect on local industry patenting (OECD, 2019).

Policy tools implemented in OECD countries and their effects in supporting science-industry knowledge transfer are presented through various methods and data sources. These include various financial resources (R&D and innovation grants), business development centers, collaborative tax incentives, doctoral or post-doctoral researchers' support, whether their orientation is the supply or demand side. A comprehensive overview of policy instruments is offered.

Among the emerging policy approaches in information transfer, knowledge creation (joint creation of industry, civil society and common laboratories, joint research projects, etc.) and researches together with science-industry collaboration, intermediary institutions that help meet the supply and demand for new technologies. Opportunities such as the creation of (R&D centers, business development centers, etc. for science-industry collaboration) and the usage of new forms of open digital innovation provided by digital platforms are seen (OECD, 2018). States can be reinforced by updating their policies to bring information together and provide convenience to target groups by overcoming situations that may cause operational difficulties and administrative problems in enhancing the innovation of complementary science. Fig. 2.4.2 presents various channels that will positively affect innovation with university-industry-state proximity in OECD countries.

In OECD Database on Governance of Public Research Policy (stip.oecd.org/resgov), governance practices that direct science-industry knowledge transfer of countries are presented. Universities and research institutions, which allow them to use their own support programs for information transfer, cooperate with industry representatives and non-governmental organizations for innovation. In OECD countries, universities and public/private R&D centers are in constant interaction with the industry, in order to increase support in national/international performance-based funding or grant mechanisms. Countries' policy tools are extremely beneficial in supporting science-industry knowledge transfer in the emergence of these opportunities and innovative opportunities.

2.2 University-Industry Collaboration in BRICS Countries

In recent years, the economies of BRICS (Brazil, Russia, India, China and South Africa) countries continue to be the subject of the world agenda with many scientific studies. BRICS countries in the developing country economy group contribute to science with original researches in various aspects of science technology and innovation studies (Gammeltoft, 2008). Young population, rich natural resources, important geographical locations, socio-economic and demographic conditions, etc. factors provide advantages for developing economies. While these five countries exhibit unified growth and potential to promote mutual growth and development together, they show many mutual developments in the fields of science, technology and innovation. (O'neill, 2001).

BRICS countries are united in national, regional and technological innovation systems, technological competence development, science technology and sustainable development, R&D, university-industry relations, science,

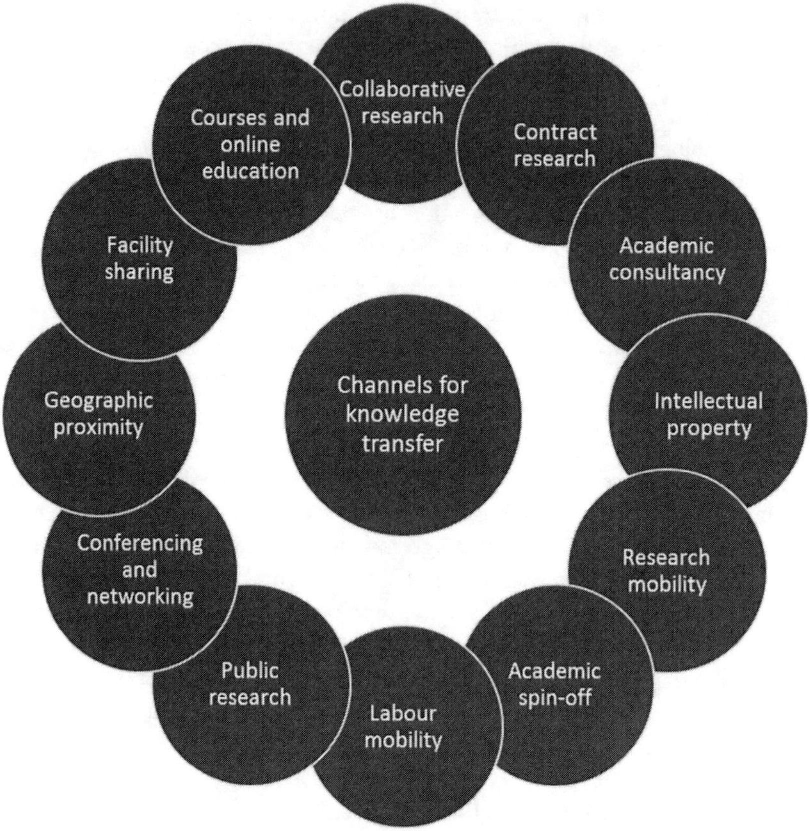

Fig. 2.4.2: Various Channels of Knowledge Transfer in Science-Industry Collaboration. (OECD, 2013)

technology and innovation policy, science and technology collaboration. Therefore, BRICS countries have recently undergone significant structural changes to become more industrialized economies (Daniels et al., 2017). However, the increasing economic inequality and population growth of these countries faces the problem of lack of access to innovation (Soares et al., 2018). Along with the economic growth of the countries, energy consumption, carbon emission and their impacts from these countries constitute a global concern. It also shows that green technological innovation can increase production-based energy efficiency and CO2 emission efficiency (Patra et al., 2017). Moreover, it has been observed in the scientific literature that there is an important gap in advancing innovation knowledge as a mechanism for inclusive development. The gap is perhaps due to the improper conceptualization of innovation to include the wider society in socio-economic and development activities.

When the role of innovation in inclusive development in the world is researched in the literature, there are important gaps not only in BRICS countries but also in other countries. Countries focus particularly on innovation in a broad sense, with less attention to development. The reason for this is that the potential that can play in development by conceptualizing innovation is not appreciated to involve the wider society in socio-economic and development activities. Also, the lack or limitation of specific public policy support in development of BRICS countries requires critical analysis of the roles that triple university-industry-state collaboration plays in innovation ecosystems. It should include an innovation review and research proposals that show the importance level for companies and nations those want to survive and thrive in today's business environment.

2.3 University-Industry Collaboration in World's Least Developed Countries (LCDs)

Investing in science, technology and innovation is the backbone of productivity-driven economic recovery and sustainable development. Low-income countries, which face serious structural obstacles in sustainable development, are highly vulnerable to economic and environmental problems. The least developed countries of the world, which lacks factors such as low production capacity, accelerating growth and inclusive policy, and promoting sustainable development, also lack the concepts of university-industry-state collaboration. (Farley, 2007). Various deficiencies of LCDs for innovation are illustrated in Fig. 2.4.3.

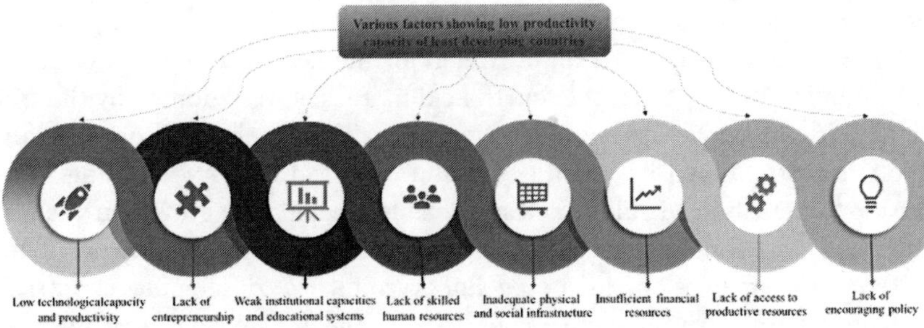

Fig. 2.4.3: Various Factors Showing Low Productivity Capacity of Least Developing Countries

One of the keys to sustainable productivity and development is a highly skilled workforce. However, this is an impressive acquisition for reaching global markets. This is especially important for least-developed countries. LDCs should attach importance to the following four elements as an effective tool to achieve sustainable development goals. First, it should develop a common and effective conceptual framework to ensure that it is economically and socially inclusive while promoting the reduction of carbon emissions (Bryant et al., 2009). Effective institutions and digital infrastructure, appropriate legal and regulatory frameworks, investment commitment and investment incentives, and future workforce should be critical components of this framework. The second is to take advantage of programs that encourage governments to promote economic, social and environmental support to achieve their goals. Third, innovation policies and strategies must therefore be inclusive, open and collaborative in order to support sustainable development. The Final step is to develop technology sharing opportunities for concrete and sustainable innovation, to enable countries at all levels of development to benefit from existing technologies and to develop a regional innovation culture.

The United Nations (UN) Technology Bank for Least-Developed Countries, as a global organization, works to increase the contribution of science, technology and innovation for sustainable development in the least-developed countries of the world. The United Nations Technology Bank actively engages with national, regional and international partners to present programs and projects that strengthen science, technology and innovation capacity in the least developed countries. UN Technology Bank supports national and regional technological efforts, strengthens cross-sectoral partnerships and helps countries identify and use appropriate technologies to transform their economies and improve livelihoods. Apart from the establishment such as UN, various organizations from different countries, humanitarian foundations and non-governmental organizations support the development of LDC countries by providing food, health and economic supports.

For 2011–2020 Year Program of Action for the Least-Developed Countries in Istanbul 9–13 May 2011, the fourth held in Turkey was adopted by the UN Conference on the Least-Developed Countries. The Istanbul Action Program (IPoA) has strengthen its institutional and technical capacity-building partnership to contribute to guided and sustainable development growth in science, technology and innovation. A wide range of actors are expected to contribute to IPoA implementation, including donor countries, developing countries, parliaments, the private sector, civil society, the UN system and international and regional financial institutions. IPoA is aware that LDCs represent the human and natural resource potential for the world's economic and will contribute to peace, prosperity and sustainable development in addressing specific development needs. The overall aim of IPoA is to overcome the structural challenges faced by LDCs to eliminate poverty and achieve internationally agreed development goals. IPoA focuses on reducing the vulnerabilities of LDCs and addresses new challenges for development, including the effects of interconnected food, fuel and economic crises and climate change, with a strong focus on structural transformation that increases production capacity. IPoA also aims to produce full and productive employment and decent work for everyone, especially young people (Hossain, 2011). This report covers the eight priority action objectives of the Action Program for the Least Developed Countries of 2011–2020, see Fig. 2.4.4 below. It also highlights activities undertaken by other stakeholders, including the United Nations system, civil society and the private sector. The outputs of the ten-year action plan will be discussed at the meetings in Doha and New York in 2021, and future action plans will be developed.

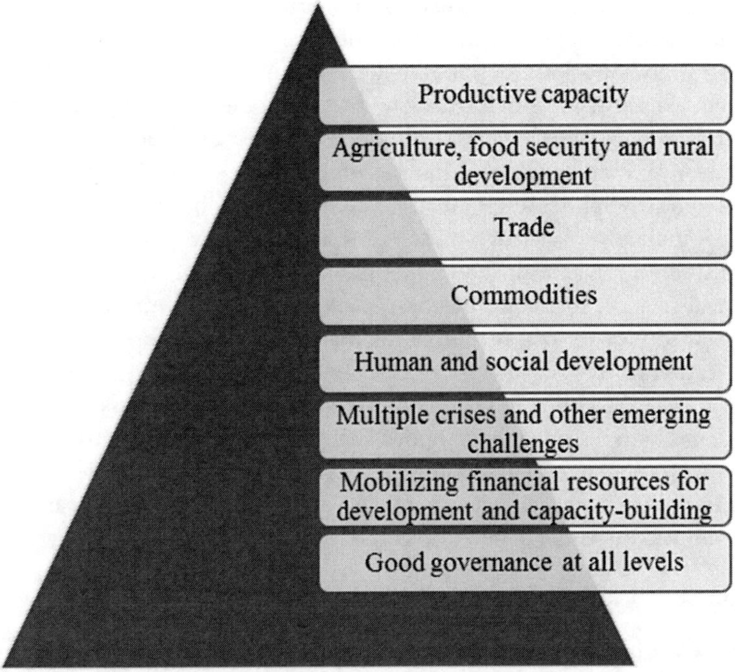

Fig. 2.4.4. Eight Priority Action Plans for the Least Developed Countries of 2011–2020

3 Key Findings

In the literature review conducted in terms of university-industry-state collaboration, R&D, patenting, sustainability, socio-economic development features of developed/developing countries in the age of technological and economic change, new evidence and indicators in national/international development are shown below.

Direct contributions of universities and public research institutions to patents grow faster than firms' inventions. Thanks to the technoparks that bring together industrialists and universities, it is possible to cooperate in high-tech R&D projects and to create more qualified inventions. Therefore, it is easier to commercialize innovative products resulting from the collaboration of universities and industry.

Universities, which have a great potential in patents, are effective in intellectual property applications through the academic rewards and regulations made in academic promotion criteria. In addition to these, increases in countries' graduate, doctorate programs and scholarship variations also affect the increase in the number of intellectual property.

Universities, public research institutions and industry's increasing brand, patent/utility, model, and design activities create innovative products with public-university-industry research collaboration. When the patent application data of the countries are analyzed, it is seen that most of all creative activities are formed by university-industry collaboration according to the sector (Tseng et al., 2020).

In some disciplines and industry sectors, labor mobility is a key channel of science-industry knowledge transfer. According to evidence based on labor force studies, it has been shown that graduates of social sciences (economics, political science, sociology, business, etc.) contribute to innovation in a wide range of service sectors, including the highly dynamic information and communication sectors.

A number of policy tools are used to support science-industry knowledge transfer. Examples include activities such as grants, tax incentives, mobility plans for researchers, fairs to meet industrialists and universities, seminars, technology markets, awareness seminars on patents, training of trainers, and inter-university patent competition.

4 Recommendations

In the R&D, innovation and patenting system of the countries, the performance of public research, the role of the industry and universities, previous studies for innovation in the university-industry-state collaboration and results obtained were evaluated. Although countries tend to use various policy tools to support the transfer of information, difficulties arise in innovative design or implementation in terms of the number of budgets or initiatives between countries. In order to transform science and technology into innovation and overcome difficulties, a number of important suggestions are presented below.

Creation of new organizations/units: These organizations should include R&D centers, management mechanisms and regional technology transfer organizations for science-industry collaboration. They should aim to build bridges between science and industry in terms of their financing structures, functions and organizational profiles. Among the new approaches, larger sectoral or regional technology transfer offices established with various universities and more specialized units should be created to meet specific business needs.

More emphasis on collaborating with innovative products: Collaborative innovation relationships, including public support for science-industry collaboration and the creation of shared knowledge of industry, civil society, and researchers, should be uncovered. There may be different forms for these, such as creating common infrastructures, sharing resources and participating in joint research projects. These are public research institutions and higher education institutions that allow researchers to temporarily join the industry for bidirectional mobility, and industry researchers to temporarily participate in university activities.

Adapting information transfer policies to digital transformation: New open digital innovation forms allow a more intense collaboration between companies and universities. These include experts' online communities, contests, open calls, and crowdsourcing. It should be able to meet technology supply and demand by combining digital platforms, global public research centers, individual scientists and freelancers to solve specific technological problems.

Governance mechanisms: For information transfer, universities and research centers should have institutional arrangements governing policy action related to publicly funded research. It can create interactions and synergies between different levels of governance, as well as create effective coordination mechanisms.

Setting up functional units: Universities and research centers, like in many OECD countries, create their own legal structures and functional units (e.g. TTO), decide on the recruitment and promotion of academic staff, and determine the share of researchers' income. Income from patent license or from research should be included in performance-based funding and contract systems.

Sustainability and innovation in exports: The private sector and civil society should participate to shape how universities interact with the industry and to be more actively involved in policy decision making, and strengthening our technology, innovation, R&D, branding strategy.

The importance of updating and digital technologies in the academic curriculum: Policies should take advantage of the knowledge transfer opportunities offered by the industry. Academic curriculum needs to be revised regularly to meet emerging industry needs. The most innovative approaches to innovations from digital technologies include expert communities, open calls and crowdsourcing. Such opportunities can help foster new collaborations and support international competitiveness of the research.

Policy approaches: New policy approaches to support science and industry linkages should gradually change from the short-term information transfer model between industry and science to a more interactive, longer-term information "innovation" model in supporting economic priorities. This should aim to address wider social challenges that involve many stakeholders from industry, civil society, research and the state.

Incubation structures: The characteristics of incubation structures that have effects similar to entrepreneurship are to contribute to regional economic growth by providing physical infrastructure and consultancy services to innovative companies that increase employment and support economic growth.

Conclusions

With the globalization of R&D and the collaboration of university-industry-state, the development of the innovation system will always increase. With international university-industry-state collaboration, foreign companies and foreign universities contribute to the establishment of the national innovation system of host countries. In addition, university-industry collaboration can be considered as part or method of international education. With the internationalization of education and R&D activities, the innovation system has the potential to become global. In the context of innovation, the innovation system will be one of the goals of future research centers. Types of university-industry-state collaboration form categorized and tested factors in future research in the context of innovation. With this research, the importance of university-industry-state collaboration is presented for the internationalization of science and technology.

Accordingly, in innovation and socio-economic development, universities and industry organizations should use national and international grants and support programs for R&D-based studies, write and execute projects.

In addition, university-industry meeting platforms should be built, industry needs analysis should be created, and the needs of industry to be resolved with the right people should be carried out.

The results show that: (1) R&D efficiency has spatial dependence and high efficiency regions have a spreading effect on surrounding areas. (2) State competition has a significant stimulating effect on R&D efficiency and/or expansion of R&D efficiency. (3) The impact of government competition on productivity is affected by the legal environment, and the incentive effect of government competition exists only in a good legal environment. The results of this study reveal an important way to increase R&D efficiency by establishing a new efficiency-oriented and environmentally managed R&D competition mechanism. R&D centers, in collaboration with university-industry-state, provide significant benefits in designing innovative products.

References

Andrews, D., & Criscuolo, C. (2013). Knowledge-Based Capital, Innovation and Resource Allocation. OECD Economics Department Working Papers, No. 1046, OECD Publishing. http://dx.doi.org/10.1787/5k46bj546kzs-en

Becker, W., & Dietz, J. (2004). R&D Cooperation and Innovation Activities of Firms-Evidence for the German Manufacturing Industry. Research Policy, 33(2), 209–223.

Bhattacharya, D., & Hossain, S. S. (2011). Least Developed Countries in the Next Decade. Retrieved from: https://www.oecd.org/development/development-philanthropy/49898821.pdf, Accessed Date: 25.09.2020

Bryant, L., Carver, L., Butler, C. D., & Anage, A. (2009). Climate Change and Family Planning: Least-Developed Countries Define the Agenda. Bulletin of the World Health Organization, 87, 852–857.

Carla, M., João J. F., & Carla, M. (2018). University–Industry Cooperation: A Systematic Literature Review and Research Agenda, Science and Public Policy, 45(5), 708–718.

Coldrick, S., Longhurst, P., Ivey, P., & Hannis, J. (2005). An R&D Options Selection Model for Investment Decisions. Technovation, 25(3), 185–193.

Daniels, C. U., Ustyuzhantseva, O., & Yao, W. (2017). Innovation for Inclusive Development, Public Policy Support and Triple Helix: Perspectives from BRICS. African Journal of Science, Technology, Innovation and Development, 9(5), 513–527.

Etzkowitz, H. (2003). Innovation in Innovation: The Triple Helix of University-Industry-Government Relations. Social Science Information, 42(3), 293–337.

Eyyuboğlu, B., & Günay Aktaş, S. (2016). Türkiye'de Teknoparkların Coğrafi Dağılım ve Yoğunluğu (2001–2015) [Analysis of Geographical Distribution and Concentration of Technoparks in Turkey (2001–2015)], Journal of East Geography, 21(35): 75–88. DOI: 10.17295/dcd.87582.

Farley, S. (2007). Donor Support to Science, Technology and Innovation for Development; Approaches in the Least Developed Countries. UNCTAD Report for the 2007 Least Developed Country Report.

Fritsch, M., & Slavtchev, V. (2007). Universities and Innovation in Space. Industry and Innovation, 14(2): 201–218.

Gammeltoft, P. (2008). Emerging Multinationals: Outward FDI from the BRICS Countries. International Journal of Technology and Globalisation, 4(1), 5–22.

Index, G. I. (2019). The Global Innovation Index 2019: Creating Healthy Lives–The Future of Medical Innovation, New York: USA, Cornell University, INSEAD, and the World Intellectual Property Organization, ISBN 979-10-95870-14-2, Retrieved from: https://www.wipo.int/publications/en/details.jsp?id=4434&plang=EN#:~:text=The%20Global%20Innovation%20Index%202019,education%2C%20infrastructure%20and%20business%20sophistication, Accessed Date: 21.09.2020

Karytinos, A., & Ingham, A. (2015). A Growing Interest for Intellectual Property in Universities. Pharmaceutical Patent Analyst, 4(2), 59–61.

Koç, K., & Mente, A. (2007). İnovasyon Kavramı ve Üniversite-Sanayi-Devlet İşbirliğinde Üçlü Sarmal Modeli [The Concept of Innovation and the Triple Helix Model in University-Industry-State Cooperation], Retrieved from: http://www.sdergi.hacettepe.edu.tr/makaleler/kkahm.pdf, Date of Access: 05.05.2020.

OECD. (2018). OECD Science, Technology and Innovation Outlook 2018. OECD Publishing.

OECD. (2019). University-Industry Collaboration: New Evidence and Policy Options. OECD Publishing.

O'Neill, J. (2001). Building better global economic BRICs. Global Economics Paper No: 66, New York: USA, Goldman Sachs & Co. Retrieved from: http://www.elcorreo.eu.org/IMG/pdf/Building_Better_Global_Economic_Brics.pdf, Accessed date: 25.09.2020

Özgüz, V., & Mandal, H. (2013). İleri Teknolojilerde Üniversite Sanayi Işbirliği Ve Kurumsal Ar-Ge Merkezlerinin Yönetişimi [University-Industry Cooperation in Advanced Technologies and Governance of Corporate R&D centers], retrieved from: sanayisurasi.gov.tr. Access Date: 22.07.2020ç.

Patra, S. K., & Muchie, M. (2017). Science, Technology and Innovation in BRICS Countries: Introduction to the Special Issue. African Journal of Science, Technology, Innovation and Development, 9(5), 499–501.

Soares, M. C. C., Scerri, M., & Maharajh, R. (Eds.). (2018). Inequality and development challenges: BRICS national systems of innovation. New Delhi: India, Routledge.

Tseng, F. C., Huang, M. H., & Chen, D. Z. (2020). Factors of University–Industry Collaboration Affecting University Innovation Performance. The Journal of Technology Transfer, 45(2), 560–577.

University, INSEAD, World Intellectual Property Organization. https://www.wipo.int/reference/en/, Date of Access: 22.07.2020.

Üçler, Y. T., & Karaçor, Z. (2014). Bölgesel Kalkinmada Üniversite-Sanayi Isbirligi: Konya Örnegi [University-Industry Cooperation in Regional Development: Konya Case.], Journal of Seluk Üniversity Social Sciences Institute, (31), 167183.

World Intellectual Property Organization, Cornell University, & INSEAD. (2017). The global innovation index 2017: Innovation feeding the world. World Intellectual Property Organization.

Internet Resources

https://stip.oecd.org/resgov/ResGov.html, Date of Access: 22.07.2020.

https://infobrics.org/documents/, Date of Access: 22.07.2020.

https://unctad.org/en/Pages/Publications/TheLeastDevelopedCountriesReport.aspx, Date of Access: 22.07.2020.

https://www.un.org/development/desa/publications/publication Access Date: 22.07.2020.

Dr. Gürçem Özaytürk and Dr. Faruk Mike

2.5 The Role of International Trade in Regional Development

Abstract: Development and underdevelopment are among the most important problems of developing countries. One of the ways for the countries to overcome this problem is to determine priority sectors for development in the new world order, which has been going through a transformation with the globalization process. In determining and implementing these sectors, it is vital to consider the internal dynamics of the countries, pay regard to the regional differences, and make choices that are suitable for their potential. This chapter aims to explain empirically the relationship between international trade and the key regional development indicators (the relationship between per capita income, education, and health) for the regions in Turkey with the highest foreign trade performance, namely TR10 (Istanbul), TR41 (Bursa, Eskişehir, Bilecik) and TR42 (Kocaeli, Sakarya, Düzce, Bolu, Yalova), concerning the Level 2 classification. The findings obtained show that international trade plays a very important and decisive role in regional development.

Keywords: Regional development, International trade, TR10-TR41-TR42 Region.

Introduction

Rather than being an approach based on central government and government intervention, urban and regional development is a process that can be implemented with the participation of national and even international actors. The fact that the outside world affects the urban and regional development of a country is not something new, which dates back to the times of urban colonialism. The development of a trade class in cities, or the sites of capitalist production, helped expanding the trade links between different areas, facilitated the division of labor between different cities, and encouraged the growth of new branches of industry. The close relationship between the cities caused the separation of production and trade, thus facilitating the distribution of production between industrial cities (Marx and Engels, 1970: 72). As the new capitalist production system became easier, it took root in the countryside, and the large cities of the Industrial Revolution emerged. The evolution of harbors and local transportation systems were shaped by the trade and investment decisions of the colonial authorities, and the geographical location of the harbors was decisive on the choice of city centers (Pernia and Quising, 2005: 80).

Today, however, the external effects on urban and regional development manifest themselves through globalization (Yeung and Lo, 1998). The process that has become evident in the international circulation and distribution of raw materials, goods and services, and information in recent years, is expressed as globalization. The restructuring of the global economy, failures in regional development policies, weakening of the power of the nation-state along with the growth of the power of the cities and regions further increase the interest in this field. Regions with intensive information and capital flows outgrow their national positions become a part of the global world. Certainly, the consequences of the liberalization of the world trade system in this period have affected the environment, economy, social and public structure as well as the cities and regions. The path to development in the 21st century passes through cities and regions that have the opportunity to trade with other production centers in their regions by crossing over their national borders, and by expanding their product range and removing the obstacles in the way of the entrepreneurs. The cities and the regions that have succeeded in this can increase their competitive power and economic weight and achieve more economic returns than many states in the global arena (Jacobs, 1984: 56). However, the globalization process pushes cities and regions that have failed to do so into the background, which results in uneven development. According to Marin (2004), who discusses this transformation in the cities and regions in detail, the developments in information, telecommunications, transportation, and production technologies are decreasing the geographical constraints and allowing the economic activities to become even more global. Thus, with the increasing foreign trade, trade relations between regions and cities are becoming more common. This situation not only increases the importance of regions and cities but also contributes to their specialization in production. Increasing specialization and advantages in production enable the development of some regions and cities, and carry them forward while widening the gap between them and the remaining regions.

At this point, two questions are thrown out for consideration. Does international trade, increasing with globalization, actually promote the spatial concentration, thereby providing a positive effect on regional development at the end of the process? Or, contrary to expectations, does international trade have a negative impact on development?

Economic activities mostly concentrate in capital metropolises, and in developing countries where the infrastructure is insufficient, foreign direct investment and trade intensify in certain regions by strengthening urban priority (Fuchs and Pernia, 1987). On the other hand, considering that spatial development patterns are generally determined by domestic market forces and that investment and trade tend to follow these patterns for reasons of efficiency; international trade is thought to have a positive effect on regional development. Therefore, this study will address the role of the international trade volume of the sub-regions of TR10-TR41-TR41, based on Turkey's Level 2 classification, in the regional development with various development variables.

1 International Trade and Development

Although growth and development are two concepts frequently used interchangeably, growth is the expansion of an economy's production capacity that can be measured numerically/quantitatively; whereas development indicates a more qualitative change (Freyssinet, 1985: 124). In this respect, it is understood that development is a concept that also includes growth since it expresses both more output and changes in the technical and the institutional structure as well.

Undoubtedly, as it enhances global efficiency in the allocation of resources, provides incomes to producers arising from specialization, and ensures the consumers to enjoy advantages due to more efficient production methods (Tupy, 2005: 2), an increase in per capita income and the country's welfare is expected with the increase in international trade. There are many studies in the literature as well, concluding that international trade positively affects economic growth and thus development (Brahmbhatt and Dadush, 1996; Dollar, 1992; Edwards, 1997; Frankel and Romer, 1996; Harrison, 1995; Mangir et al., 2017; Sachs and Warner, 1995).

On the other hand, discussing international trade as import and export, Nourzad and Powell (2003) have shown that while exports trigger growth, imports trigger development more. They have based their conclusion on that public health will benefit more from the imported medical supply/equipment and better trained medical staff, that the imported modern agricultural machinery, technical services, and farming methods will increase the capacity of food production in the country, and that the student exchanges and travels abroad for educational purposes will improve the quality of education, and thus the imported goods will contribute to the efficient use of both physical and human capital.

Contrary to this view, Awokuse (2007) has argued that the increase in exports is the factor that provides positive externalities, and therefore the key to economic growth is export. Brazzel and Hicks (1968), who base regional development on export-based theories, also think that the increase in exports will increase the need for intermediate goods and services by the exporting industries, and this increase will enhance the total value added of the region by promoting household consumption.

Eusufzai (1996) has not addressed the issue concerning the export/import distinction but evaluated the index of openness. In his study, Eusufzai has shown that from among the variables used as indicators of openness and development, the relationship between the human development index and the ratio of the population with access to clean water resources is positive; whereas there is a negative relationship concerning the mortality variable under the age of five. Reaching similar results in their study, Güngör and Kurt (2007) established the existence of a long-term relationship between openness and development, and mutual causality relations between the human development index, the gross domestic product calculated with reference to the purchasing power parity, and the education index, which are the variables of openness and development.

However, although the increase in international trade is a part of the development strategy, it cannot completely replace it (Rodrik, 1999: 14). Since development is a more comprehensive concept consisting of social, cultural, and political variables providing a continuous and cumulative increase in the real national income of a society, Adelman and Yeldan (2000: 143) refer to five phenomena for its realization. These are sustainable growth, structural change in production and consumption patterns, technological progress, social, political and institutional modernization, and most importantly, a broad improvement in living standards. In this context, the regional development can be said to be a phenomenon dependent on the internal dynamics that can be realized by increasing the socio-economic and demographic indicators, job opportunities, living standards and the quality of life of the people living in the region (Şahin, 2017: 56). In short, although it is insufficient to consider international trade as a development indicator only on the grounds of its inducing growth, it will be more accurate to treat the externalities created by the increase in international trade and the increase in income together in assessing the impact of international trade on development.

2 TR10-TR41-TR42 Regions

The starting point for regional development is generally the imbalances arising from natural or geographical conditions. Industrialization/growth experienced in the core/central regions starts at and spreads from a certain region or city to its surroundings. This is because the feedback effect of these core/central regions is positive, and thus stimulates and drives the social change.

Sprawling technological and social innovations and intensifying economic activities increase the efficiency of capital in that region and lead to the development of the region with the external benefits and internal economies they provide (Gök, 2012: 1–2). One of the best examples of such a core/central region is Istanbul.

In Istanbul, a metropolitan city where the social, economic, and spatial infrastructure opportunities of the industrial sector are clustered, agglomeration trends have caused excessive accumulation in some economic sectors and the fact that these sectors have surpassed the economic watersheds has created a need to move towards new areas. According to Ewing (1997), this process initially caused the areas of interaction to widen or overstep the administrative boundaries and to form new agglomeration centers across the administrative borders thanks to the support of developments in transportation and communication technologies. As a result, many branches of industry originating from Istanbul have expanded in the east, west, and south directions and sprawled to many areas within the Marmara Region, where they brought about important changes.

With a view to aligning the regional development policies of Turkey with the EU's regional development policy and with a cabinet decision in 2002, the Nomenclature of Territorial Units for Statistics was prepared nationwide. The nomenclature prepared identified 12 regions as Level-1, 26 regions as Level-2, and 81 regions (province) as Level-3. Classified under the Level-2 Territorial Units for Statistics, TR10 includes Istanbul province; TR41 covers Bursa, Eskişehir, and Bilecik provinces, and TR 42 includes Kocaeli, Sakarya, Düzce, Bolu, and Yalova provinces. These three regions rank in the top three in terms of Turkey's industry and international trade volume.

Although 49.4 % of the total exports from Turkey, and 52.2 % of imports take place in Istanbul, with their trade surplus TR41 and TR42 regions also make a substantial contribution to the national economy. In 2019 alone, exports amounted to $ 12.1 billion and imports to $ 8.7 billion in the TR41 region. Automotive, textile ready-to-wear, food, basic metal industry, cement, and soil products, chemical-plastic industry products are among the most significant export items. While Bursa shines out in international direct investments, which are important in terms of exports and employment, Bilecik and Eskişehir also have significant potential. Similarly, of the 15.66 billion dollars of the total exports of Turkey in 2019, TR42 region had a share of 9 % of (1.405 billion dollars). According to customs data, the region realized 2.70 billion dollars of export, amounting to 17,3 % of the total exports of Turkey.

3 Data and Analytical Framework

This study aims at examining the impact of international trade on regional development in Turkey for TR10-TR41-TR42 regions via panel causality analysis. The main reason for preferring these regions is that they are the most developed regions of Turkey in terms of industry and commerce. The study focuses on the role of international trade on regional development in these three sub-regions. In this context, the study will attempt to explain the relationship between the three main indicators of development and international trade (export and import). These development indicators in question consist of economic growth (EG), education level (E), and developments in the health sector (H). The models to be applied accordingly are as follows:

$$\text{Model 1}: EG = f(X, M) \tag{1}$$

$$\text{Model 2}: E = f(X, M) \tag{2}$$

$$\text{Model 3}: H = f(X, M) \tag{3}$$

In this study, economic growth (EG) is represented by gross domestic product per capita (US \$); education level (E) is represented by the total number of high school or equivalent graduates (aged 15 and over); and the health sector (H) is represented by the total number of beds. X and M represent total export (US \$) and total import (US \$) values, respectively. Analysis periods cover different period intervals for each model.[1] In this respect, in line with the availability of data, the analysis consists of observations covering the years of 2004–2018 for the economic growth model, the years of 2008–2018 for the education level model, and the years of 2002–2018 for the health sector model. All series have been obtained from the Turkish Statistical Institute. The series are incorporated into the analysis by taking their logarithms.

4 Econometric Methodology

4.1 Cross-Sectional Dependence

In panel data analysis, the preference between the first and second generation tests is determined according to whether the cross-sectional dependence exists

1 There are serious difficulties in obtaining regional development indicators. In this sense, our aim has been to carry out the analysis in the best possible way depending on the availability of data.

between the sections. In this sense, disregarding the cross-sectional dependence in the analysis may lead to a loss of productivity on the part of the estimators and to obtain invalid test statistics. In this respect, LM test (Breusch and Pagan, 1980), CD and CDLM tests (Peseran, 2004) and LM-Adj test (Peseran et al., 2008) are widely used to investigate the cross-sectional dependence in the literature.

In the context of the seemingly unrelated regression estimation Breusch ve Pagan (1980) propose an LM statistic (where N is constant and $T \rightarrow \infty$):

$$LM = T\sum_{i=1}^{N-1}\sum_{j=i+1}^{N}\hat{\rho}_{ij}^{2} \tag{4}$$

where $\hat{\rho}_{ij}$ refers to the correlation coefficient obtained from the error terms. The LM is asymptotically distributed under the assumption of the N (N-1)/2 degree of freedom of the chi-square. However, this test is not an effective estimator when N → ∞. To address this shortcoming, Pesaran (2004: 5) has proposed a standard LM statistic:

$$CD_{lm} = \sqrt{\frac{1}{N(N-1)}}\left(\sum_{i=1}^{N-1}\sum_{j=i+1}^{N}\left(T\hat{\rho}_{ij}^{2}-1\right)\right), N(0,1) \tag{5}$$

In the case where T → ∞ and then N → ∞, the CD_{lm}test shows asymptotically standard normal distribution. However, Pesaran (2004) has stated that in cases where N is large and T is small, significant size deterioration will occur in LM and CD_{lm} tests and developed an alternative version to eliminate this deficiency:

$$CD = \sqrt{\frac{2}{N(N-1)}}\left(\sum_{i=1}^{N-1}\sum_{j=i+1}^{N}\sqrt{T_{ij}\hat{\rho}_{ij}^{2}}\right), N(0,1) \tag{6}$$

The CD test shows asymptotically standard normal distribution in cases where N → ∞ and T → ∞, regardless of any order. Also, this test can be applied in cases where N and T have small samples. Finally, setting forth that the LM test was deviated when the group mean was zero and the individual mean was different from zero, Pesaran, Ullah, and Yamagata (2008: 2) proposed the bias-adjusted version (LM_{adj}) of the LM test:

$$LM_{adj} = \sqrt{\frac{2}{N(N-1)}} \left(\sum_{i=1}^{N-1} \sum_{j=i+1}^{N} \frac{(T-k)\hat{\rho}_{ij}^2 - \mu_{T_{ij}}}{\upsilon_{T_{ij}}} \right), N(0,1) \tag{7}$$

where $\mu_{T_{ij}}$ represents the mean, and $\upsilon_{T_{ij}}$ represents the variance. The test statistics to be obtained here show asymptotically standard normal distribution.

4.2 Emirmahmutoğlu and Kose (2011) Panel Causality Analysis

Extending the lag augmented vector autoregressive (LA-VAR) approach, Emirmahmutoğlu and Kose (2011) have proposed a panel causality analysis based on meta-analysis in heterogeneous mixed panels. Basically, it has three important advantages: (i) it does not require the series to be stationary under the VAR system and thus enables causality analysis to be applied for panels consisting of stationary, non-stationary, integrated and non-integrated series. (ii) it allows us to avoid pre-test bias regarding stationarity and cointegration testing. Finally, (iii) causality estimates sensitive to cross-section dependence can be obtained through the bootstrap method. In this sense, under the null hypothesis of $H_0 : A_{1,2,ij} = 0$, the $Var\,(k_i + dmax_i)$ model in heterogeneous mixed panels is estimated through Equation (8):

$$z_{i,t} = \mu_i + A_{i1} z_{i,t-1} + \ldots + A_{ik} z_{i,t-k_i} + \sum_{j=k_i+1}^{k_i+dmax_i} A_{ij} z_{i,t-1} + u_{i,t} \tag{8}$$

where i represents the individual cross-section size, and t is the time dimension. After forecasting the model, Fisher test statistics are used:

$$Fisher = -2\sum_{i=1}^{N} ln\,(p_i)\; i = 1, 2, \ldots, N \tag{9}$$

where p_i, i shows the p-value of the cross-section unit belonging to the Wald statistics. If the $k_i + dmax_i$ lag level VAR model is taken into account in heterogeneous mixed panels, the following equations can be obtained:

$$x_{i,t} = \mu_i^x + \sum_{j=1}^{k_i+dmax_i} A_{11,ij} x_{i,t-j} + \sum_{j=1}^{k_i+dmax_i} A_{12,ij} y_{i,t-j} + u_{i,t}^x \tag{10}$$

$$y_{i,t} = \mu_i^y + \sum_{j=1}^{k_i+dmax_i} A_{21,ij} x_{i,t-j} + \sum_{j=1}^{k_i+dmax_i} A_{22,ij} y_{i,t-j} + u_{i,t}^y \tag{11}$$

Tab. 2.5.1: Cross-Sectional Dependence Test Results (Model 1). Source: Authors

Methods	Economic Growth ↔ Export		Economic Growth ↔ Import	
	Test Statistics	Prob.	Test Statistics	Prob.
CDLM1 Test	13.687	0.003	18.240	0.000
CDLM2 Test	4.363	0.000	6.222	0.000
CDLM3 Test	3.525	0.000	3.976	0.000
LM-Adj Test	5.406	0.000	5.306	0.000

Note: Hypotheses for cross-sectional estimations: H_0: There is no cross-sectional dependence between the series, H_1: There exists the cross-sectional dependence between the series.

where $dmax_i$ represents the maximum degree of integration in the system for each i. In Equation (10), the causality relationship from y to x is tested, whereas in Equation (11) the causality relationship from x to y is tested.

5 Analysis Results

The findings will be discussed under three headings: (i) economic growth and international trade, (ii) education level and international trade, and (iii) health sector and international trade, respectively.

5.1 Economic Growth and International Trade

Table 2.5.1 shows the test results for the cross-sectional dependence between economic growth and international trade (export and import) parameters. Accordingly, all test results for both export and import models reject the H_0 hypothesis at 1% significance level and reveal that there is a cross-sectional dependence between the series. This indicates that the condition required for the panel causality analysis developed by Emirmahmutoglu and Kose (2012) is met. Panel causality test results are given in Tab. 2.5.2.

The Fisher statistic in Tab. 2.5.2 mainly reflects the causality analysis findings between economic growth and international trade for the TR10-TR41-TR42 regions. Accordingly, test results reveal that there is a bidirectional causality relationship between the total import value (M) and economic growth (EG) for the TR10-TR41-TR42 regions. This situation indicates an important point. TR10-TR41-TR42 regions constitute Turkey's most important industrial production center. Raw material and energy needs, which are an indispensable element of the production process, are imported from abroad to a large extent. In this

Tab. 2.5.2: Panel Causality Test Results (Model 1). Source: Authors

Causality	Regions	Wald	p-value	Fisher Statistics
Export → EG	TR10	6.343	0.096	5.520
	TR41	0.638	0.888	(0.479)
	TR42	0.108	0.742	
Import → EG	TR10	1.273	0.736	11.721
	TR41	8.165	0.043	(0.068)
	TR42	0.132	0.091	
EG → Export	TR10	1.411	0.716	5.142
	TR41	0.559	0.235	(0.526)
	TR42	0.455	0.455	
EG → Import	TR10	3.082	0.379	34.487
	TR41	15.681	0.001	(0.000)
	TR42	22.009	0.000	

Note: The analyses were carried out by taking into account the Akaike Information Criterion (AIC). Values in parentheses reflect probability values.

sense, it is considered that the industrial production realized through imported inputs contributes significantly to the growth process in the Marmara Region.

5.2 Education Level and International Trade

Tab. 2.5.3 shows the cross-sectional dependence test results for educational level and international trade (export and import). Accordingly, CDLM1, CDLM2, and CDLM3 test results reject the H_0 hypothesis at the significance level of 1 % for both export and import models and reveal that there is a cross-sectional dependence between the series. On the other hand, LM-Adj Test results reject H_0 hypothesis at the significance level of 5 % for the import model and 10 % for the export model. This enables the application of the panel causality analysis developed by Emirmahmutoğlu and Kose (2012), in a way similar to the economic growth model. Panel causality test results for Model 2 are given in Tab. 2.5.4.

The Fisher statistic in Tab. 2.5.4 mainly reflects the causality analysis findings for the relationship between education level and international trade for the TR10-TR41-TR42 regions. Accordingly, the findings reveal the existence of a bidirectional causal relationship between the total import value (M) and the education level (E) for the TR10-TR41-TR42 regions. It is noteworthy that, similar to the economic growth model (Model 1), import value

Tab. 2.5.3: Cross-Sectional Dependence Test Results (Model 2). Source: Authors

Methods	Education ↔ Export		Education ↔ Import	
	Test Statistics	Prob.	Test Statistics	Prob.
CDLM1 Test	21.732	0.000	21.154	0.000
CDLM2 Test	7.647	0.000	7.411	0.000
CDLM3 Test	4.631	0.000	4.595	0.000
LM-Adj Test	1.531	0.063	1.783	0.037

Note: Hypotheses for cross-sectional estimations: H_0: There is no cross-sectional dependence between the series, H_1: There exists the cross-sectional dependence between the series.

Tab. 2.5.4: Panel Causality Test Results (Model 2). Source: Authors

Causality	Regions	Wald	p-value	Fisher Statistics
Export → Education	TR10	3.218	0.200	13.213 (0.040)
	TR41	5.113	0.024	
	TR42	2.514	0.284	
Import → Education	TR10	47.786	0.000	70.141 (0.000)
	TR41	18.625	0.000	
	TR42	3.730	0.155	
Education → Export	TR10	5.948	0.051	9.149 (0.165)
	TR41	1.418	0.234	
	TR42	0.294	0.863	
Education → Import	TR10	27.067	0.000	44.299 (0.000)
	TR41	16.743	0.000	
	TR42	0.489	0.783	

Note: The analyses were carried out by taking into account the Akaike Information Criterion (AIC). Values in parentheses reflect probability values.

also has a significant impact on determining the level of education in the TR10-TR41-TR42 regions. Especially technology and innovation transfers from foreign countries are thought to have a significant impact on the level of education in the region in question. On the other hand, it is observed in Tab. 2.5.4 that there is a unidirectional causality relationship from the total export value to the education level. The results show that international trade affects the education level in TR10-TR41-TR42 regions through both export and import channels.

5.3 Health Sector and International Trade

Finally, the results of cross-sectional dependence and causality analysis for the relationship between the health sector and international trade (export and import) are given in Tab. 2.5.5 and Tab. 2.5.6, respectively. Accordingly, all cross-sectional dependence test results reject the H_0 hypothesis at 1% significance level for both export and import models and reveal that there is a cross-sectional dependence between the series. Causality analysis findings point to the existence of a unidirectional causality relationship only from the health sector to the total export value. The findings reveal that international trade in general does not have any impact on the health sector in the TR10-TR41-TR42 regions.

Tab. 2.5.5: Cross-Sectional Dependence Test Results (Model 3). Source: Authors

Methods	Health ↔ Export		Health ↔ Export	
	Test Statistics	**Prob.**	**Test Statistics**	**Prob.**
CDLM1 Test	28.873	0.000	28.303	0.000
CDLM2 Test	10.563	0.000	10.330	0.000
CDLM3 Test	5.370	0.000	5.302	0.000
LM-Adj Test	10.104	0.000	12.456	0.000

Note: Hypotheses for cross-sectional estimations: H_0: There is no cross-sectional dependence between the series, H_1: There exists the cross-sectional dependence between the series.

Tab. 2.5.6: Panel Causality Test Results (Model 3). Source: Authors

Causality	Regions	Wald	p-value	Fisher Statistics
Export → Health	TR10	2.253	0.324	7.449
	TR41	1.367	0.242	(0.281)
	TR42	1.043	0.307	
Import→ Health	TR10	0.145	0.704	3.714
	TR41	0.000	0.999	(0.715)
	TR42	1.491	0.222	
Health → Export	TR10	13.336	0.001	14.506
	TR41	0.096	0.756	(0.024)
	TR42	0.113	0.737	
Health → Import	TR10	1.417	0.234	4.058
	TR41	0.026	0.871	(0.669)
	TR42	0.212	0.645	

Note: The analyses were carried out by taking into account the Akaike Information Criterion (AIC). Values in parentheses reflect probability values.

Conclusion

Economic growth and development is undoubtedly the main goal of every country. Regional development, on the other hand, is the basic building block of a country's development policies. However, with the globalization process, all economic activities that have gained an international dimension have not only changed the definition of the concept of the region but also transformed the approaches in the field of regional development. One of the best examples of this is international trade. The purpose of this study has been to investigate the impact of international trade on regional development.

With reference to the panel causality analysis proposed by Emirmahmutoğlu and Kose (2011), this study has examined the impact of international trade on the regional development for TR10-TR41-TR42 regions in Turkey. In this context, the relationship between three main indicators of development (economic growth, education level, and health sector) and international trade (export and import) has been investigated. The findings obtained can be divided into three parts: (i) there is a bidirectional causality relationship between economic growth and imports; (ii) there is a bidirectional causality relationship between educational level and imports, and a unidirectional causality relationship from exports to the level of education; and finally (iii) international trade does not have a significant impact on the health sector.

It has been found that especially, the total import value has a significant impact on the economic growth and education level in the Marmara Region. Imports of raw materials and intermediate goods, which are the main input of industrial production, is thought to have contributed significantly to the growth process in the region. On the other hand, technology and innovation transfers from foreign countries are estimated to be an important determinant on the level of education.

Especially technology and innovation transfers from abroad are thought to have a significant impact on the level of education in the region in question. Accordingly, it is recommended that policymakers should focus on international trade policies concerning the regional development strategies.

References

Adelman, I., & Yeldan, E. (2000). The End of the Developmental State?, *Structural Change and Economic Dynamics*, 11, 95–109.

Awokuse, T. O. (2007). Causality between Exports, Imports, and Economic Growth: Evidence from Transition Economies. *Economics Letters*, 94.

Brahmbhatt, M., & Dadush, U. (1996). Disparities in Global Integration. *Finance and Development*, 33(3), 47–50.

Brazzel, J. M., & Hicks, W. W. (1968). Exports and Regional Economic Growth: An Evaluation of the Economic Base and Staple Models. *Land Economics*, *44*(4), 503–509.

Breusch, T. S., & Pagan, A. R. (1980). The Lagrange Multiplier Test and Its Applications to Model Specification in Econometrics. *The Review of Economic Studies*, 47(1), 239–253.

Dollar, D. (1992). Outward-Oriented Developing Economies Really Do Growth More Rapidly: Evidence from 95 LDCs, 1976–1985. *Economic Development and Cultural Change*, 40(3), 523–544.

Edwards, S. (1997). Openness, Productivity and Growth: What Do We Really Know?. *NBER Working Papers*, No: 5978.

Emirmahmutoglu, F., & Kose, N. (2011). Testing for Granger Causality in Heterogeneous Mixed Panels. *Economic Modelling*, 28(3), 870–876.

Eusufzai, Z., (1996). Openness, Economic Growth, and Development: Some Further Results. *Economic Development and Cultural Change*, 44(2), 333–338.

Ewing, R. (1997). Is Los Angeles-Style Sprawl Desirable? *Journal of the American Planning Association*, 63(1): 107–126.

Frankel, J. A., & Romer, D. (1996). Trade and Growth: An Empirical Investigation. *NBER Working Papers*, No: 5476.

Freyssinet, J. (1985). Azgelişmişlik iktisadı. (Çev. T. Öcal, M. A. Kılıçbay). Ankara: Gazi Üniversitesi İ.İ.B.F. Yayın No: 36,

Fuchs, R. J., & Pernia, E. M. (1988). External Economic Forces and National Spatial Development: Japanese Direct Investment in Pacific Asia. Ed.: Roland J.Fuchs, In *Urbanization and Urban Policies in Pacific Asia*, Pages: 88–111. New York: USA, Routledge Taylor & Francis Group, e-book ISBN: 9780429266898, https://doi.org/10.4324/9780429266898

Gök, A. (2012). Bölgesel Kalkınmanın Dış Ticarete Etkisi ve GAP Örneği [The Effect of Regional Development on Foreign Trade and the Example of GAP]. *Turkey Economic Association Discussion Paper, Retrieved from: http:// www. tek. org. tr/dosyalar/gap. pdf.*

Güngör, B., & Kurt, S. (2007). Dışa Açıklık Ve Kalkınma İlişkisi (1968–2003): Türkiye Örneği [The Relationship between Opennes and Development (1968–2003): The Case of Turkey], *Journal of Ataturk University Economics and Administrative Sciences*, 21(2): 197–210.

Harrison, A. (1995). Openness and Growth: A Time-Series, Cross-Country Analysis for Developing Countries. *NBER Working Paper Series*, No: 5221.

Jacobs J. (1984). Cities and the Wealth of Nations, New York: Random House Publishers.

Mangir, F., Kabaklarli, E., & Ayhan, F. (2017). An Analysis for the Relationship between Trade Openness and Economic Growth: Evidence for Ten African Countries. *Journal of Management and Economics Research*, 15(1), 58–71. DOI: 10.11611/yead.373442.

Marin, M. (2004). Globalleşme Sürecinde Kent ve Bölgelerin Mekansal Ekonomilerdeki Rolü ve Ekonomik Coğrafya Eşitsizliği: Bir Yerleşim Kuramı Yaklaşımı [The Role of Cities and Regions in Spatial Economies in the Globalization Process and Economic Geography Inequality: A Settlement Theory Approach], Urban Economic Research Symposium, Pamukkale University, Denizli-Turkey, 20–39.

Marx, K., & Engels, F. (1970). *The German Ideology.* (Vol. 1). International Publishers Co.: New York.

Nourzad, F., & Powell, J. J. (2003). Openness, and Development: Evidence from a Panel of Developing Countries. *Scientific Journal of Administrative Development*, 1(1), 72–93.

Pernia, E. M., & Quising, P. F. (2005). Trade Openness and Regional Development in a Developing Country. In *Globalization and Urban Development* (79–94). Springer, Berlin, Heidelberg.

Pesaran, H. M. (2004). General Diagnostic Tests for Cross-Sectional Dependence in Panels. *University of Cambridge, Cambridge Working Papers in Economics*, 435.

Pesaran, M. H., Ullah, A., & Yamagata, T. (2008). A Bias-Adjusted LM Test of Error Cross-Section Independence. *The Econometrics Journal*, 11(1), 105–127.

Rodrik, D. (1999). Yeni Küresel Ekonomi ve Gelişmekte Olan Ülkeler: Dışa Açılma Nasıl Gerçekleştirilmeli? [The New Global Economy and Developing Countries: How to Achieve Outward Opening], Sultan Gül (Trns.), First Issue. Istanbul: Sabah Books.

Sachs, J. D., & Warner, A. (1995). Economic Reform and the Process of Global Integration, *Brookings Papers on Economic Activity*, 1, ss.1–118.

Şahin, D. (2017). Bölgesel Kalkınmada Dış Ticaretin Rolü: TR81 Bölgesi Örneği [The Role of Foreign Trade in Regional Development: Tr81 Region Sample]. *International Journal of Management Economics and Business, 13*(5), 55–67.

Tupy, M. L. (2005). Trade Liberalization and Poverty Reduction in Sub-Sahara Africa, *Policy Analysis*, No: 557.

Yeung, Y. M., & Lo, F. C. (1998). Globalization and World City Formation in Pacific Asia. *Globalization and the World of Large Cities*, in: F. Lo and Y. Yeung (Eds) Globalization and the World of Large Cities, pp. 132–154. Tokyo: United Nations University Press.

Dr. Başak Gök and Prof. Dr. Hadi Gökçen

2.6 Regional Development and Distance Education: Performance Evaluation of University Distance Education Programs[1]

Abstract: Universities contribute to both regional and global development with the knowledge they produce and the qualified manpower they raise. Universities open formal and distance education (DE) programs and develop new programs to meet the needs of individuals and the community. In order to develop new programs and make the existing programs more effective, the performance of these programs should be determined. In this chapter, evaluation of the performance of DE is presented. DE performance is calculated based on service quality and effectiveness. We use DE-SERVQUAL (Distance Education Service Quality) scale and efficiency analysis as measurement tools. The chapter sample consists of students enrolled in the distance education program and the universities they enrolled in Turkey. We found that DE performance is generally medium and low in Turkey. The qualitative increase in DE program diversity is as important as the quantitative increase. It is expected to contribute to decision making units both in terms of improving the quality of the service provided and the effective use of university scarce resources.

Keywords: Institutional evaluation, Performance evaluation, Distance education.

Introduction

Universities are public institutions that are established to meet the higher education needs of the society, conduct research, and to produce and disseminate information. Universities work to achieve their goals through formal, open and distance education programs. Along with scientific and educational activities, universities play an important role in regional development, intellectual capital, international recognition, and building knowledge and a knowledge-based society.

Universities contribute to regional economic growth, prosperity and human capital by taking a role in the evaluation of regional resources. Human capital is crucial for development and sustainable competitive advantage in globalized world.

1 This study was produced from the doctoral thesis entitled "Evaluation of service quality and efficiency of distance education programs in universities".

The increase of human capital provides both global and regional development. In order to ensure sustainable development and competitiveness in the knowledge-based global economy, the focus should be on training high quality people (Nage-Sibande and Morolong, 2018: 496). Additionally, The World Bank Report describes investment in human capital as a good investment (Psacharopoulos and Patrinos, 2018). Therefore, universities contribute to countries both in meeting the need for higher education and raising quality manpower, by opening formal and distance education programs (Chawinga and Zozie, 2016: 5).

Universities, that are part of the service sector, are non-profit institutions. In Turkey, universities are public institutions structured as state and foundation. According to data from 2017, 30% of total education expenditure and education expenditure per student in Turkey, were at the higher education level (TUİK, 2019). During the 2017–2018 academic year, while 7198987 students were receiving higher education services in Turkey, 1.25% of those students (90675 students) were enrolled in distance education programs (YÖK, 2019).

It is important for the countries to manage the performance of the services they provide as well as to plan their economic resources properly. Performance management is defined as information on the inputs, outputs and results, regular production, collection, analysis, reporting and use of data related to the functioning of public institutions and organizations (Thomas, 2006: 10). Distance education is a field of study that is explored and tried to be developed due to developing technology and communication channels. Zawacki-Richter and Naidu (2016: 262) determined the distance education study themes by analyzing the studies in the literature in 5-year periods. These themes have been grouped as professionalization and institutional consolidation/fortification (1980–1984), instructional design and educational technology (1985–1989), quality assurance in distance education (1990–1994), student support, and early stages of online learning (1995–1999), the emergence of the online university (2000–2004), cooperative learning and online interaction forms (2005–2009) and interactive learning, mass online open courses (MOOC) and open education resources (2010–2014). The increase in the need for education, the development in communication technology and the competition in education as in every field affect the operations and the planning related to distance education. As the institutional resources are limited, providing high-performance services is among the goals of each institution. Therefore, distance education programs have to evaluate the performance related to the service they offer.

There are a limited number of studies in literature showing how evaluation affects programs and policies and what kind of difference it makes (Sridharan and Nakaima, 2011: 140–141). Although studies to evaluate the performance of distance education programs are not among the research trends determined by Zawacki-Richter and Naidu (2016: 262), it is an issue that should be given importance in the popularization and development of distance education. The importance of distance education has become more apparent especially in COVID-19 pandemic. In this study, a proposal is presented to evaluate the performance of distance education programs. The performance of distance education programs is determined based on the quality of distance education service and efficiency score.

1 Conceptual Framework

Performance management involves collecting information about the current and future status of the enterprise, comparing this information and making arrangements to improve performance continuously, in order to reach its goals (Karahan and Özgür, 2011: 34). Performance measurement and management is very important for efficient and effective management of any institution (Melnyk, Bititci, Platts, Tobias and Andersen, 2014: 173). Performance measurement in the public sector can be defined as reporting data that sets financial and non-financial targets. Matei and Matei (2008: 38) say that performance measurement in public sector is determined by whether the public production and public output quality reaches the targets or not. Public production includes products and services; the quality of the outputs includes service quality and customer satisfaction.

It is difficult to select the indicators and define the targets used in the performance measurement in the public service sector (Garcia-Aracil and Palomares-Montero, 2010: 218; Propper and Wilson, 2003: 252). Fountain (2001: 57) stated that it may not be appropriate to use private sector performance indicators in public services. While indicators such as profit and market share in the private sector facilitate performance measurement, it is more difficult to determine the indicators defining the targets in the public service sector. Carlin (2004: 278) distinguishes the public sector from traditional institutions in performance measurement due to the multi-dimensional nature of the measurement targets and the insufficiency of data collection systems. Fulfilling non-economic social benefits in the public sector is part of the multi-dimensional nature of measurement targets. However, the sufficient system is not available in the public sector to collect data on all outputs (Carlin, 2004: 278).

A common method in the literature was not accepted on performance measurement, and different models were used. Some of the methods used in performance measurement are balanced scorecard, benchmarking, data envelopment analysis (DEA) and Malmquist method (Ensslin, Ensslin, Matos, Dutra and

Ripoll-Feliu, 2015: 1012; Zhonghua and Yee, 2012: 795). Performance measurement criteria may differ depending on the conceptual area. Andersen, Boesen and Pedersen (2016: 858) grouped 110 performance criteria used in performance measurement of public institutions under 5 groups according to conceptual areas. These are classified as stakeholders, formality, subjectivity, process focus type, and product focus type and analysis unit. In addition to that, efficiency and efficiency criteria are also frequently used in performance measurement studies.

The most general definition of the service is the benefits that the customers get. Quality is the ability of a product or service to respond to customer requests. Quality, which has a multi-dimensional structure, is a concept that cannot be easily defined and measured. The increase in quality directly affects customer satisfaction. And increasing customer satisfaction provides competitive advantage (Kenyon and Sen, 2015; 51).

Due to services are abstract, service quality is also abstract. Therefore, the term "perceived service quality" is frequently used instead of service quality. The degree and direction of the difference between the existent status of perceptions and expectations of the customers regarding the service they receive is expressed as the perceived service quality (Parasuraman, Zeithaml and Berry, 1988: 19).

There are different approaches in evaluating service quality, and the SERVQUAL scale is widely used. The SERVQUAL scale consists of the dimensions of physical appearance, reliability, enthusiasm, security and empathy, and has a 7-point Likert structure. The service quality score is determined by the difference between the perception of the existent perceived status and the expected status of the service (Parasuraman et al., 1988: 23, 30). Service quality score (SQ) is calculated as follows.

$$SQ = SQ_{Perceived} - SQ_{Expected} \quad (1)$$

With the degree of importance given to the service quality dimension by the customers, weighted service quality score is also calculated. Each dimension has a value between 0–1, with the total importance of the dimensions that form the service quality being 1. Service quality score as "SQ", importance level as "a"; the weighted service quality score is expressed with "a SQ" and is calculated according to the following equation.

$$a\,SQ = a^{*}\,SQ \quad (2)$$

When determining the quality of service in higher education, it is first necessary to define the producer and consumer sides. Universities can be defined as units that develop education programs and produce education services in line with the demands and needs of the society, in other words as producers. Although many stakeholders such as teaching staff, parents, government, employers, local people and society are affected by the education service provided by the university, the most important consumer of this service is the student (Gürbüz and Erglenen, 2008: 3).

Although SERVQUAL scale has a wide usage area, it may not meet all the needs in some areas. Therefore, researchers have also developed measuring tools suitable for the study area in order to measure service quality. Service quality measurement tools compatible with the characteristics of higher education and web services are HEdPERF (Abdullah, 2006: 579), E-selfqual (Ding, Hu and Sheng 2011: 514), E-S-QUAL (Parasuraman, Zeithaml and Malhotra, 2002: 17), HEDQUAL (İçli and Anıl, 2014: 40), Sitequal (Yoo and Donthu, 2001: 9), Webqual (Barnes and Vidgen, 2001: 23), WebqualTM (Loiacono, Watson and Goodhue, 2002: 433) in the literature.

The dimensions that make up the quality of service in the tools used in the literature to measure the quality of distance education services offered by universities are as follows. Gök (2017: 147) determined the dimensions of distance education service quality as, e-learning environment, accessibility, trust and enthusiasm; Simmons (2007: 166) as, efficiency, system availability, fulfillment, privacy, enthusiasm, compensation (recovery) and communication; Udo, Bagchi and Kirs (2011: 1276) as, assurance, empathy, enthusiasm, reliability and website content; Uppal, Ali and Gulliver (2017: 422) as, assurance, reliability, empathy, sensitivity, concrete characteristics and learning content; Martinez-Argülles, Castan and Juan (2010: 155) as, learning processes, management processes, learning materials and resources, user interface, interaction, fees and compensation.

Efficiency analysis is a widely used method to compare and measure the relative efficiency of co-decision units with multiple inputs and outputs. It shows the ways of determining the location of the business in the current competitive environment and producing more outputs with the inputs available.

Data envelopment analysis is an analytical technique for defining resource use among similar organizations. It contributes to increase the efficiency of the institution and be able to make full use of its potential (Abbot and Doucouliagos, 2003: 91). The foundations of DEA were laid in 1957 by Farrell (1957: 265), using single input and output in the evaluation of efficiency; and it emerged in 1978 as a result of the evaluation of the relative technical efficiency of multiple inputs and outputs by Charnes, Cooper and Rhodes (1978: 443). DEA can also be used in banks, hospitals, universities, airports, tax offices, libraries, schools or their departments, environmental and energy organizations (Avkıran, 2001: 59) and non-profit public institutions (Sözen, Alp and Kılınç, 2012: 194).

DEA is applied as Banker, Charnes and Cooper (BCC) model, Charnes, Cooper and Rhodes (CCR) model, and additive and multiplicative models, for inputs and outputs (Karahan and Özgür, 2009: 46). In all these methods, linear programming transformation can be used considering input or output orientation. The common feature of DEA methods is that they find which decision making unit (DMU) constitutes the efficiency limit and detect the active and inactive DMUs according to this efficiency limit. In DEA models, input-oriented (BCC) models are preferred to measure the same output with the least amount of input, and output-oriented models (CCR) are preferred to measure the maximum output with the same amount of input.

In the analysis of the efficiency, DMUs are evaluated according to the input and output variables and compared relatively. There are different approaches for the relationship between the number of DMU and the number of input and output variables to be used in the analysis when conducting the evaluation of the efficiency (Ramanathan, 2003: 173). The number of DMU being greater than the sum of the number of input and output variables (Avkıran, 2001: 68); the number of DMU being at least 2–3 times the number of input and output variables (Ramanathan, 2003: 174); the number of DMU being at least 3 times higher than the total of input and output variables (Cooper et al., 2007: 116; Vasslioglou and Giokas, 1990: 592) approaches take place in literature.

Higher education can be considered as an input-output transformation process (Garcia-Aracil and Palomares-Montero, 2010: 2018). Universities are a big economic enterprise with the use of both money and human resources. Like all profits based enterprises, universities should define their efficiencies and produce more efficient outputs. The outputs produced by universities are different from outputs of the profit based enterprises. The measurement of efficiency is more difficult as universities are not for profit, input and output values do not have a market value, and a wide variety of outputs are produced from a wide variety of inputs (Johnes, 2006: 273). Therefore, efficiency can be defined according to specific areas. While evaluating the efficiency of universities, the input and output variables used may differ depending on the area (education, research, general, public service). The number of students is often used as the output variable, and the number of academic staff is frequently used as the input variable (Flegg, Allen, Field and Thurlow, 2004; Agasisti and Johnes, 2009).

2 Methodology

In this study, data was collected by survey research method. The survey research method aims to collect and define the data of the group under the circumstances related to the subject (Büyüköztürk et al., 2008: 16; Yazıcıoğlu and Erdoğan, 2014: 37).

To determine the universe of the research, the web pages of the universities released in the web page of Higher Education Council (YÖK) in the 2014–2015 academic year in Turkey, have been analyzed. As a result of this analysis, it has been observed that there are 65 universities that offer distance education programs. All of these universities were contacted by e-mail or telephone. 46 universities shared the number of students enrolled in their distance education program, which is 56417. Universities that offer education services through distance education programs are approximately the 70% of all universities. In line with these data, the number of students receiving distance education services, who constitute the research universe has been taken as 100000.

The number of samples representing the universe should be at least 383 at 100000 universe size and 0,05 significance level (Yazıcıoğlu and Erdoğan, 2014: 89). In the research, 724 volunteer students who enrolled distance education program answered the scale. The answers of the participants who filled the scale incompletely and showed deviation according to the data set were removed, and the analysis was conducted with the 64% (457 participants) of those responses. Due to the fact that distance education is carried out by more than one unit in some universities, each unit providing distance education service is considered as a separate DMU. The responses of 457 students who were receiving distance education services in 9 DMUs that participated in the study voluntarily, were evaluated.

2.1 Data Collection Tools

2.1.1 DE-SERVQUAL Scale

DE-SERVQUAL measures students' perceptions of distance education service quality. The scale consists of 4 parts in which the demographic information, the importance of the dimensions that constitute the quality of distance education service, the expectations of the students from the distance education service and the perceptions about the present state of the distance education they receive, are explored. Perceptions in the scale were explored by grading 7 point Likert type with 24 items. The perception of distance education consists of the dimensions of e-learning environment, trust, accessibility and enthusiasm (Appendix). The construct validity of the scale was found by confirmatory factor analysis, and calculated as $\chi2/df=3,733$, GFI=0,851, IFI=0,919, CFI=0,919, RMSEA=0,077. The Cronbach Alpha internal consistency coefficient is 0,960 and the alpha coefficients of each dimension are 0,905 for the e-learning environment; it is 0,755 for trust; 0,829 for accessibility and 0,937 for enthusiasm, it is quite good for the confidence factor and high for other factors and the whole scale (Gök, 2017: 94).

2.1.2 Efficiency Analysis Data Form

In order to define the efficiency of distance education programs, input-output variables were determined and an efficiency analysis data form including these variables was prepared. The efficiencies of DMUs were defined with the variables of the number of academic staff, the total number of students, the number of graduate students, and program diversity.

Distance education performance has been calculated based on service quality and efficiency. Distance education performance score is expressed with the symbol "DE-P". The normalized service quality score NSQ, which is used in the calculation of DE-P score, was obtained through DE-SERVQUAL; and the efficiency score (EA) was obtained through DEA.

2.1.3 Calculating NSQ

Since DE-SERVQUAL is a 7-point Likert, the service quality score is between +6 and -6 and is expressed by SQ. The weighted service quality score, which is determined according to the importance given by the participants to the dimensions that constitute distance education service quality, is defined as aSQ. The SQ and aSQ calculation is included in Equation 3 and Equation 4.

The score range obtained from the service quality scale may vary according to the rating number of the Likert scale. Therefore, service quality score has been normalized. In the study, the SQ score obtained through the DE-SERVQUAL scale was converted to NSQ, which has a value between 0–1 and used in calculations. NSQ was obtained through the following equation.

$$\mathrm{NSQ} = \frac{\mathrm{SQ} + 6}{6 - (-6)} = \frac{\mathrm{SQ} + 6}{12} \tag{3}$$

The weighted normalized service quality score (aNSQ) is valued between 0–1 and is calculated as follows.

$$\mathrm{aNSQ} = \mathrm{a} * \mathrm{NSQ} \tag{4}$$

2.1.4 Calculating EA

In the study, the efficiency scores of each DMU were determined by output-oriented CCR. The value obtained is a relative efficiency score and can only be compared to the other DMUs with which it is evaluated together.

Tab. 2.6.1: Models and Variables Used in Efficiency Analysis. Source: Authors

Model	Input variable	Output variable
CCR output orientation	Academic staff/Number of students Program diversity	Number of graduate students

The number of input and output variables to be used in efficiency analysis has been determined according to the approach of analyzing at least 3 times more DMU than the number of variables (Cooper et al., 2007: 116; Vasslioglou and Giokas, 1990: 592). As there are 9 DMUs participated in the study, it was decided to use a total of 3 input and output variables in the analysis. The models and variables used in defining the efficiency analysis are in Tab. 2.6.1.

The output-oriented CCR mathematical model that defines the efficiency score is given below and the indices in the model and their explanations are as follows.

$$\max \varphi + \varepsilon \left(\sum_{i=1}^{m} s_i^- + \sum_{r=1}^{s} s_r^+ \right) \tag{5}$$

Subject to

$$\sum_{j=1}^{n} x_{ij}\lambda_j + s_i^- = x_{io}, i = 1, 2, \ldots, m$$
$$\sum_{j=1}^{n} y_{rj}\lambda_j + s_r^+ = \varphi y_{ro}, r = 1, 2, \ldots, s$$
$$\lambda_j,\ s_i^-,\ s_r^+ \geq 0; \quad \forall\ i,\ j,\ r$$

X_{io}: The o., the efficiency of which is evaluated, belongs to DMU i. amount of input

y_{ro}: The o., the efficiency of which is evaluated, belongs to DMU r. amount of output

X_{ij}: j. belongs to DMU i. amount of input

y_{rj}: j. belongs to DMU r. amount of output

u_r: Weight given to r. output by o.DMU

ν_i: Weight given to i. input by o.DMU

m: Number of input

s: Number of output

n: Number of DMU

s^-: Input redundancies

s^+: Output deficiencies

θ^*: Efficiency score

When we define the efficiency score as "θ", the DMUs that take the value $\theta^*=1$, form the boundary points. In cases where some boundary points are weakly efficient, although $\theta^*=1$, at least one slack variable has not taken the value 0. For a DMU to be relatively efficient, it must both be $\theta^*=1$ and all slack variables $(s_i^-,\ s_r^+)$ must take the value 0. s^- shows the input redundancies and s^+ shows the output deficiencies. In cases where the slack variables are not 0, the output-oriented CCR can be expressed by using the s_i^- *ve* s_r^+ slack variables to convert the inequalities in the model to equality.

In the model, when the optimal goal value of the DMU is taken as q^* and the weights of the optimal solution are taken as v^* and μ^*, if there is at least one optimal solution as $q^* = 1, \quad v^* > 0$ ve $\mu^*>0$, that DMU is efficient. The model where the optimal goal value is not θ^* and the slack variables are not 0 is shown. For the DMU to be efficient, there must be $\theta^*=1$ optimal solution.

The result is expressed with θ^* in problems solved by linear programming. In the output-oriented CCR model, the result is $\theta^*\geq 1$. Inefficient DMUs need to increase their output at this rate. By regulating the θ^* score, the efficiency score is obtained as $\theta = \frac{1}{\theta^*}$. The efficiency score varies between 0 and 1.

2.1.5 *Calculating DE-P*

The distance education performance score is defined as DE-P. DE-P has been calculated with NSQ and EA scores that take values between 0–1. While defining DE-P, additive and multiplicative calculation proposal has been presented. These have been calculated with the following equations depending on NSQ and EA.

$$\mathrm{DE-P\,(Additive)} = (\mathrm{NSQ} + \mathrm{EA})\,/2 \tag{6}$$

$$\mathrm{DE-P\,(Multiplicative)} = \mathrm{NSQ} * \mathrm{EA} \tag{7}$$

The weighted DE-P scores have been calculated according to equation 8 and 9.

$$\mathrm{DE-P\,(Additive)} = (\mathrm{aNSQ} + \mathrm{EA})\,/2 \tag{8}$$

$$\text{DE} - \text{P}\,(\text{Multiplicative}) = \text{aNSQ} * \text{EA} \tag{9}$$

Levels were defined for DE-P scores that were obtained by multiplicative and additive calculations. DE-P score levels were defined by dividing into 3 equal parts in the lowest and highest mark range that can be scored. Table 2 shows the DE-P score levels. Research results have been interpreted according to the levels defined in Tab. 2.6.2.

3 Findings

The units of universities offering distance education services are defined as DMU, and service quality scores of each DMU are given in Tab. 2.6.3.

The normalized service quality score, aNSQ, which includes the levels of importance given by the students to the dimensions that constitute the service quality, got a value between 0,35 and 0,53. DMU-6 (0,53) had the highest NSQ score. It was followed by DMU-2 (0,48), DMU-9 (0,47), DMU-1 (0,46), DMU-3 (0,46), DMU-4 (0,46), DMU-7 (0,39), DMU-5 (0,36) and DMU-8 (0,35). The NSQ score was, DMU-6 (0,51), DMU-2 (0,49), DMU-9 (0,49), DMU-4 (0,47), DMU-5 (0,47), DMU-7 (0,47), DMU-1 (0,47), DMU-3 (0,46) and DMU-8 (0,46) in descending order (Tab. 2.6.3).

Input and output variables used to define the efficiency of DMUs and the values of these variables are given in Tab. 2.6.4.

In the proposed model, the number of academic staff per student and program diversity are accepted as input variable, and the number of graduate students are output variable. Mathematical calculations for DMU-1 are as follows. It was calculated below.

$$\max z = \varphi + s_1^- + s_2^- + s^+$$

s.t.

$$\begin{aligned} 0,3276511 \quad & \lambda_1 + 0,06257379 \quad \lambda_2 + 0,070882203 \quad \lambda_3 + 0,008533333 \\ & \lambda_4 + 0,074733096 \quad \lambda_5 + 0,063448276 \quad \lambda_6 + 0,021237642 \\ & \lambda_7 + 0,002197802 \quad \lambda_8 + 0,11805556 \quad \lambda_9 + s_1^- = 0,03276511 \end{aligned}$$

$$16\lambda_1 + 5\lambda_2 + 9\lambda_3 + 15\lambda_4 + 5\lambda_5 + 4\lambda_6 + 7\lambda_7 + 7\lambda_8 + 5\lambda_9 + s_2^- = 16$$

Tab. 2.6.2: DE-P Score Levels. Source: Authors

DE-P	NSQ		aNSQ		EA		DE-P		DE-P level –Weighted DE-P level		
	Lowest	Highest	Lowest	Highest	Lowest	Highest	Lowest	Highest	Low (L)	Medium (M)	High (H)
DE-P(Additive)	0	1	0	1	0	1	0	1	0–0,33	0,34–0,66	0,67–1
DE-P(Multiplicative)	0	1	0	1	0	1	0	1	0–0,33	0,34–0,66	0,67–1

Tab. 2.6.3: Distance Education Service Quality Scores of DMUs. Source: Authors

DMU	Service quality scores		Normalized service quality scores	
	SQ	aSQ	NSQ	aNSQ
DMU-1	-0,46	-0,45	0,46	0,46
DMU-2	-0,06	-0,25	0,49	0,48
DMU-3	-0,43	-0,51	0,46	0,46
DMU-4	-0,38	-0,43	0,47	0,46
DMU-5	-0,45	-1,79	0,47	0,36
DMU-6	-0,10	-0,41	0,51	0,53
DMU-7	-0,32	-1,29	0,47	0,39
DMU-8	-0,41	-1,62	0,46	0,35
DMU-9	-0,09	-0,37	0,49	0,47

Tab. 2.6.4: DMU Efficiency Analysis Input and Output Variables. Source: Authors

DMU	Input variable		Output variable
	Number of academic staff/ Number of students	Program diversity	Number of graduate students
	x_1	x_2	y_1
DMU-1	0,03276511	16	958
DMU-2	0,06257379	5	208
DMU-3	0,070882203	9	843
DMU-4	0,008533333	15	338
DMU-5	0,074733096	5	66
DMU-6	0,063448276	4	293
DMU-7	0,021237642	7	302
DMU-8	0,002197802	7	109
DMU-9	0,118055556	5	70

$$958\lambda_1 + 208\lambda_2 + 843\lambda_3 + 338\lambda_4 + 66\lambda_5 + 293\lambda_6 + 302\lambda_7 + 109\lambda_8 + 70\lambda_9 - s^+ = 958\varphi$$

$$\lambda_1, \lambda_2, \lambda_3, \lambda_4, \lambda_5, \lambda_6, \lambda_7, \lambda_8, \lambda_9, s_1^-, s_2^-, s^+ \geq 0$$

$$\theta^* = 1 \; and \; \theta = \frac{1}{\theta^*} = 1$$

Tab. 2.6.5: DMU Efficiency Scores. Source: Authors

DMU	**Efficiency score**
DMU-1	1
DMU-2	0,44
DMU-3	1
DMU-4	1
DMU-5	0,14
DMU-6	0,78
DMU-7	0,66
DMU-8	1
DMU-9	0,15

If we use variables and calculate for DMU-2 at Table 4, we find θ^* and θ values are as follows.

$$\theta^* = 2,251303 \; and \; \theta = \frac{1}{\theta^*} = 0,444128$$

CCR output-oriented efficiency score is calculated for all DMUs and presented in Tab. 2.6.5.

In Table 5, DMU-1 (1), DMU-3 (1), DMU-4 (1) and DMU-8 (1) are efficient. DMU-6 (0,78) is at the closest ranking to the efficiency limit and followed by DMU-7 (0,66), DMU-2 (0,44), DMU-9 (0,15) and DMU-5 (0,14).

DE-P was calculated based on service quality and efficiency analysis scores. The values used in the additive and multiplicative calculation of the performance score of distance education programs, DE-P and its score level are as in Tab. 2.6.6.

The DE-P score in the additive performance model is observed to be high in DMU-1 (0,73), DMU-3 (0,73), DMU-4 (0,74) and DMU-8 (0,73). The additive performance score of DMU-2 (0,47), DMU-6 (0,65), DMU-7 (0,57) and DMU-9 (0,34) are medium; and DMU-5 (0,31). The weighted total performance score is high in DMU-1 (0,73), DMU-3 (0,73), DMU-4 (0,73) and DMU-8 (0,68). DMU-2 (0,46), DMU-6 (0,66) and DMU-7 (0,53) have medium level additive performance score, while DMU-5 (0,25) and DMU-9 (0,33) have low additive performance score (Tab. 2.6.6).

According to multiplicative performance score model, DMU-1 (0,46), DMU-3 (0,46), DMU-4 (0,47), DMU-6 (0,40) and DMU-8 (0,46) have medium level score. DMU-2 (0,22), DMU-5 (0,07), DMU-7 (0,31) and DMU-9 (0,09) have

Tab. 2.6.6: DE-P Scores and Levels. Source: Authors

DMU	Efficiency score (EA)	Service quality scores		DE-P (Additive)				DE-P (Multiplicative)			
		NSQ	aNSQ	Score	Level	Weighted score	Level	Score	Level	Weighted score	Level
DMU-1	1	0,46	0,46	0,73	H	0,73	H	0,46	M	0,46	M
DMU-2	0,44	0,49	0,48	0,47	M	0,46	M	0,22	L	0,21	L
DMU-3	1	0,46	0,46	0,73	H	0,73	H	0,46	M	0,46	M
DMU-4	1	0,47	0,46	0,74	H	0,73	H	0,47	M	0,46	L
DMU-5	0,14	0,47	0,36	0,31	L	0,25	L	0,07	L	0,05	L
DMU-6	0,78	0,51	0,53	0,65	M	0,66	M	0,40	M	0,41	M
DMU-7	0,66	0,47	0,39	0,57	M	0,53	M	0,31	L	0,26	L
DMU-8	1	0,46	0,35	0,73	H	0,68	H	0,46	M	0,35	M
DMU-9	0,19	0,49	0,47	0,34	M	0,33	L	0,09	L	0,09	L

low level performance scores. According to the weighted multiplicative performance model, DMU-1 (0,46), DMU-3 (0,46), DMU-4 (0,46), DMU-6 (0,41) and DMU-8 (0,35) have medium level score. DMU-2 (0,21), DMU-5 (0,05), DMU-7 (0,26) and DMU-9 (0,09) have low level performance scores (Tab. 2.6.6).

4 Discussion and Recommendations

Distance education serves many purposes such as responding to the learning needs of individuals, providing equal opportunities, and improving qualified manpower. It is inevitable that distance education will continue to be a preferred education platform in the future as it contributes to both personal development and knowledge economy. Therefore, the units that offer distance education services should measure and evaluate their performance in order to be able to provide better quality and efficient service.

Performance evaluation of higher education service is different from the business world. In our world where the resources are not unlimited, universities are trying to provide high-performance services with scarce resources such as faculty and administrative staff, the variety of programs offered and the number of student quotas. In this study, the performance of distance education programs of universities was defined depending on the quality of the service provided and the efficiency. The proposed model is expected to contribute to managers in studies related to distance education and strategic decisions.

Institutional performance measurement is used in establishing a connecting among planning, decision, action and results (Micheli and Mari, 2014: 147). While defining the performance of the university, it is important to evaluate both quantitative and qualitative measurements in a balanced way by including them in the calculation. In the university performance measuring research of Kallio, Kallio and Grossi (2017: 295) emphasized the importance of quantitative and qualitative performance evaluation. Also Duque (2014: 14) stated that inclusion of components related to service marketing in evaluation of service performance will shed light on decision-makers in understanding the key factors related to the service and the relationship between them and in strategic decisions.

Performance evaluations of education services offered by universities are generally based on student-based data such as student employment results and student satisfaction levels (Harris et al, 2019: 2). In this study, in the proposal presented to calculate the distance education performance of universities, the distance education performance is affected by service quality and efficiency. We used both quantitative and qualitative variables to evaluate distance education performance via wider perspective by using distance education service quality and efficiency scores, and we calculated the DE-P score as additive and multiplicative. While comparing additive and multiplicative calculations, it was observed that the multiplicative DE-P score was lower than the additive. Mathematically, since the DE-P score is in the range of 0–1, it is inevitable that the multiplication score is less than the additive score. This situation must be taken into consideration in the evaluation and choosing the most appropriate method in line with the purposes should be given due importance. While the DE-P score level is low, medium and high in additive model; it is in medium and low in the multiplicative model (Table 6).

If the service quality is low and the efficiency is high at the distance education program, improvements should be made that match the expectations of the students who are customers. Similarly, if the perception of service quality is high and program efficiency is low, there should be efforts to use resources more efficiently in the institution.

In the study, the service quality and efficiency score have the same weight in the additive and multiplicative calculation of DE-P. DMUs can also evaluate their performance by assigning different weights to service quality and efficiency score in line with the goals. A clear definition of the founding purpose, targets and expected results in distance education units will enable putting forward and evaluating the performance criteria more precisely. Yet, performance can be calculated from a wider perspective by adding other outputs such as service quality and efficiency score that affect performance, to the model.

Number of DMU is very important while measuring performance. The number of variables used in defining the efficiency depends on the number of DMUs involved in the study. By increasing the number of DMUs, the efficiency can be evaluated from a wider perspective by using more input and output variables. Additionally, satisfaction, perception or rankings from alumni is valuable and, they would be good choice for output variable. But we couldn't access these variables.

References

Abbott, M., & Doucouliagos, C. (2003). The efficiency of Australian universities: A data envelopment analysis. Economics of Education Review, 22(1), 89–97. https://doi.org/10.1016/S0272-7757(01)00068-1

Abdullah, F. (2006). The development of HEdPERF: A new measuring instrument of service quality for the higher education sector. International Journal of Consumer Studies, 30(6), 569–581. https://doi.org/10.1111/j.1470-6431.2005.00480.x

Agasisti, T. & Johnes, G. (2009). Beyond frontiers: Comparing the efficiency of higher education decision-making units across more than one country, Education Economics, 17(1), 59–79. https://doi.org/10.1080/09645290701523291

Andersen, L. B., Boesen, A., & Pedersen, L. H. (2016). Performance in public organizations: Clarifying the conceptual space. Public Administration Review, 76(6), 852–862. https://doi.org/10.1111/puar.12578

Avkıran, N. K. (2001). Investigating technical and scale efficiencies of Australian universities through data envelopment analysis. Socio-Economic Planning Sciences, 35(1), 57–80. https://doi.org/10.1016/S0038-0121(00)00010-0

Barnes, S. J., & Vidgen, R. (2001). An evaluation of cyber-bookshops: The WebQual method. International Journal of Electronic Commerce, 6(1), 11–30. https://doi.org/10.1080/10864415.2001.11044225

Büyüköztürk, Ş., Kılıç Çakmak, E., Akgün, Ö. E., Karadeniz, Ş., & Demirel, F. (2008). Bilimsel araştırma yöntemleri[Scientific research methods]. (2nd ed). Ankara: Pegem Akademi.

Carlin, T. M. (2004). Output-based management and the management of performance: Insights from the Victorian experience. Management Accounting Research, 15(3), 267–283. https://doi.org/10.1016/j.mar.2004.04.002.

Charnes, A., Cooper, W. W., & Rhodes, E. (1978). Measuring the efficiency of decision making units. European Journal of Operational Research, 2(6), 429–444. https://doi.org/10.1016/0377-2217(78)90138-8

Chawinga, W. D., & Zozie, P. A. (2016). Increasing access to higher education through open and distance learning: Empirical findings from Mzuzu University. Malawi. International Review of Research in Open and Distance Learning, 17(4), 1–20. https://doi.org/10.19173/irrodl.v17i4.2409

Cooper, W. W., Seiford, L. M., & Tone, K. (2007). A comprehensive text with models, applications, References and DEA-Solver Software. (2nd ed.). New York: Springer. https://doi.org/10.1007/978-0-387-45283-8

Ding, D. X., Hu, P. J. H., & Sheng, O. R. L. (2011). E-SELFQUAL: A scale for measuring online self-service quality. Journal of Business Research, 64(5), 508–515. https://doi.org/10.1016/j.jbusres.2010.04.007

Duque, L. C. (2014). A framework for analysing higher education performance: Students' satisfaction, perceived learning outcomes, and dropout intentions, Total Quality Management & Business Excellence, 25: 1–2, 1–21. https://doi.org/10.1080/14783363.2013.807677

Ensslin, S. R., Ensslin, L., Matos, L. S, Dutra, A., & Ripoll-Feliu, V. M. (2015). Research opportunities in performance measurement in public utilities regulation. International Journal of Productivity and Performance Management, 64(7), 994–1017. https://doi.org/10.1108/IJPPM-05-2014-0067

Farrell, M. J. (1957). The measurement of productive efficiency. Journal of the Royal Statistical Society. Series A (General), 120(3), 253–290. https://doi.org/10.2307/2343100

Flegg, A. T., Allen, D. O., Field, K. & Thurlow, T. W. (2004). Measuring the efficiency of British universities: A multi-period data envelopment analysis, Education Economics, 12(3), 231–249. https://doi.org/10.1080/0904529042000258590

Fountain, J. E. (2001). Paradoxes of public sector customer service. Governance: An International Journal of Policy and Administration, 14(1), 55–73. https://doi.org/10.1111/0952-1895.00151

Garcia-Aracil, A., & Palomares-Montero, D. (2010). Examining benchmark indicator systems for the evaluation of higher education institutions. Higher Education, 60(2), 217–234. https://doi.org/10.1007/s10734-009-9296-8

Gök, B. (2017). Üniversitelerde uzaktan eğitim programlarının hizmet kalitesi ve etkinliğinin değerlendirilmesi [Evaluation of service quality and effectiveness of distance education programs in universities.]. Gazi University Informatics Institute. Unpublished Doctoral Thesis. Ankara.

Gürbüz, E., & Ergülen, A. (2008). Yükseköğretim kurumlarında hizmet kalitesi ölçü ve modelleri [Service quality measures and models in higher education institutions]. Ankara: Detay Yayıncılık.

Harris, W. E., Langan, A. M., Barrett, N., Jack, K., Wibberley, C., & Hamshire, C. (2019). A case for using both direct and indirect benchmarking to compare university performance metrics. Studies in Higher Education, 44(12), 2281–2292. https://doi.org/10.1080/03075079.2018.1490893.

İçli, G. E., & Anıl, N. K. (2014). The HEDQUAL Scale: A new measurement scale of service quality for MBA programs in higher education. South African Journal of Business Management, 45(3), 31–44.

Johnes, J. (2006). Data envelopment analysis and its application to the measurement of efficiency in higher education. Economics of Education Review, 25(3), 273–288. https://doi.org/10.1016/j.econedurev.2005.02.005

Kallio, K. M., Kallio, T. J., & Grossi, G. (2017). Performance measurement in universities: ambiguities in the use of quality versus quantity in performance indicators. Public Money and Management, 37(4), 293–300. https://doi.org/10.1080/09540962.2017.1295735

Karahan, A., & Özgür, E. (2011). Hastanelerde performans yönetim sistemi ve veri zarflama analizi [Performance management system and data envelopment analysis in hospitals]. (2nd ed.). Ankara: Nobel Yayın.

Kenyon, G. N., & Sen, K. S. (2015). Perception of quality: Mapping product and service quality consumer perception. In The aspects of quality. Londra: Springer.

Loiacono, E. T., Watson, R. T., & Goodhue, D. L. (2002). WebQual TM : A measure of web site quality. Marketing Theory and Applications, 13(3), 432–438. https://doi.org/10.1590/S0104-530X2005000200011

Martinez-Argüelles, M., Castán, J., & Juan, A. (2009). How do students measure service quality in e-learning? A case study regarding an internet-based university. Electronic Journal of e-Learning, 8(2), 151–160.

Matei, A., & Matei, L. (2008). Statistic instruments for performance evaluation in the public sector. A case study for Romania. International Review on Public and Nonprofit Marketing, 5(1), 35–52. https://doi.org/10.1007/s12208-008-0003-8

Melnyk, S. A., Bititci, U., Platts, K., Tobias, J., & Andersen, B. (2014). Is performance measurement and management fit for the future? Management Accounting Research, 25(2), 173–186. https://doi.org/10.1016/j.mar.2013.07.007

Micheli, P., & Mari, L. (2014). The theory and practice of performance measurement. Management Accounting Research, 25(2), 147–156. https://doi.org/10.1016/j.mar.2013.07.005

Nage-Sibande, B., & Morolong, B. L. (2018). A trend analysis of opportunities and challenges of open and distance learning provision in dual-mode institutions. Distance Education, 39(4), 495–510. https://doi.org/10.1080/01587919.2018.1457951

Parasuraman, A., Zeithaml, V. A., & Berry, L. L. (1988). SERVQUAL: A multiple-item scale for measuring customer perceptions of service quality, Journal of Retailing, 64(1), 12–40. https://doi.org/10.1016/S0148-2963(99)00084-3

Parasuraman, A., Zeithaml, V. A., & Malhotra, A. (2002). E-S-QUAL: A multiple-item scale for assessing electronic service quality. Journal of Servive Research, 7(10), 1–21. https://doi.org/10.1177/1094670504271156

Propper, C., & Wilson, D. (2003). The use and usefulness of performance measures in the public sector. Oxford Review of Economic Policy, 19(2), 250–267. https://doi.org/10.1093/oxrep/19.2.250

Psacharopoulos, G. & Patrinos, H. A. (2018). Returns to Investment in Education: A Decennial Review of the Global Literature. Policy Research Working Paper; No. 8402. World Bank, Washington, DC. © World Bank. https://openknowledge.worldbank.org/handle/10986/29672 License: CC BY 3.0 IGO.

Ramanathan, R. (2003). An introduction to data envelopment analysis: A tool for performance measurement, New Delhi: Sage Publications.

Simmons, K. O. (2007). Distance learner expectations for quality, technology-enabled, support service. Walden University Applied Management and Decision Sciences. Doctoral Thesis. Minnesota.

Sözen, A., Alp, I., & Kılınç, C. (2012). Efficiency assessment of the hydro-power plants in Turkey by using data envelopment analysis. Renewable Energy, 46, 192–202.

Sridharan, S., & Nakaima, A. (2011). Ten steps to making evaluation matter. Evaluating and Program Planning, 34, 135–146.

Thomas, P. (2006). Performance measurement, reporting, obstacles and accountability: Recent trends and future directions. Australia and New Zealand School of Government Monograph. Canberra: ANU E-Press.

TUİK (2019). "Education Statistics", http://www.tuik.gov.tr/PreTablo.do?alt_id=1018 (Accessed 22 February 2019).

Udo, G. J., Bagchi, K. K., & Kirs, P. J. (2011). Using SERVQUAL to assess the quality of e-learning experience. Computers in Human Behavior, 27, 1272–1283.

Uppal, M. A., Ali, S., & Gulliver, S. (2018). Factors determining e-learning service quality. British Journal of Educational Technology, 49(3), 412–426.

Vasslioglou, M., & Giokas, D. (1990). A study of the relative efficiency of bank branches: An application of data envelopment analysis. The Journal of Operational Research Society, 41(7), 591–597.

Yazıcıoğlu, Y., & Erdoğan, S. (2014). SPSS uygulamalı bilimsel araştırma yöntemleri [SPSS applied scientific research methods]. (4th ed). Ankara: Detay Yayıncılık.

YÖK (2019), "Report on Students Number in Turkey", https://istatistik.yok.gov.tr/ (Accessed 22 February 2019).

Yoo, B., & Donthu, N. (2001). Developing a scale to measure perceived quality of an internet shopping site (SITEQUAL). Quarterly Journal of Electronic Commerce, 2(1), 31–47.

Zawacki-Richter, O., & Naidu, S. (2016). Mapping research trends from 35 years of publications in distance education. Distance Education, 37(3), 245–269.

Zhonghua, C., & Yee, W. (2012). Research frontiers in public sector performance measurement. Physics Procedia, 25, 793–799.

Dr. Arif İğdeli

2.7 The Regional Distribution of Technoparks and Their Impact on Innovation

Abstract: Rapid advances have been inevitable in the innovation process today, where the transfer of knowledge to technology is shortened. The way to achieve this progress for countries is to invest in innovation and encourage R&D expenditure. Universities, which are the production centers of science, are the best places to invest in innovation. Companies are needed to transform the academic knowledge emerging in universities that have the necessary infrastructure for innovation into practice and commercialize. Policy makers who are aware of this need, have accelerated the commercialization of academic knowledge by establishing technoparks, strengthening the bond between universities and companies. Technoparks have contributed to regional development by increasing the innovation capacity of the regions. This chapter aims to determine the impact of the number of active technoparks on innovation capacity in regions of Turkey. In accordance with this purpose, the distribution of the number of active technopark between NUTS I and NUTS II regions of Turkey are presented with the aid of the figures. According to the findings, there are significant differences between number of active technoparks in the West and East regions of Turkey. In addition, according to the findings there is a distinction in the number of patent applications between the West and East of Turkey. These differences between regions are similar in number of active technoparks and patent applications. This similarity indicates the relationship between the number of active technoparks and patent applications in the regions

Keywords: Technoparks, Regional analysis, Regional distribution, Innovation.

Introduction

The concept of development, which has an important place in the implementation and development of regional policies, emerged especially after the Second World War and has undergone serious changes in its definition, goals and tools during the period. Development, which is expressed as the rise of countries or regions from the current situation to a better state, was explained only with economic indicators in the past, but also with social, cultural and environmental indicators today. In short, the concept of development, which was expressed only with the changes in the Gross Domestic Product (hereafter GDP) of countries or individuals in the past, is now expressed as the development of countries or individuals in the economic, social and cultural field, the increase in institutional capacity, the progress of human capital and the development of environmental sensitivity (Pektaş & Demirkol, 2018: 79).

The change in the concept of development over time has shown has also affected the regional policies implemented by the countries and brought the concept of regional development to the agenda. Regional development is defined as policy measures aimed at developing sustainable economic growth and living standards through the efficient use of regional and local resources. Factors such as the economic structure of the underdeveloped regions, insufficient capital, high population growth rate and inadequate job opportunities, high net immigration rate point to the necessity of regional development in order to rid these regions from their disadvantaged position (Tutar & Demiral, 2007: 67). Regional development, which is also expressed as a set of strategies and actions aimed at eliminating the imbalance between the regions. It has goals such as reducing unemployment, increasing the competitiveness and profitability of businesses in the region, attracting investments in the region, establishing and developing the infrastructure of the region, and preventing income inequality between regions. Significant changes have been observed in the regional development policies implemented to achieve these goals in the last four decades (Kandemir & Ergin, 2018: 2648–2649). While it is thought that the driving force of regional growth was large infrastructure investments in the traditional understanding of regional development pre-1970, the driving force of regional growth in new regional development understanding is considered to be factors such as human capital, innovation, collective learning, interdependence and local culture (Akpınar, 2013: 30).

New actors were needed in regional development with the abandonment of the traditional regional development approach and the adoption of the new regional development approach. Technoparks emerging as a result of the needs contribute to regional development through innovation by facilitating technology transfer between companies in the region. Technoparks ensure the commercialization of academic knowledge by realizing the cooperation between the state, university and industry. Technoparks, which are the interface of cooperation between university and industry, aim to produce high value-added technology-intensive products in their regions. Technoparks established for this purpose have been successful in increasing the innovation capacity of the regions in the countries. This success caught the attention of policy makers and led to the spread of technoparks around the world.

The motivation factor of the research is to evaluation the success level of technoparks in increasing the innovation capacity of regions. Depending on the basic motivation, it is aimed to determine the regional distribution of technoparks and to evaluate the impact of the technoparks on the innovation capacity of regions. For this purpose, the distribution of the number of active technoparks between NUTS1 and NUTS II regions is presented with maps. Patent application numbers were used as an innovation indicator in evaluating the impact of technoparks on the innovation capacity of regions, due to the inaccessibility of regional data such as R&D expenditure, high technology exports, number of researchers and technicians. This research consists of four section. In the second section following the introduction, the definition, goals and objectives of technoparks are presented. In the third section, the impact of technoparks on regions and evaluation criteria are given. In the following chapter, the regional distribution of active technoparks is presented with maps and the relationship between the number of active technoparks and the patent applications in the regions is evaluated by comparing the maps. In the conclusion part, the findings of the research are discussed and suggestions are offered to policy makers in line with the findings.

1 Definition and Purposes of Technopark

As an important actor of the new regional development understanding, the diversity in the aims and activities of the technoparks makes it difficult to agree on a common definition of the technopark concept. The most common definitions used in the literature regarding technopark are given below.

The UK Science Parks Association defines the technopark as an organization that has ties to universities and R&D centers, and has technology transfer activities that support the formation and development of knowledge-based businesses in the region (Alkibay, 2012: 67). According to the International Science Parks Association (IASP), technopark is an initiative designed to encourage the establishment and growth of industry initiatives based on knowledge and high technology, associated with one or more universities and R&D centers, officially or on an activity basis, and will provide support in technology transfer to tenant companies (Keleş & Tunca, 2010: 3).

Amoroso and Soriano (2019: 1) define the technopark as the structures that encourage the housing and growth of startups by facilitating the flow of information between universities, R&D institutions and markets, known as the triple helix. In line with these definitions, technopark can be described as organizations that meet the need for technology transfer from other companies through positive externalities in order to survive and develop in the region. During the Second World War, the close collaboration between scientists and engineers played an important role in victory, which led to the rapid acceptance of the idea of concentrating companies in the same region in the United States. The success of Standford Research Park and Research Triangle Park in the United States has triggered the spread of technoparks around the world (Amoroso & Soriano, 2019: 1). Countries that aim to export technology instead of importing have created the infrastructure of technoparks and supported their development in order to capture and accommodate technological developments (Kandemir & İlter, 2019: 1219). In addition to the success of the technoparks in the United States, there are many reasons that enable the establishment and spread of technoparks around the world. The reasons for the establishment and spread of technoparks around the world are listed below (Çilingir, 2011: 205; Alkibay et al., 2012: 67; Rodriguez-Pose & Hardy, 2014: 19; Cansız, 2017: 26–28; Bayzin & Şengür, 2019: 300):

i. Seeking a solution to unemployment and stagnant economy by increasing competition
ii. Facilitating the commercialization of information
iii. Decreasing in employment in the traditional manufacturing industry
iv. Increasing participation of local governments in economic development
v. Accelerating technological developments and technology production
vi. Increasing the development level of countries and preventing brain drain
vii. Increasing opportunities for cooperation between institutions that have the same goals and problems
viii. Supporting innovation-based entrepreneurship
ix. Contribution to regional development

The history of the technoparks whose reasons for their establishment are given above, started in 1952 with the efforts of a group of researchers who wanted to commercialize their research under the leadership of Stanford University (Zuhal, 2017: 57). Following this technopark, also known as the Slicon Valley, the Research Triangle Park was established seven years later in North Carolina. The pioneering technoparks established to improve the cooperation between the university and the industry could not show the expected contribution and development until the 1970s in regions where industrial production is intense. The stagnation in industrial branches and increase in unemployment caused due to the increase in oil prices during the 1970s pushed countries to seek solutions to overcome the economic crisis (Yalçıntaş, 2014: 91). Developed countries, especially the United States and Japan, considered the way to overcome the economic crisis through the close cooperation established between research institutions and companies. With the cooperation, researches have been carried out in new fields such as software, biotechnology, space technologies, automation, robotic coding and information technologies. As a result of these researches, low-cost new products have been created and the market has revived (Keleş & Tunca, 2010: 4–5). After the United States, the technoparks are established in England. Hariot-Watt University Technopark and Cambridge Technopark are pioneering technoparks in England in 1972 (Tepe & Zaim, 2016: 22).

The fact that the reputation of these pioneering technoparks exceeds the borders of the region has transformed the technoparks from a tool used in the industrialized regions of developed countries to a tool that policy makers over the world wish to bring to their own countries (Rodriguez-Pose & Hardy, 2014: 2). As a result, the establishment of technoparks has accelerated all over the world since the 1980s. Countries that have just completed their industrialization process such as China, South Korea and India, which have realized the success of technoparks, have started the establishment of technoparks in the 1990s to support economic growth and development (Eyyuboğlu & Aktaş, 2017: 78).

The history of the establishment of technoparks in Turkey extends to the cooperation between Istanbul Technical University (ITU) and the Istanbul Chamber of Commerce (ITO) in the mid-1980s. This technopark, operating in 1986, has become a technology development center with the agreement signed between ITU and the Small and Medium Enterprises Support and Development Administration (SMESDA) in the following years (Yanıktepe et al., 2016: 5). Technoparks have come up to the agenda as a policy in the V. Five Year Development Plan for the first time in Turkey and have continued to take place as a policy tool in following development plans. DPT received proposals for the establishment of technoparks in Turkey, by inviting experts from the United Nations. As a result of these proposals, it has been decided to establish five technoparks in Turkey such as ITÜ, ODTÜ, Ege University, Anadolu University, and Tubitak MAM Research Center, by the cooperation with DPT, United Nations Development Program and United Nations Industrial Development Organization (UNIDO) (Keleş & Tunca, 2010: 5–6). Then, the Ministry of Industry and Trade published the regulations on technoparks in 1996. METU and TUBITAK MAM Research Center approved as the first technoparks in Turkey after the approving the applications within the frameworks of this regulation (Çilingir, 2011: 207). Technoparks gain their legal identity with the Technology Development Zones law enacted by the Turkish Grand National Assembly (TBMM) in 2001. As a result of this law, financial incentives for entrepreneurs, employees and managing companies within the body of technoparks were provided in order to facilitate the establishment and development of technoparks as well as defining the establishment and management of technoparks (Demirli, 2014: 98). The establishment and expansion of technoparks in Turkey has been the 2001–2020 period. Compared to the industrialized countries, Turkey is quite late in the establishment of technoparks. However, Turkey has exerted great efforts during the 2001–2020 period and accelerate the establishment of technoparks in order to close the gap between these countries. While the number of technoparks was 2 in 2001 when the law was enacted, the number of technoparks is 84 in 2020. The 70 of 84 technoparks are currently in active and the others are in the installation phase (TGBD, 2020).

Policy makers have chosen to use the term technology development zones instead of technoparks in Turkey. In addition to technology development zones, concepts such as science research park, innovation center, technopole, center of excellence and industrial park are frequently used in the literature instead of technoparks (Rodriguez-Pose & Hardy, 2014: 16; Zuhal, 2017: 56). Underlying the naming and defining of technoparks in different ways are the country's development models, opportunities, industrial model, geographical structure, administrative and legal systems, socio-cultural structures and differences in the level of technological development (Gül & Çakır, 2014: 82; Tepe & Zaim, 2016: 21). Although the naming of technoparks is different between countries, their aims and basic philosophy are similar between countries. The purposes of technoparks are generally listed as follows: (Technology Development Zones Law 2001; Wallsten, 2004: 4; Rodriguez-Pose & Hardy, 2014: 17; Nosonov & Letkina, 2019: 4214):

a. Stimulate information and technology flows between companies and research institutions
b. Communicate between companies, entrepreneurs and technicians
c. Promote a culture of innovation, creativity and quality
d. Focus on the benefit of people as well as companies and research institutions
e. Encourage the establishment of new technology-based companies
f. Establish to the connections between startups, global innovative companies and research institutions
g. Capture the advanced technology by accelerating the entry of foreign capital into the country
h. Promote the technology-intensive production and entrepreneurship
i. Create universal technical solutions, technologies and models
j. Ensure that financial flows, technical and intellectual resources are concentrated in the region for the implementation of innovative projects

k. Play a catalyst role in regional economic development

The aims and applications of technoparks have started to differ over time. In addition to their purposes and practices, differences are observed between technoparks in many factors such as the scale of technoparks, concrete infrastructure, intangible support forms, various targeted industries, types of supported companies and the nature of leading stakeholders (Çilingir, 2011: 206; Rodriguez-Pose & Hardy, 2014: 4). Technoparks are divided into five groups in line with the differentiation. These are (Kıncal, 2014; 7–8):

a. Technoparks established directly by the governments
b. Technoparks established by universities
c. Technoparks established with the cooperation of companies with strong financial structure and research institutions
d. Technoparks established by local governments
e. Technoparks established with the cooperation of public and private sectors

Although there is a difference between the types of technoparks listed above, there are common features that should be found in technoparks generally. These common features are listed as transferring technology from research institutions to companies, supporting startups and increasing the innovation capacity of the region (Cansız, 2017: 33). Firstly, technology transfer from research institutions to companies is possible with the close relationship between universities and technoparks. An intermediary is required for transferring the information produced by universities to firms and bringing them into the economy. Technoparks meet this requirement by establishing close relationships between firms and universities (Olcay & Bulu, 2016: 72). As a result of the establishment of the link between universities and technoparks, academicians have the opportunity to work in technopark firms. This situation accelerates technology transfer from universities to companies (Pekol & Erbaş, 2011: 41). In addition, the link between universities and technoparks facilitates the efficient use of resources, the sharing of infrastructure and the emergence of new ideas (Cansız, 2017: 32).

2 The Impact of Technoparks on Regions and Evaluation Criterias

Technoparks are thought to play a catalyzt role in the development of the regional economies. Technoparks create significant positive external effects for the economy of the region by encouraging the establishment and clustering of specific sector companies in the region (Yanıktepe et al., 2016: 3). These effects are attracting long-term foreign capital to the region, stimulating the local economy, contributing to industrialization, increasing the competitiveness of the regions, increasing the technology production capability of the regions, opening the region to international markets (Kıncal, 2014: 17–18; Kayalıdere, 2014: 85; Yıldız & Aykanat, 2015: 1197; Eyyuboğlu & Aktaş, 2017: 78). In addition to these, technoparks also contribute to the creation of an environmentally friendly, clean and beautiful lifestyle, to increase the cultural activities in the region, to increase the employment level in the region by conducting researches in the regions needed by the industry (Keleş & Tunca, 2010: 9). In short, technoparks offer opportunities not only for the economic development but also social and cultural development of the region. Evaluation criteria have been developed by researchers to measure the effects of technoparks on firms, universities and regions and the success of technoparks. These criteria are listed as follows (Kiper, 2010: 51):

a. Projects realized with the cooperation of firms and research institutions in technopark
b. Number of commercialized scientific thoughts
c. Number of patents
d. License and product-service sales
e. Consultancy services offered to companies in the industry
f. Number of academic staff working in technopark firms
g. The width and depth of the connections formed outside the research institutions of technoparks

It is very difficult to measure the effects of technoparks on regional development. The reason for this difficulty is attributed to three main factors. These are (Amoroso & Soriano, 2019: 2–3);

a. Lack of firm-level quantitative data
b. It is only possible to make comparison between firms inside and outside the technopark
c. The functional diversity of technoparks creates heterogeneous parking groups with different focuses and purposes.

The lack of quantitative data of the technopark firms in Turkey is the most important constraints of the research. This constraint makes it difficult to measure the effects of technoparks on the innovation levels of regions. The effects of technoparks on the innovation levels of the regions are analyzed with regional data instead of company data due to this constraint. The number of academic staff employed by the technopark firms in Turkey, consulting services offered to companies and the commercialization of scientific thought regional data are not inaccessible. Therefore, the effects of technoparks on the innovation levels of the regions will be evaluated by comparing the number of active technoparks and patent applications in the regions.

3 Regional Distribution of Technoparks and Their Impact on Innovation

Technoparks, which are an important tool of the new regional development policies adopted after the failure of traditional regional development policies, have shown a serious development throughout the world in the last fifty years. Turkey has achieved this development later than the developed countries. Therefore, technoparks have been established and become widespread in the 2000s. The development of total and active technoparks in Turkey are presented by Fig. 2.7.1.

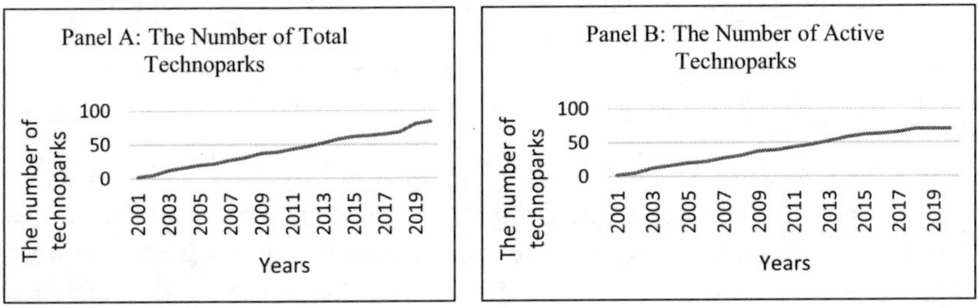

Fig. 2.7.1: The Number of Total and Active Techno Parks in Turkey. Source: Ministry of Industry and Technology (2020)

According to Fig. 2.7.1, the total and active technoparks tends to increase in Turkey between 2001 and 2020 periods. The number of total technoparks, which was two in 2001, reached 84 in 2020. However, while 70 of these technoparks are active, 14 of them are in the installation phase. Firms in active technoparks serve in different sectors. The sectoral distribution of firms in technoparks is summarized in Tab. 2.7.1.

According to Tab. 2.7.1, technopark firms mostly operate in the software sector. After the software sector, technopark firms are active in research and experimental areas related to natural sciences and engineering. Tab. 2.7.1 shows that technopark firms mostly operate in technology-intensive sectors. This situation indicates that technoparks will increase region's innovation skills.

Tab. 2.7.1: Sectoral Distribution of Firms in Technoparks in 2020

1 Sectors	2 Percentage
3 Software activities	4 44.04
5 Research and experimental development activities	6 7.24
7 Computer consulting activities	8 3.20
9 Biotechnology activities	10 2.92
11 Engineering and consultancy activities for the manufacturing industry	12 1.62
13 Engineering consulting services	14 1.53
15 Consultancy services for energy projects	16 1.37
17 Computer service activities	18 1.36
19 Computer hardware activities	20 1.27
21 Manufacture of electronic tools and circuits	22 1.17
23 Manufacture of installed electronic card	24 1.08
25 Manufacture of pharmaceutical products	26 1.00
27 Manufacture of medical equipment and supplies	28 1.00
29 Other	30 32.2

Source: Ministry of Industry and Technology (2020)

The success of technoparks in increasing the innovation capacity of the regions is evaluated by comparing the number of active technoparks with the number of patent applications in the regions. The distribution of the number of active technoparks was carried out NUTS I and NUTS II classifications. The distribution of the number of active technoparks between NUTS I and NUTS II regions in 2020 is mapped in Fig. 2.7.2.

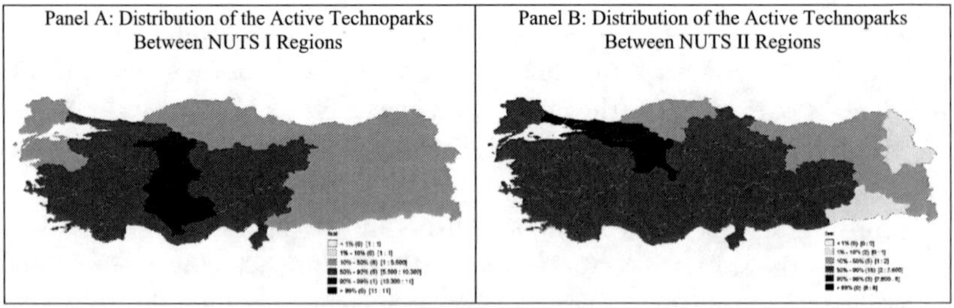

Fig. 2.7.2: Distribution of the Number of Active Technoparks in 2020 among NUTS I and NUTS II Regions. Source: Ministry of Industry and Technology (2020)

The distinction draws attention between the West and East regions of Turkey in Panel A which reflects the distribution of the number of active technoparks between NUTS I and NUTS II region. According to Panel A and Panel B, the number of active technopark in the West Regions is above the average of Turkey, while the number of active technopark in the East region is under the average of Turkey. The highest number of active technoparks is Western Anatolia, including the capital of Turkey in Panel A. While the highest number of active technoparks are TR10, TR42 and TR51 covering industrial cities such as İstanbul, Kocaeli and Ankara. There is no distinction between the East regions of Turkey in terms of the number of active technoparks. However, TRA2 and TRC3 regions dissociate the other regions in Panel B. These findings show that NUTS II classification reflects the economic indicators of the regions more detailed than the NUTS I classification.

The impact of active technoparks on the innovation capacity of the regions is determined by the comparing Figure 2.7.2 and Figure 2.7.3. The distribution of the patent application numbers between NUTS I and NUTS II regions in 2020 is pictured in Fig. 2.7.3. Figure 2.7.3 should be copied after this paragraph

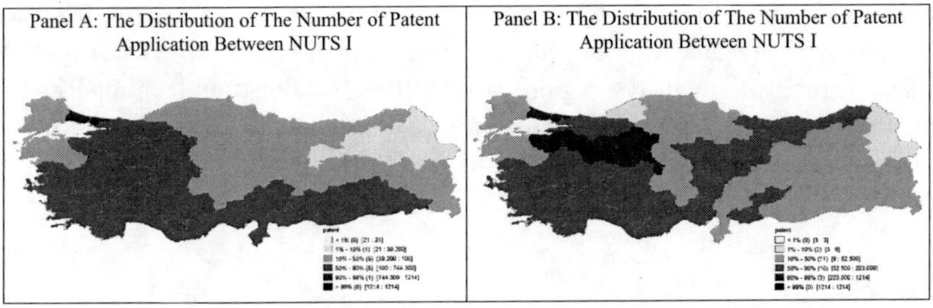

Fig. 2.7.3: The Distribution of the Patent Application Numbers between NUTS I and NUTS II Regions. Source: Turkish Patent and Trademark Office (2020)

According to Panel A and Panel B, the West Regions of Turkey is above the average of Turkey in terms of the number of patent applications, while the East regions of Turkey is below the average of Turkey in terms of the number of patent applications. According to Panel A, the highest number of patent applications is İstanbul region, while the lowest number of patent applications is the Northeastern Anatolia region. The highest number of patent applications are in İstanbul region can be explained the majority of industrial organizations in the private sector agglomerated in this areas. The fact that Northeastern Anatolia region has the least number of patent applications is similar to Figure 2.7.2.

Panel A. Northeastern Anatolia region is at the bottom of the ranking among NUTS II regions in terms of the number of active technoparks and patent applications. This finding indicates the correlation between the number of active technoparks and patent applications in the regions.

According to Panel B, TR10, TR41 and TR51 regions have the highest number of patent applications, while TR81 and TRA2 regions have the lowest number of patent applications. Figure 2.7.3 Panel B findings resemble Figure 2.7.2 Panel B findings. The high level of the number of active technoparks and patent applications in the regions where industrial centers are located indicates the relationship between technopark and innovation. It is not possible to base the economic disparities between the East and West Regions of Turkey only on the number of active technoparks in the regions. Because the development gap between the Eastern and Western regions of Turkey is based on quite old. However, it can be considered that the number of active technoparks causes the development difference between the regions to widen further. It is no coincidence that the TRA2 region has the lowest number of active technoparks and patent applications among NUTS II regions of Turkey. These findings reveal the relationship between the number of active technoparks and patent applications. In line with these findings, it can be concluded that technoparks will increase the innovation capacities of the underdeveloped regions by making the research institutions in the regions. In addition, establishing technoparks in regions which are undeveloped in terms of development will make it attractive for investors to come these regions due to the new incentives offered by technoparks.

Conclusion

The failure of traditional regional approaches, which argue that large infrastructure investments in developed countries are the engine of regional development, have led policy makers to seek new solutions. Developed countries have adopted a new understanding of regional development that prioritizes factors such as human capital, innovation, collective learning, interdependence and local culture in stimulating their stagnating economies. The new understanding of regional development aims at interregional competition by strengthening the relationship between actors such as research institutions, companies and local people in the region. With the adoption and spread of the new regional development approach, new regional actors were also needed. Technoparks are one of the institutions that meet this need. Technoparks, which enable the commercialization of academic knowledge, especially by providing cooperation between government-research institutions and industry, contribute to development by increasing the innovation capacity of the region. The purpose of the research is to determine whether the technoparks are successful to upgrade innovation capacities in NUTS I and NUTS II regions of Turkey. In line with this purpose, the distribution of the active number of technoparks between NUTS I and NUTS II regions is presented with maps. Then, the distribution of the number of patent applications, which is one of the outputs of the innovation, between NUTS I and NUTS II regions was determined with the help of maps. The relationship between the active number of technoparks and the number of patent applications in the regions was evaluated by comparing the maps.

According to the findings, the West Regions of Turkey is above the average of Turkey in terms of active technoparks, while the East regions of Turkey is below the average of Turkey in terms of active technoparks. In addition, the findings show that the highest number of technoparks are located in industrial centers of Turkey such as İstanbul, Ankara and Kocaeli. The distribution of the active number of technoparks between NUTS I and NUTS II regions is mostly similar. However, there are some differences between the distributions. The most striking of these differences is that TR10 and TR41 regions where covering İstanbul and Kocaeli provinces are in the upper group in the distribution of NUTS I regions compared to distribution of NUTS II regions in terms of the number of active technoparks. This situation indicates that NUTS II classification offers more detailed results than the NUTS I classification in reflecting the economic indicators of the region.

According to another finding obtained in the study, the distribution of the number of active technoparks and the patent applications between NUTS I and NUTS II regions are similar. There is a distinction between the East and West Regions of Turkey in terms of the number of active technoparks as well as the number of patent applications. In addition, regions covering industrial centers such as Istanbul and Ankara are among the top group in the number of active technoparks and patent applications, while the TRA2 region, which covers the provinces of Ağrı, Ardahan, Iğdır and Kars, is in the lowest group in the number of active technoparks and patent applications. Based on the findings, it cannot be considered that the distribution of the active number of technoparks creates the difference of patent application between the regions. Because the history of the development gap between regions in Turkey is based on the past. However, in line with the findings, it can be stated that the regional distribution of the number of active technoparks plays a role in expanding the difference between regions.

In line with the research findings, policy makers should give priority the East regions of Turkey on establishment of technoparks. The regions where innovation capacity is quite low compared to the average of Turkey may withdraw investment in the establishment of technoparks for the needs. In addition, the concentration of technoparks in these regions will allow academic staff to work in technopark companies, preventing human capital migration between regions. Researchers who intend to investigate this issue in the future can add a different dimension to the relationship between the number of active technoparks and the patent applications by using company data instead of regional data.

References

Akpınar, R. (2013). Türkiye'de Değişen Bölgesel Kalkınma Politikaları[Changing Regional Development Policies in Turkey]. *The Black Sea Journal of Social Sciences*, 4(6), 29–46.

Alkibay, S., Orhaner, E., Korkmaz, S. & Sertoğlu, A. E. (2012). Üniversite Sanayi İşbirliği Çerçevesinde Teknoparklar, Yönetimsel Sorunları Ve Çözüm Önerileri[Technoparks within the Framework of University-Industry Cooperation, Managerial Problems and Suggested Solutions]. *Atatürk University Journal of Economics and Administrative Sciences*, 26(2), 65–90.

Amoroso, S. & Soriano, F. H. (2019). An International Perspective on Science and Technology Parks Amoroso, S., Link, A. N. &Wright, M. (Ed.), Science and Technology Parks and Regional Economic Development (1–8. ss.). Springer Nature.

Bayzin, S. & Şengür, M. (2019). Üniversite Sanayi İşbirliğinde Teknoparkların Rolü[Role of Technoparks in University-Industry Cooperation]. *The International Journal of Economic and Social Research*, 15(3), 299–313.

Cansız, M. (2017). 2023'e Doğru Türkiye Teknoparkları[Technoparks in Turkey Towards 2023]. Ankara: Republic of Turkey Ministry of Development.

Çilingir, Ç. (2011). Bölgesel Kalkınmada Teknoloji Geliştirme Bölgeleri[Technology Development Zones in Regional Development]. 5th Regional Development and Governance Symposium: Governance of Industrial Policy, 27–28 January 2011, Ankara, TEPAV, 203–212.

Demirli, Y. (2014). Türkiye'de Teknoparklara Yönelik Teşvikler Ve Teknoparkların Bilim Ve Teknoloji Kapasitesinin Gelişimine Etkisi[The Incentives for Technoparks in Turkey and Contribution to Development of the Science and Technology Capacity]. *Journal of Public Finance*, 166, 95–115.

Eyyuboğlu, B. B. & Aktaş, S. G. (2017). Türkiye'de Teknoparkların Coğrafi Dağılımı Ve Yoğunluğu (2001–2015)[Analysis of Geographical Distribution and Concentration of Technoparks in Turkey]. *Eastern Geographical Review*, 35, 75–88.

Gül, T. G. & Çakır, S. (2014). Teknoparklar ve Teknoloji Üretimi: İzmir Teknoloji Geliştirme Bölgesi Örneği[Technoparks and Technology Production: The Case of İzmir Technology Development Region]. *Knowledge Economy& Knowledge Management*, 9(1), 79–90.

Kandemir, O. & Ergin, Ü. (2018). Bölgesel Gelişme Bağlamında Kalkınma Ajanslarının Faaliyetleri: TR82 Bölgesi (Kastamonu, Sinop, Çankırı) Örneği[Activities of Development Agencies in the Context of Regional Development: Case of TR82 Region (Kastamonu, Sinop, Çankırı)]. *Journal of Human and Social Science Researchers*, 7(4), 2646–2671.

Kandemir, T. & İlter, B. (2019). Girişimcilik Faaliyetlerinde Teknoparkların Önemi: Afyon-Uşak Zafer Teknoloji Geliştirme Bölgesi örneği[Importance of technopark In Entrepreneurship Activities: Afyon-Uşak Zafer Technology Development Zone example]. *Afyon Kocatepe University Journal of Social Sciences*, 21(4), 1216–1229.

Kayalıdere, G. (2014). Türkiye'nin Teknoloji Politikalarında Teknoparkların Önemi Ve Teknoparklara Yönelik Vergi Avantajları[The Importance of Technoparks Within Technology Policy of Turkey and Tax Advantages for Technoparks]. *Gazi University Journal of Social Science*, 1(1), 75–96.

Keleş, M. K. & Tunca, M. Z. (2010). Türkiye'deki Teknokentlerin Mevcut Durumun İncelenmesi [An Investigation of the Technoparks in Turkey]. *Journal of Süleyman Demirel University Institute of Social Sciences*, 1(11), 1–22.

Kıncal, A. (2014). Bütüncül Bir Yaklaşımla Teknoparkların Ülke Ekonomisi Üzerindeki Etkileri[The Effects of Technoparks on the National Economy with a Holistic Approach],https://www.academia.edu/2063768/Teknoparklar%C4%B1n_Ekonomik_Etkileri (Date of Access: 10.07.2020).

Kiper, M. (2010). Dünya'da ve Türkiye'de Üniversite- Sanayi İşbirliği[The University-Industry Cooperation in the World and Turkey]. Ankara: Turkey Technology Development Foundation.

Nosonov, A. & Letkina, N. (2019). Technoparks as Centers of Regional Economic Development. *International Journal of Innovative Technology and Exploring Engineering*, 8(12), 4213–4218.

Olcay, G. A. & Bulu, M. (2016). Technoparks and Technology Transfer Offices as Drivers of an Innovation Economy: Lessons from Istanbul's Innovation Spaces. *Journal of Urban Technology*, 23(1), 71–93.

Pekol, Ö. & Erbaş, B. Ç. (2011). Patent Sisteminde Türkiye'deki Teknoparkların Yeri [Technoparks in Turkey: Patent System Perspective]. *Ege Academic Review*, 11(1), 39–58.

Pektaş, E. K. & Demirkol, A. (2018). Kalkınma Ajanslarının Bölgesel Kalkınma Sürecindeki Rolü Ve Etkileri: Zafer Kalkınma Ajansı Örneği[The Role And Impacts of Development Agencies on Regional Development Process: The

Case of Zafer Development Agency]. *MCBÜ Journal of Social Sciences*, 16(2), 77–98.

Republic of Turkey Industry and Trade Ministry (2020). The Statistics of Technology Development Zones, https://www.sanayi.gov.tr/istatistikler/istatistiki-bilgiler/mi0203011501 (Access date: 10.07.2020).

Rodriguez-Pose, A. & Hardy, D. (2014). Technology and Industrial Parks in Emerging Countries: Panacea or Pipedream. New York: Springer

Technology Development Zones Law (2001). Technology Development Zones Implementation Regulation, https://www.resmigazete.gov.tr/eskiler/2014/03/20140312-2.htm (Date of Access: 13.07.2020).

Tepe, S. & Zaim, A. H. (2016). Türkiye ve Dünya'da Teknopark Uygulamaları: Teknopark İstanbul Örneği[Technopark Applications in Turkey and the World: A Case Study of Technopark Istanbul]. *Istanbul Commerce University Journal of Science*, 29: 19–43.

TGBD (2020). Technology Development Zones Association, https://www.tgbd.org.tr/ (Date of Access: 13.07.2020).

Turkish Patent and Trademark (2020). The Distribution of Patent Applications with Respect to Cities. https://www.turkpatent.gov.tr/TURKPATENT/statistics/ (Access date: 05.07.2020).

Tutar, F. & Demiral, M. (2007). Yerel Ekonomilerin Yerel Aktörleri: Bölgesel Kalkınma Ajansları [Local Actors of The Local Economy: Regional Development Agencies]. *Eskişehir Osmangazi University Journal of Economic and Administrative Sciences*, 2(1), 65–83.

Wallsten, S. (2004). Do Science Parks Generate Regional Economic Growth? An emprical Analysis of Their Effects on Job Growth and Venture Capital. Joint Center for Regulatory Studies Working Paper, 1–17.

Yalçıntaş, M. (2014). Üniversite- Sanayi-Devlet İşbirliğinin Ülke Ekonomilerine Etkileri: Teknopark İstanbul Örneği[The Effects of University-Industry-Government Collaboration On Economies: The Example of Technopark İstanbul]. Journal of Financial Research and Studies, 5(10), 83–106.

Yanıktepe, B., Çavuş, M. F., & Aksoy, A. (2016). Technoparks as an Actor of Regional Development: An Evaluation of Turkey. *Journal of Applied Economic Science*, 10(1), 1–8.

Yıldız, T. & Aykanat, Z. (2015). Clustering and Innovation Concepts and Innovative Clusters: An application on Technoparks in Turkey. *Procedia-Social and Behavioral Sciences*, 195, 1196–1205.

Zuhal, M. (2017). Ulusal Yenilik Sistemlerinde Teknoparkların Önemi: Türkiye Deneyimi[The İmportance of Technoparks İn National İnnovation Systems: A Case of Turkey]. *The Journal of Scientific Researches*, 2(7), 52–66.

Dr. Zuhal Önez Çetin

2.8 Financial and Technical Supports of Regional Development Agencies in Turkey: The Case of Two Provinces from Different Development Agencies

Abstract: In Turkey, Regional Development Agencies (RDA) have been providing technical and financial supports at the regional level. In the context of the study, financial and technical supports of the Development Agencies have been searched with the case of two provinces in Turkey, which are determined according to the well-being index for provinces of TurkStat (2015), and the first province is Bolu from Marka East Marmara Development Agency (TR42) having a good well-being overall index of '3' in comparison to the other selected province of Şanlıurfa having the total well-being overall index of '73' from Karacadağ Development Agency (TRC2). The projects in Bolu and in Şanlıurfa that gained financial and technical support of the agencies within the scope of the financial and technical programs of Development Agencies at the provincial level have searched from the noble project lists' announcements of each Development agency, to find out the fundamental areas of the successful projects that are supported by the agencies in each province.

Keywords: Development agency, Well-being index for provinces, Financial and technical support, Bolu, Şanlıurfa.

Introduction

By the 1950s/1960s onwards, development agencies formed a part of regional policy in many countries located in the Western Europe, and recently, that approach attract the attention in Central and East Europe as a potential way in dealing with the complexities of industrial restructuring (Danson, Halkier, and Damborg, 1998: 14). The fundamental targets that are given to Regional Development Agencies are pointed out as coordinating regional economic development and regeneration, developing the competitiveness at the region, and alleviating the inequalities in the economic growth between and within regions (Blackman and Ormston, 2005: 378).

Moreover, in the period, from 1960s to the 2000s, basic elements that make up the regional development policies in Turkey was to ensure rapid development of the regions that were underdeveloped and to enable a balanced development among the regions by means of investments, after the 2000s, there has been a transformation in regional policies with the aims of taking advantage of the existing potential of all regions and spreading development across the country and Development Agencies, which are the institutional expressions of this transformation, take the potential of the regions as the main subject and add all sides to the development (The Ministry of Development, 2018a: 1). The development understanding with development agencies in Turkey can be expressed to move toward a new model, this new model is moving from the development understanding that is planned at the center and implemented by central institutions, to a new development understanding model where regional competitiveness can be increased and central, local government and private sector can work together (Eryılmaz and Tuncer, 2013: 178).

In the 8th Five-Year Development Plan Regional Development Specialization Commission Report (State Planning Organization, 2000: 44–45), at the title of 'Recommendations on Principle, Strategy and Tools of 8th Five-Year Development Plan', in the sub-title of 'policies, strategies and tools', there are important explanations about the region, it is clarified that "regional plans should direct structural change, therefore; a) Regions should be provided to specialize in the sectors in which they have comparative advantage in line with the national plan preferences, and therefore their relative priorities should be determined at the national and international level, b) Regions need to be evaluated as parts of a whole within the scope of Country Regulation, c) No region is without problems, the recent natural disasters have strikingly once again revealed that serious settlement/site selection errors have been made in our most developed region and in the metropolis we hope to add to the world, all regions should be planned without making any development distinction, d) Special development strategies should be determined for border regions."

The important factor on the establishment of development agencies and its legal structure, is the EU membership process and developments in the EU membership process, and the issues EU attaches importance to reach the EU targets are the development of the member countries at the regional level and their regional cohesion and closing the gap between regions (Turkish Court of Accounts, 2019: 9). At Turkey Accession Partnership Document with the title of Council Decision of 8 March 2001 on the Principles, Priorities, Intermediate Goals And Conditions located at the Accession Partnership with the Republic of Turkey, under the title of "Regional Policy And Coordination of Structural Elements", the sub-themes of, Preparation of a NUTS (naming of regional units for statistical purposes) classification which is in harmony with community rules, adopting a strategy for the target of the development of a regional policy which is effective; finally, in terms of project selection in Turkey's planning process starting to establish regional policy criteria have been clarified (Turkey Accession Partnership Document, 2001: 6)[1].

At the Law No 5449 (2006) on the Services of Development Agencies, at the title of aim and scope, in the Article 1 clarified that "The purpose of this Law; to regulate the principles and procedures regarding the establishment, duty and powers and coordination of development agencies to be established in order to accelerate regional development, to ensure sustainability, to reduce interregional and intraregional development disparities in line with the principle and policies envisaged in the national development plan and programs, by improving the cooperation between public, private and non-governmental organizations, ensuring the proper and effective use of resources and mobilizing local potential". [2]

In the 9th Development Plan Regional Development Specialization Commission Report (State Planning Organization, 2008: 18) development agencies are clarified as "Development Agencies are local governance and regional strategy design institutions where decisions and policies regarding regional development practices are taken and implemented by those living in the region (especially key actors and stakeholders) within a participatory structure". Besides, some of the functions of the development agencies are pointed out as; regional planning, supporting with regional development purpose, research, analysis and reporting having the target of regional development, promotion, the development of cooperation among public, private and non-governmental organizations (Turkish Court of Accounts, 2019: 11).

Within the context of the study, two provinces have been selected according to the well-being index for provinces of TurkStat (2015), the first selected province of Bolu from Marka East Marmara Development Agency (TR42) has a good well-being overall index of '3' in comparison to the second selected province of Şanlıurfa that has the total well-being overall index of '73' from Karacadağ Development Agency (TRC2). In the study, the projects in Bolu and in Şanlıurfa that achieved financial and technical support of the agencies within the scope of the financial and technical programs at the provincial level have searched from the noble project lists' announcements of each Development agency, to find out the fundamental areas of the successful projects that are supported by the agencies in each province (only the successful projects of the provincial

1 For details, see, <https://www.ab.gov.tr/katilim-ortakligi-belgeleri_46226.html>.
2 For details, see, <https://www.resmigazete.gov.tr/eskiler/2006/02/20060208-1.htm>.

institutions and organizations that achieve financial and technical support have been examined, in order to limit the study; the feasibility support programs have not been examined and the projects of the district level institutions and organizations are not included in the research). In the study, the terms mainly covering from 2018 to 2019 have been searched, and the financial and technical supports of the Agencies in Bolu and Şanlıurfa have demonstrated with the charts that are prepared from the noble project lists' announcements of the websites of each agency at that related period. The projects that gained financial and technical support in Bolu and in Şanlıurfa have demonstrated in detail in for making a comparison between the provinces.

1 The Supports of Regional Development Agencies in Turkey

The development agencies can provide financial and technical support to the actors located in the region, the areas have been identified in the regional plan and programs and the annual work program and related application guides with the targets such as to speed up the development process in the region and implementing the activities that are important in the region, in line with the previously determined eligibility criteria (The Ministry of Development, 2018b: 13). In that scope, the Development Agencies provide financial and technical support in Turkey, and the categories of those supports have been explained at the Tab. 2.8.1. As follows;

2 The Selection of the Provinces from Regional Development Agencies

2.1 Turkey Statistical Institute Well-Being Index for Provinces

Turkey Statistical Institute (TurkStat/ Türkiye İstatistik Kurumu) has made the study of well-being index for provinces, within the context of this index study, it is targeted to create an indicator system that will create a base for following the city within the framework of all aspects and improving the life in the province (TurkStat, 2016a: 1). Moreover, related to well-being index for provinces study, the targeted index features are clarified as "individual, household and result oriented, allowing to measure the life level of those living in that province and monitor it over time, represented by policy sensitive, improvable indicators, and reducing the different quality of life dimensions that make up good life to a single dimension" (TurkStat, 2016b: 1). In well-being index for provinces involves 11 dimensions including different dimensions of life and these dimensions are listed as follows; housing, working life, income and wealth, health, education

Tab. 2.8.1. The Financial and Technical Supports of Development Agencies

1. FINANCIAL SUPPORT	The financial support to which the agency can ensure is stated as; direct financing support, interest support and interest-free credit support (The Ministry of Development, 2018b: 14).
A) Direct Financing Support	Direct financing support is explained in the Article 12, item 2 of the Regulation on Development Agencies Project and Activity Support (2008: 5) as follows, "Direct financing support consists mainly of the support provided by the agency through the call for proposals. However, the agency (Abolished phrase/: RG (Official Newspaper)-15/9/2017-30181) (. . .) without making a call for project proposals and by easing some of its obligations on project preparation or directly managing the project preparation process, (Different phrase: RG (Official Newspaper)-15/9/2017- 30181) can provide direct support in the form of feasibility support and guided project support".
B) Interest support and interest-free credit support:	The definition of interest support is expressed in the Article 29 of the Regulation on Development Agencies Project and Activity Support (2008: 17), item 1 as follows; "(Different: RG (Official Newspaper)-15/9/2017-30181) Interest support is the financial support for the projects specified in the application guide, which requires the Agency to meet the interest expenses to be paid in return for the loans to be received from the relevant intermediary institutions". Interest-free credit support is expressed in the Article 30 of the Regulation on Development Agencies Project and Activity Support (2008: 17), item 1 as follows; "Interest-free credit support is the financial support the agency will provide by providing interest-free credit through intermediary institutions to projects that comply with the application guide".
2. TECHNICAL SUPPORT	The technical support to be provided by the agency has to include the following activities and studies, provided that it is not associated with a call for proposal published by the agency (The Ministry of Development, 2018b: 107); "Activities of local governments primarily to implement planning activities and regional plans and programs, or to increase local development capacity, and it must cover the work of other applicants that can contribute to local and regional development".

Sources: (The Regulation on Development Agencies Project and Activity Support, 2008; The Ministry of Development, 2018b).

Tab. 2.8.2: Rankings and Index Values of Well-Being Index for Provinces, 2015 (TurkStat, 2015)

	BOLU		ŞANLIURFA	
	Rank	**Index**	**Rank**	**Index**
Overall Index	3	0,6553	73	0,3540
Housing	3	0,9247	73	0,2835
Work Life	26	0,6240	76	0,2221
Income and Wealth	9	0,5803	78	0,0938
Health	2	0,8023	74	0,4324
Education	14	0,6480	78	0,2440
Environment	18	0,6820	63	0,5327
Safety	28	0,6780	31	0,6626
Civic Engagement	59	0,3814	69	0,3239
Access to Infrastructure services	35	0,4546	56	0,3704
Social Life	3	0,6441	71	0,2988
Life Satisfaction	14	0,7895	56	0,4302

For Details, see, <http://www.tuik.gov.tr/PreTablo.do?alt_id=1106#>.
Source: (TurkStat, 2015). This Chart is prepared according to TurkStat (2015) data at <http://www.tuik.gov.tr/ PreTablo.do?alt_ id=1106#>.

and environment, security, civic participation, access to infrastructure services, social life and life satisfaction; these listed dimensions are expressed with 41 indicators, the well-being index for provinces taking a value between 0 and 1, explains a better life level as the index approaches 1 (TurkStat, 2016a: 1). The main criteria which are used for determining well-being index for provinces indicators are pointed as follows; "being suitable for the main goal, benefit and result oriented; reflecting the good life where individuals live, can be improved by policy changes, can reflect distinctions between provinces, the direction of contribution can be clearly determined, easy to understand, to be accurate and strong, to be updated periodically" (TurkStat, 2016b: 1–2).

As it is observed from the Tab. 2.8.2 above which is prepared according to the TurkStat (2015) statistics of well-being index for provinces, two provinces from different regional development agencies have been selected having different rank and indexes as to the well-being index for provinces in Turkey, which are Bolu from East Marmara Development Agency (TR42) and Şanlıurfa from Karacadağ Development Agency (TRC2).

3 Case Provinces' Projects that Gained Financial and Technical Support

3.1 The Province of Bolu and the Projects that Gained Financial and Technical Support of Development Agency

The provinces within the scope of the duty of MARKA East Marmara Development Agency include Kocaeli, Düzce, and Yalova, Sakarya, Bolu (MARKA East Marmara Development Agency, 2019a: 6). The MARKA East Marmara Development Agency has made progress in producing information, and the main studies that have made this progress are stated as 2 regional plan, regional innovation strategy, 292 reports, statistical database and MARKAStat application, detailed sector reports, and within the scope of these studies, the Agency provides financial and technical supports and the purpose of these supports is expressed as the triggering of regional development (MARKA East Marmara Development Agency, 2019b: 2).

When the province of Bolu is evaluated in general economic terms, the sectors are expressed as follows: the agricultural sector has a share of 13%, the industrial area has a share of 33%, and the service sector has a share of 54% in the economy of Bolu (MARKA East Marmara Development Agency, 2018: 6). There are four Organized Industrial Zones in Bolu, but two of them are active, and it is possible to list these Organized Industrial Zones as follows; Bolu Mixed and Textile Specialized Organized Industrial Zone (active) and Gerede Organized Industrial Zone (active), Gerede Leather Specialized Organized Industrial Zone and Yeniçağa Organized Industrial Zone (MARKA East Marmara Development Agency, 2014: 31). Moreover, the activities carried out by MARKA East Marmara Development Agency are summarized as 120,072,426₺ support has been provided to 483 projects and the support provided within the scope of 22 project call for proposals and 6 direct activity support program in the priority fields and issues, a total project volume of 216,854,562₺ has been created, 404 projects have been financed with a budget of 3,258,534₺ and this support provided within the scope of the technical supports provided to meet the institutional necessities of local actors (MARKA East Marmara Development Agency, 2019b: 2).

As it is seen from the Tab. 2.8.3, in the province of Bolu, in the year of 2020, there are two successful projects that achieved technical support of the MARKA East Marmara Development Agency at the provincial level. In the year 2019, seven projects gained the technical support of the agency[3], four projects also

---

3 For details, see, "2019 Yılı Teknik Destek Programı Başvuru Sonuçları", <http://www.marka.org.tr/sayfa/657/664/2019-yili-teknik-destek-programi-basvuru-sonu%C3%A7lari>.

Tab. 2.8.3: Financial and Technical Supports to the Projects of Bolu

2020 Year Technical Support Program	**Project Name**	**Applicant Name**
January-February	Palliative And Post-Life Care Training And Counseling Service For Healthcare Professionals	Bolu Provincial Health Directorate
	Bolu Health Tourism Brands with Hiser	Bolu Chamber of Commerce And Industry
2019 Year Financial Support Program	**Project Name**	**Applicant Name**
A)	Financial Support Program for Improving Vocational Education for Manufacturing Industry	
1.	Improving Production Skills and Professional Competencies of Food Processing Department Students with Innovative Approaches	Baibü Yeniçağa Yaşar Çelik Vocational School
2.	For Industry 4.0 (Improving Vocational Education)	İzzet Baysal Vocational and Technical Anatolian High School
B)	Development of Production Infrastructures Small Scale Infrastructure Financial Support Program	
	Production of Long And High Performance Boron Based Mgb2 Superconducting Wire For Cryogenic Electromagnets	Bolu Technology Development Zone Inc.
C)	Culture and Tourism Small Scale Infrastructure Financial Support Program	
	I Discover Bolu at Bolu Info Point (BIP)	Bolu Municipality
2019 Year Technical Support Program	**Project Name**	**Applicant Name**
January-February	To Healthy Generations with Qualified Maternity Services	Bolu Provincial Health Directorate
	Energy Manager and Energy Identity Specialist Training	Bolu Provincial Directorate of National Education
May-June	Bolu Product Space Analysis Study	Bolu Chamber of Commerce and Industry

Tab. 2.8.3: Continued

2020 Year Technical Support Program	**Project Name**	**Applicant Name**
July-August	Geographical Sign Registration Increases the Competitiveness of Honey of Bolu and the Region	Bolu Province Bee Breeders Association
September-October	Applied SPSS And Statistics Training For Healthy Analysis	Bolu Provincial Health Directorate
	Cooperation And Cooperative Education Based On Local Development	Bolu Municipality
November-December	Reaching Smart Urban Consciousness with the EU Project	Bolu Municipality
2018 Year Financial Support Program	**Project Name**	**Applicant Name**
Financial Support Program for Improving Vocational Education for Manufacturing Industry	Development of Production and Design Skills of Leather, Textile, Shoe and Fashion Design Students	Abant İzzet Baysal University Gerede Vocational School
Development of Production Infrastructures Small Scale Infrastructure Financial Support Program	Bolu Develops with Quality Feed Production for Sustainable Food	Bolu Chamber of Agriculture
	Family Tree of Food	Abant İzzet Baysal University Yenigıdam
Tourism Financial Support Program	Tourism is Developing with New Investments in Bolu	Aysel-İsa Okur Kayı Apart Hotel
	Innovative Approaches in Alternative Tourism	Grand Kartal Tourism and Trade Inc.
	Bolu's First 2 Star Business Hotel	Mustafa Karabaş
	Bolu Thermal Hotel Development Project	Bolsantur Bolu Construction Industry and Tourism Inc.
	Bolu Hilton Hotel Increases Service Capacity And Diversity With "Gurme Restaurant"	Hampton By Hilton

(continued on next page)

Tab. 2.8.3: Continued

2020 Year Technical Support Program	Project Name	Applicant Name
2018 Year Technical Support Program		
July-August	STEM (Science, Technology, Engineering, Mathematics) Trainer Training	Bolu Provincial National Education Directorate
	SEBEN Fossil Research Forest Promotion Center Garden Landscape Planning	Directorate of West Black Sea Forestry Research Institute
	Sample Type Barn Plan Project Supply to Our Animal Breeders in Bolu Province	Bolu Provincial Agriculture and Forestry Directorate
	Bolu New Generation Design And Production Workshop Installation Consultancy Service	Bolu Municipality
September-October	Bolu's Tourism Value Increases with Cross-Border Stakeholders	Bolu Municipality
November-December	Netcad and Geographic Information System Training	Bolu Environment and Urbanisation Provincial Directorate
	Health Tourism Will Find Life in Bolu	Bolu Provincial Health Directorate
	Bolu Continues to Register Brand Products	Bolu Chamber Of Commerce And Industry
	Nature Conservation and National Parks Technical Staff Receives Arcgis Training	Bolu Nature Conservation and National Parks Branch Directorate

This Chart has been prepared according to the announcements located at the website of MARKA East Marmara Development Agency <http://www.marka.org.tr/anasayfa> related to financial and technical support programs' application results, and the references of all announcements that are used at the preparation of this chart have been demonstrated at the references of the study in detail.

achieved financial support, and the Agency has made financial support under the programs of 'Financial Support Program for Improving Vocational Education for Manufacturing Industry', 'Development of Production Infrastructures Small Scale Infrastructure Financial Support Program', and 'Culture and Tourism

Small Scale Infrastructure Financial Support Program'[4]. In the year 2018, there are eight successful projects that gained financial support of the Agency in the province of Bolu under the programs of 'Financial Support Program for Improving Vocational Education for Manufacturing Industry', 'Development of Production Infrastructures Small Scale Infrastructure Financial Support Program', and 'Tourism Financial Support Program'.[5] Besides, in the year 2018, there are nine successful projects that gained technical support of the Agency.[6] When examining the proportions of the successful projects in Bolu, the highest ratio is observed at the technical support with nine successful projects in the year 2018 and at the financial support with eight successful projects in the year 2018 in the province of Bolu.

The successful projects that gained technical supports of the Agency during the year 2019 are mainly on training (education) and consultancy such as 'Energy Manager and Energy Identity Specialist Training', 'Applied SPSS And Statistics Training For Healthy Analysis', 'Cooperation And Cooperative Education Based On Local Development' and 'Reaching Smart Urban Consciousness with the EU Project'.[7]Additionally, in the year 2019 'Financial Support Program for Improving Vocational Education for Manufacturing Industry', there are also successful projects on training such as 'Improving Production Skills and Professional Competencies of Food Processing Department Students with Innovative Approaches' and 'For Industry 4.0 (Improving Vocational Education)'.[8] Besides, there are also projects related to health in Bolu such as

4 For details, see, "2019 Yılı Mali Destek Programları Başvuru Sonuçları", <http://www.marka.org.tr/sayfa/657/727/2019-yili-mali-destek-programlari-basvuru-sonu%C3%A7lari>.

5 For details, see, "2018 Yılı Mali Destek Programları Başvuru Sonuçları", < http://www.marka.org.tr/sayfa/621/624/2018-yili-mali-destek-programlari-basvuru-sonu%C3%A7lari>.

6 For details, see, "2018 Yılı Teknik Destek Programı Başvuru Sonuçları", <http://www.marka.org.tr/sayfa/621/644/2018-yili-teknik-destek-programi-basvuru-sonu%C3%A7lari>.

7 For details, see, "2019 Yılı Teknik Destek Programı Başvuru Sonuçları", <http://www.marka.org.tr/sayfa/657/664/2019-yili-teknik-destek-programi-basvuru-sonu%C3%A7lari>.

8 For details, see, "2019 Yılı Mali Destek Programları Başvuru Sonuçları", <http://www.marka.org.tr/sayfa/657/727/2019-yili-mali-destek-programlari-basvuru-sonu%C3%A7lari>.

the successful project 'Palliative And Post-Life Care Training And Counseling Service For Healthcare Professionals' of Bolu Provincial Health Directorate[9] that gained technical support in 2020, and the project of "To Healthy Generations with Qualified Maternity Services" of Bolu Provincial Health Directorate that achieved technical support in 2019[10]. Moreover, in the year 2018, the highest number of the successful projects are at the Tourism Financial Support Program and secondly, at the Development of Production Infrastructures Small Scale Infrastructure Financial Support Program. [11] The technical supports of the Agency to the successful projects in Bolu during the year 2018 are mainly on training (education) and consultancy such as 'STEM (Science, Technology, Engineering, Mathematics) Trainer Training', 'Netcad and Geographic Information System Training', 'Nature Conservation and National Parks Technical Staff Receives Arcgis Training' and 'Bolu New Generation Design And Production Workshop Installation Consultancy Service'.[12] Many institutions and organizations' projects have facilitated from the MARKA East Marmara Development Agency technical and financial supports, some of the institutions that gained technical supports can be listed as Bolu Provincial Health Directorate, Bolu Chamber of Commerce and Industry, Bolu Provincial Directorate of National Education, and Bolu Municipality.[13] Besides, some of the institutions that gained financial support can be listed as Baibü Yeniçağa Yaşar Çelik Vocational School, İzzet Baysal Vocational and Technical Anatolian

9 For details, see, "2020 Yılı Teknik Destek Programı Ocak-Şubat Dönemi Başvuru Sonuçları", <http://www.marka.org.tr/haber/detay/2663/2020-yili-teknik-destek-programi-ocak-subat-donemi-basvuru-sonu %C3%A7lari>.

10 For details, see, "2019 Yılı Teknik Destek Programı Ocak-Şubat Dönemi Başvuru Sonuçları", <http://www.marka.org.tr/haber/detay/2621/2019-yili-teknik-destek-programi-ocak-subat-donemi-basvuru-sonu%C3%A7lari>.

11 For details, see, "2018 Yılı Mali Destek Programları Başvuru Sonuçları",< http://www.marka.org.tr/sayfa/621/624/2018-yili-mali-destek-programlari-basvuru-sonu%C3%A7lari>.

12 For details, see, "2018 Yılı Teknik Destek Programı Başvuru Sonuçları", <http://www.marka.org.tr/sayfa/621/644/2018-yili-teknik-destek-programi-basvuru-sonu%C3%A7lari>.

13 For details, see, "2019 Yılı Teknik Destek Programı Başvuru Sonuçları", <http://www.marka.org.tr/sayfa/657/664/2019-yili-teknik-destek-programi-basvuru-sonu%C3%A7lari>.

High School, Bolu Technology Development Zone Inc.[14], and Bolu Chamber of Agriculture[15].

3.2 The Province of Şanlıurfa and the Projects that Gained Financial and Technical Support of Development Agency

Karacadağ Development Agency covers the provinces of Diyarbakır and Şanlıurfa in the TRC2 Region, and the official opening date of the Development Agency is 5 December 2009 and the opening of Şanlıurfa Investment Support Office is 7 March 2010 (Karacadağ Development Agency, 2019: 10). Karacadağ Development Agency prepared the 2014–2023 Regional Plan in accordance with the national plan, programs and other national strategy documents, and regional plan has been prepared within the framework of a participatory approach, taking into account the local potential and needs and four major development axes were adopted in the Regional Plan, these axes are expressed as follows; "Urban Economies and Economic Growth, Human Development and Social Capital, Quality of Life and Spatial Organization, Sustainable Development and Green Growth" (Karacadağ Development Agency, 2018: 2). Besides, there are two important support programs of Karacadağ Development Agency which are Social Support Program and Attraction Centers Support Program.

Firstly, the purpose of the Social Support Program, which will be implemented in Diyarbakır and Şanlıurfa in the TRC2 Region for the year 2020, is also explained as follows; "Increasing employability through projects to be carried out, enabling disadvantaged sections of society to participate more in economic and social life, and contributing to children, youth and women in the region to express themselves better through cultural, art and sports activities" (Karacadağ Development Agency, 2020: 136–137). Secondly, the goal of the Attraction Centers Support program is expressed as "Increasing the production, export, employment, productivity, technology and innovation capacities with high added value of cities that are regional centers of attraction in

14 For details, see, "2019 Yılı Mali Destek Programları Başvuru Sonuçları", <http://www.marka.org.tr/sayfa/657/727/2019-yili-mali-destek-programlari-basvuru-sonu%C3%A7lari>.

15 For details, see, "2018 Yılı Mali Destek Programları Başvuru Sonuçları",< http://www.marka.org.tr/sayfa/621/624/2018-yili-mali-destek-programlari-basvuru-sonu%C3%A7lari>.

relatively underdeveloped regions and regions that giving migration in order to ensure a more balanced settlement order throughout the country and to direct migration gradually" (Karacadağ Development Agency, Attraction Centers Support Program, 2020).

As it is seen at the Tab. 2.8.4, within the context of the 2019 year Technical Program on September and October term, there have been many successful Projects that gained technical support mainly on training (education) and consultancy such as 'School Education KA2 Strategic Partnership Projects Preparation Consultancy', 'Certified Basic First Aid Training', 'Food Safety and Hygiene Training', 'Netcad Training', 'Mind And Intelligence Games Trainer Training', 'Corporate Identity Development Training', 'Increasing the Capacity of Şanlıurfa Project Team'.[16] Moreover on July and August term, there are also projects on training that gained success such as; GAP Agricultural Research Institute Directorate has 'Project Preparation and Implementation Training for National and International Grant Providers'; Şanlıurfa Food, Agriculture and Livestock Provincial Directorate has 'Netcad Training'; and Şanlıurfa Chamber of Commerce and Industry has 'Documentation Development And Training', and lastly, General Directorate of Şanlıurfa Water and Sewerage Administration (ŞUSKİ) has 'Our Staff Progress With Autocad And Corporate Development Training' projects. [17] Moreover on May and June term, there are also projects related to training that gained success such as Şanlıurfa Chamber of Commerce and Industry has 'Strengthening Institutional Capacity of ŞUTSO Women Entrepreneurs Board', Şanlıurfa Regional Directorate of Forestry has 'We Professionalize by Using Netcad Software in Forestry Project Applications' and lastly, Şanlıurfa Provincial Health Directorate has 'Kidney Transplant Preparation Training' projects.[18] Besides, in the year 2019, the projects in Şanlıurfa that gained financial support program covers the

16 For details, see, "2019 Yılı Teknik Destek Programı, eylül-ekim dönemi değerlendirme sonuçları" Asil Liste <https://www.karacadag.gov.tr/duyuru/1267/2019-yili-teknik-destek-programi-eylul--ekim-donemi-degerlendirme-sonuclari-aciklandi/>, pp.1–2.

17 For details, see, "2019 Yılı Teknik Destek Programı Temmuz-Ağustos Dönemi Değerlendirme Sonuçları"- Asil Liste, <https://www.karacadag.gov.tr/duyuru/1262/2019-yili-teknik-destek-programi-temmuz--agustos-donemi-degerlendirme-sonuclari/>, pp.1–2.

18 For details, see, "2019 Yılı Teknik Destek Programı Mayıs-Haziran Dönemi Sonuçları Açıklandı"- Asil Liste, < https://www.karacadag.gov.tr/duyuru/1253/2019-yili-teknik-destek-programi-mayis-haziran-donemi-sonuclari-aciklandi/>, pp. 1–2.

Tab. 2.8.4: Financial and Technical Supports to the Projects of Şanlıurfa

2019 Year Technical Support Program	**Project Name**	**Applicant Name**
September-October	School Education KA2 Strategic Partnership Projects Preparation Consultancy	Şanlıurfa Provincial Directorate of National Education
	Certified Basic First Aid Training	Harran University
	Food Safety and Hygiene Training	Union of Chambers of Craftsmen and Artisans
	Netcad Training	General Directorate of Şanlıurfa Water and Sewerage Administration (ŞUSKİ)
	Mind And Intelligence Games Trainer Training	Şanlıurfa Provincial Directorate of National Education
	Corporate Identity Development Training	Şanlıurfa Chamber of Independent Accountants and Financial Advisors
	Increasing the Capacity of Şanlıurfa Project Team	Şanlıurfa Governorship
July-August	Project Preparation and Implementation Training for National and International Grant Providers	Gap Agricultural Research Institute Directorate
	ŞUTSO Institutionalization Project	Şanlıurfa Chamber of Commerce and Industry
	Netcad Training	Şanlıurfa Food, Agriculture and Livestock Provincial Directorate
	Documentation Development And Training	Şanlıurfa Chamber of Commerce and Industry
	Our Staff Progress With Autocad And Corporate Development Training	General Directorate of Şanlıurfa Water and Sewerage Administration (ŞUSKİ)
May-June	Kidney Transplant Preparation Training	Şanlıurfa Provincial Health Directorate
	Strengthening the Institutional Capacity of the ŞUTSO Women Entrepreneurs Board (KGK)	Şanlıurfa Chamber of Commerce and Industry
	We Professionalize by Using Netcad Software in Forestry Project Applications	Şanlıurfa Regional Directorate of Forestry

(*continued on next page*)

Tab. 2.8.4: Continued

2019 Year Technical Support Program	**Project Name**	**Applicant Name**
2019 Year Financial Support Program	Project Name	Applicant Name
A) Integrated Resource Efficiency Financial Support Program In Agricultural Industry	Yakut Yarn Reduces Production Cost, Increases Competitive Power	Yakut Yarn Industry and Trade Limited Company
	Increasing Resource Efficiency in Vegetable Oil Production	Eyvan Textile Engineering Construction Tourism, Industry and Trade Limited Company
	Optimization of Production Tools and Raw Material Sourcing in Crude Oil Processing Plant	İzkaş Oil Industry and Trade Limited Company
	Biogap Produces Environmentally Friendly Products With Energy Efficient Applications in Manufacturing Processes	Biogap Food Pharmaceuticals and Agricultural Products Industry and Trade Limited Company
	Improving Raw Material/ Energy Efficiency And Improving Product Quality in Çırçır-Prese Plant	Yıldızsoy Textile, Industry and Trade Limited Company
	Increasing Machine Equipment/Energy Efficiency in Çırçır-Prese Plant, Continuing Applications	Korak Yarn Industry and Trade Inc.
	Efficient Use of Resources and Development of Corporate Infrastructure in Cotton Processing Plant	Akkoza Cotton Industry and Trade Limited Company

Tab. 2.8.4: Continued

2019 Year Technical Support Program	**Project Name**	**Applicant Name**
B)Industrial Infrastructure Financial Support Program	High Technology Vocational Training for Manufacturing Industry	Şanlıurfa Provincial Directorate of National Education
	Şanlıurfa Organized Industrial Zone Directorate 2nd Section Electric Power Line Infrastructure Project	Şanlıurfa Organized Industrial Zone Directorate
	Sanlıurfa Food Specialization Organized Industrial Zone Infrastructure and Superstructure Preparations Making	Şanlıurfa Food Specialized Organized Industrial Zone
C)Increasing Preschool Education Standards Financial Support Program	Our Future is Getting Stronger with Smart Kindergartens	Şanlıurfa Provincial Directorate of National Education
	Montessori Development Workshops	Şanlıurfa Provincial Directorate of National Education
2018 Year Technical Support	Project Name	Applicant Name
May-June	Orff Training for Preschool Teachers	Şanlıurfa Provincial Directorate of National Education
	Creative Drama Education in Education Museums	Şanlıurfa Provincial Directorate of National Education
	Increasing Institutional Quality Management Systems of Şanlıurfa Chamber of Commerce and Industry and Getting Consultancy Technical Support	Şanlıurfa Chamber of Commerce and Industry
	EU Project Preparation Technical Support	Şanlıurfa Chamber of Commerce and Industry

(*continued on next page*)

Tab. 2.8.4: Continued

2019 Year Technical Support Program	**Project Name**	**Applicant Name**
July-August	Project Writing Workshop with Logical Framework Approach	Şanlıurfa Provincial Directorate of National Education
	Effective Communication Techniques Training	Şanlıurfa Provincial Health Directorate
September-October	Business Ethics And Corporate Culture Training	Şanlıurfa Provincial Directorate of National Education
	Protocol Rules And Effective Communication And Official Correspondence Procedures And Principles	Şanlıurfa Provincial Culture and Tourism Directorate
	Project for Increasing the Value of Handicraft Products for Tourism and Promotion Existing in Şanlıurfa Province	Şanlıurfa Province Culture Education Art and Research Foundation
November-December	Inclusive Education Trainer Training	Şanlıurfa Provincial Directorate of National Education
	Suruç Solid Waste Transfer Station Feasibility Works Making	Şanlıurfa Metropolitan Municipality
	Communication Skills, Teamwork, Problem Solving Skills, Individual Awareness Training for Institution Managers and Employees	Şanlıurfa Labor and Employment Institution Provincial Directorate
	Capacity of Şuski Staff Increases	General Directorate of Şanlıurfa Water and Sewerage Administration
2018 Year Financial Support Program	Project Name	Applicant Name
A) Tourism Routes And Smart Cities Financial Support Program	Tourism Route Project from the Archeology Museum to the Hanlar Region	Şanlıurfa Province Culture Education Art and Research Foundation
	Şanlıurfa Meets With Smart Tourism	Şanlıurfa Provincial Culture And Tourism Directorate
	Tourism Road Project from Edessa to Fırat	Şanlıurfa Metropolitan Municipality

Tab. 2.8.4: Continued

2019 Year Technical Support Program	**Project Name**	**Applicant Name**
B) Industrial Infrastructure Financial Support Program	Making the Preparation of Sanliurfa Food Specialized Organized Industrial Zone Treatment Plant	Şanlıurfa Food Specialized Organized Industrial Zone
	University Industry Cooperation Center (ÜSİM)	Şanlıurfa Technology Development Zone Founder and Operator Inc.
	Technical Equipment and Furnishing of Şanlıurfa Fair Center	Şanlıurfa Metropolitan Municipality
	Şanlıurfa Organized Industrial Zone 3rd Section Additional Area East Side Drinking Water Main Network Infrastructure	Şanlıurfa 1. Organized Industrial Zone Directorate
	Small Industrial Building Cooperative Infrastructure Project	S. S. Şanlıurfa Sheet Metal And Machine Manufacturers Expertise Small Industry Building Coop.

This Chart has been prepared according to the announcements located at the website of Karacadağ Development Agency <https://www.karacadag.gov.tr/duyurular/1/duyurular/> related to financial and technical support programs' application results, and the references of all announcements that are used at the preparation of this chart have been demonstrated at the references of the study in detail.

programs of 'Integrated Resource Efficiency Financial Support Program in Agricultural Industry', 'Industrial Infrastructure Financial Support Program' and 'Increasing Pre-School Education Standards Financial Support Program'.[19] Most of the successful projects gained financial support are at the program of Integrated Resource Efficiency Financial Support Program in Agricultural Industry at the provincial level in the year 2019. [20] In the Year 2018, there are 13

19 For details, see, "2019 Yılı Mali Destek Programları Sonuçlandı", <https://www.karacadag.gov.tr/duyuru/1259/2019-yili-mali-destek-programlari-sonuclandi/>.

20 For details, see, "T.C. Karacadağ Kalkınma Ajansı, Program Yönetim Birimi, 2019 Yılı Tarıma Dayalı Sanayide Entegre Kaynak Verimliliği Mali Destek Programı Asil Proje Teklifleri Listesi", <https://www.karacadag.gov.tr/Duyuru/Dosya/www.karacadag.gov.tr_1259_FF2E65FY_ekv_asil_liste.pdf>, pp. 1–2.

projects that gained technical support, and 8 projects that gained financial support. In 2018, Şanlıurfa Provincial Directorate of National Education has many successful projects that gained technical support of the Agency on training such as 'Business Ethics and Corporate Culture Training' (September-October Term)[21], 'Project Writing Workshop with Logical Framework Approach' (July-August)[22], 'Orff Training for Preschool Teachers' and 'Creative Drama Education in Education Museums' (May-June)[23]. In 2018, Şanlıurfa Chamber of Commerce and Industry has also achieved technical support of the Agency with the projects on 'Increasing Institutional Quality Management Systems of Şanlıurfa Chamber of Commerce and Industry and Getting Consultancy Technical Support' and 'EU Project Preparation Technical Support' (May-June period).[24] Besides, in the year 2018, the projects at the provincial level that achieved success in financial support program covers the programs of 'Tourism Routes and Smart Cities Financial Support Program' and 'Industrial Infrastructure Financial Support Program'. Three of the projects that achieved financial support are at the Tourism Routes and Smart Cities Financial Support Program and five of them are at Industrial Infrastructure Financial Support Program.[25] In that scope, lots of institutions and organizations gained financial support, some of the institutions and organizations can be listed as Şanlıurfa Province Culture, Education, Art and Research Foundation, Şanlıurfa Provincial Culture and Tourism Directorate, Şanlıurfa Metropolitan Municipality. [26]

---

21 For details, see, Asil Liste TRC2/18/TD: Teknik Destek Programı (2018 Yılı Eylül-Ekim Dönemi)", <https://www.karacadag.gov.tr/Duyuru/Dosya/www.karacadag.gov.tr_1180_BS5U55OX_td_asil_liste.pdf>.

22 For details, see, "Asil Liste TRC2/18/TD: Teknik Destek Programı (2018 Yılı Temmuz Ağustos Dönemi)", <https://www.karacadag.gov.tr/Duyuru/Dosya/www.karacadag.gov.tr_1164_WK0R69NA_asil_liste_temmuz_agustos.pdf >.

23 For details, see, "Asil Liste TRC2/18/TD: Teknik Destek Programı (2018 Yılı Mayıs-Haziran Dönemi)", <https://www.karacadag.gov.tr/Duyuru/Dosya/www.karacadag.gov.tr_1160_RI2D07SD_asil_liste_mayis_haziran.pdf>.

24 For details, see, "Asil Liste TRC2/18/TD: Teknik Destek Programı (2018 Yılı Mayıs-Haziran Dönemi)", <https://www.karacadag.gov.tr/Duyuru/Dosya/www.karacadag.gov.tr_1160_RI2D07SD_asil_liste_mayis_haziran.pdf>.

25 For details, see, "2018 Mali Destek Programları Sonuçlandı", <https://www.karacadag.gov.tr/duyuru/1156/2018-mali-destek-programlari-sonuclandi/>.

26 For details, see, "2018 Mali Destek Programları Sonuçlandı", <https://www.karacadag.gov.tr/duyuru/1156/2018-mali-destek-programlari-sonuclandi/>.

As it is seen from Tab. 2.8.5 which is prepared according to the announcements located at the websites of MARKA East Marmara Development Agency and Karacadağ Development Agency, in the year 2019, in Bolu, there are no much differences as to the numbers of the successful projects that gained financial support of the Agency, the highest number of successful project are at the 'Financial Support Program for Improving Vocational Education for Manufacturing Industry'[27], however, in Şanlıurfa, most of the successful projects that achieved financial support of the Agency are at 'Integrated Resource Efficiency Financial Support Program In Agricultural Industry'[28]. Besides, when evaluating the number of successful projects in the year 2019, Şanlıurfa has more successful projects that gained financial support in comparison to successful projects in Bolu at the provincial level. In the year 2018, both provinces have the same total number of successful projects that achieved financial support at the provincial level; and most of the successful projects are at 'Tourism Financial Support Program' in Bolu[29], and in Şanlıurfa, most of the successful projects are at 'Industrial Infrastructure Financial Support Program'[30].

As it is seen from Tab. 2.8.6 which is prepared according to the announcements located at the websites of MARKA East Marmara Development Agency and Karacadağ Development Agencies, in the year 2019 and 2018, there are more successful projects that gained technical support of the Agency in Şanlıurfa in comparison to number of the successful projects that achieved technical support of the Agency in Bolu at the provincial level.

---

27 For details, see, "2019 Yılı Mali Destek Programları Başvuru Sonuçları", <http://www.marka.org.tr/sayfa/657/727/2019-yili-mali-destek-programlari-basvuru-sonu%C3%A7lari>.

28 For details, see, "T.C. Karacadağ Kalkınma Ajansı, Program Yönetim Birimi, 2019 Yılı Tarıma Dayalı Sanayide Entegre Kaynak Verimliliği Mali Destek Programı Asil Proje Teklifleri Listesi", <https://www.karacadag.gov.tr/Duyuru/Dosya/www.karacadag.gov.tr_1259_FF2E65FY_ekv_asil_liste.pdf>, pp. 1–2.

29 For details, see, "T.C. Doğru Marmara Kalkınma Ajansı, 2018 Yılı Proje Teklif Çağrısı, Turizm Mali Destek Programı, Başarılı Proje Listesi", <http://www.marka.org.tr/Uploads/Files/ 2018_MDP_ SONUCLAR /TUR%C4%B0ZM.PDF>.

30 For details, see, "2018 Yılı Sanayi Altyapısı Mali Destek Programı Asil Proje Teklifleri Listesi", <https://www.karacadag.gov.tr/Duyuru/Dosya/www.karacadag.gov.tr_1156_YR4F20KY_ek_1_sanayi_asil_2018web.pdf>.

Tab. 2.8.5: The Number of Successful Projects that Gained Financial Support in the Provinces of Bolu and Şanlıurfa According to the Financial Support Programs

Years	Financial Support Programs That The Projects Gaıned Financial Support In Bolu	The Number of Successful Projects Gained Financial Support in Bolu	Financial Support Programs That The Projects Gaıned Financial Support In Şanlıurfa	The Number of Successful Projects Gained Financial Support in Şanlıurfa
2019	a) Financial Support Program for Improving Vocational Education for Manufacturing Industry	2	a) Integrated Resource Efficiency Financial Support Program In Agricultural Industry	**7**
	b) Development of Production Infrastructures Small Scale Infrastructure Financial Support Program	1	b) Industrial Infrastructure Financial Support Program	3
	c) Culture and Tourism Small Scale Infrastructure Financial Support Program	1	c) Increasing Preschool Education Standards Financial Support Program	2
2018	a) Financial Support Program for Improving Vocational Education for Manufacturing Industry	1	a) Tourism Routes And Smart Cities Financial Support Program	3
	b) Development of Production Infrastructures Small Scale Infrastructure Financial Support Program	2	b) Industrial Infrastructure Financial Support Program	**5**
	c) Tourism Financial Support Program	**5**		

The chart is prepared according to the announcements located at the websites of MARKA and Karacadağ Development Agencies <http://www.marka.org.tr/anasayfa> and <https://www.karacadag.gov.tr/>. The Year 2020 is not included for the comparison of the cities, at the announcements of the Karacadağ Development Agency there is no information about the financial and technical support programs for the year 2020.

Tab. 2.8.6: The Number of Successful Projects that Gained Technical Support in the Provinces of Bolu and Şanlıurfa

Years	The Number of Successful Projects that Gained Technical Support	
	BOLU	ŞANLIURFA
2019	7	15
2018	9	13

The chart is prepared according to the announcements located at the websites of MARKA and Karacadağ Development Agencies <http://www.marka.org.tr/anasayfa> and <https://www.karacadag.gov.tr/>

Conclusions

In the study, two provinces of Bolu and Şanlıurfa, having different well-being index for provinces (TurkStat, 2015) have examined according to the financial and technical supports of the Agencies towards the successful projects at the provincial level. It has found out that each province have different programs within the scope of the financial programs, and in Bolu, these are 'Financial Support Program for Improving Vocational Education for Manufacturing Industry', 'Development of Production Infrastructures Small Scale Infrastructure Financial Support Program', 'Culture and Tourism Small Scale Infrastructure Financial Support Program' for the year 2019, and in Şanlıurfa these programs are 'Integrated Resource Efficiency Financial Support Program In Agrıcultural Industry', 'Industrial Infrastructure Financial Support Program' and 'Increasing Preschool Education Standards Financial Support Program' for the year 2019. Besides, most of the successful projects in Şanlıurfa gained financial support at 'Integrated Resource Efficiency Financial Support Program in Agricultural Industry' in 2019 and 'Industrial Infrastructure Financial Support Program' in 2018, and in Bolu, most of the successful projects achieved financial support at 'Financial Support Program for Improving Vocational Education for Manufacturing Industry' in 2019 and 'Tourism Financial Support Program' in 2018. Moreover, it has also found out that in the year 2019 and 2018, the successful projects at the provincial level that gained technical support in Şanlıurfa are higher in number in comparison to the successful Projects that achieved technical support of the Agency in Bolu. To conclude, while Bolu and Şanlıurfa have different ranks and indexes according to the well-being index for provinces, there are many successful projects that gained technical and financial support of the Agency in Şanlıurfa and in Bolu. The supports of Development Agencies are significant for the development of the cities and also regions in Turkey.

References

Blackman, T., and Ormston, C. (2005). "Discourses of accountability: Policy scrutiny of an English Regional Development Agency", Regional Studies, 39:3, 375–386.

Danson, M., Halkier, H. and Damborg, C. (1998). "Regional Development Agencies in Europe: An Introduction and Framework for Analysis", Part 1, Introduction, Chapter 1, (Edited by Henrik Halkier, Mike Danson and Charlotte Damborg), In Regional Agencies in Europe, Regional Studies Association, pp.13–25. <https://books.google.com.tr/books?hl=tr&lr=&id=ebBBDSTRmIC&oi=fnd&pg=PA11&dq=regional+development+agencies&ots=Bk4258FdBI&sig=lqtP4rVTZbAjnqnORCA2VXn3ug&redir_esc=y#v=onepage&q=regional%20development%20agencies&f=false> (Accessed in 05.06.2020).

Eryilmaz, B. and Tuncer, A. (2013). "Avrupa Birliği Uyum Sürecinde Bölgesel Kalkınma Politikaları: Bölgesel Kalkınma Ajansları ve Türkiye Uygulaması" (Regional Policies in the European Union Harmonization Process: Regional Development Agencies and Turkey Application), Journal of Academic Reviews, 8(1), pp. 165–189.

Karacadağ Development Agency, (2018). Work Program for 2018 (1 January–31 December 2018), <https://www.karacadag.gov.tr/Planlama/ Dosya/www.karacadag.gov.tr _17_K5J31HR_ karacadag_ka_ajansi_ 2018_calisma_programi_31.01.2018.pdf> (Accessed in 10. 07.2020).

Karacadağ Development Agency, (2019). 2019 Activity Report. <https://www.karacadag.gov.tr/Dokuman/Dosya/TX7L07YP_2019yilifaaliyetraporu.pdf> (Accessed in 10. 07.2020).

Karacadağ Development Agency, (2020). Work Program Draft for 2020 (1 January–31 December 2020). <https://www.karacadag.gov. tr/Kurumsal/Dosya/ JJ5B2 3HY_ka_cp_2020.pdf> (Accessed in 10. 07.2020).

Karacadağ Development Agency, Attraction Centers Support Program, (2020). Attraction Centers Support Program, <https://www.karacadag.gov.tr/destekler/4/cazibe-merkezlerini-destekleme-programi/> Accessed in 10. 06.2020).

MARKA East Marmara Development Agency (2014). Bolu Investor Guide. <http://www.marka.org.tr/uploads/files/Yatirimci_rehberleri/Bolu%20Tan%C4%B1t%C4%B1m%20Kitap%C3%A7%C4%B1%C4%9F%C4%B1%20T%C3%BCrk%C3%A7e.pdf> (Accessed in 10. 06.2020).

MARKA East Marmara Development Agency (2018). Bolu Provincial Investment Support and Promotion Strategy and 2018 Action Plan, Ocak 2018. <http://www.marka.org.tr/ Uploads/ Files/Yatirim_Raporlari/Bolu%20 Yat%C4%B1r%C4%B1m%20Destek% 20ve%20Tan%C4%B1t%C4%B1m%20 Stratejisi%20ve%202018%20y%C4%B1l%C4%B1%20Eylem%20 Plan%C4%B1%20(2018).pdf> (Accessed in 10. 06.2020).

MARKA East Marmara Development Agency (2019a). 2019 Activity Report (01.01.2019–31.12.2019), <http://www.marka.org.tr/uploads/files/ Faaliyet%20_raporu/2019_Y%C4%B1l%C4%B1_Faaliyet_Raporu.pdf> (Accessed in 10.06.2020).

MARKA East Marmara Development Agency (2019b). Work Program Summary for 2019 (1 January 2019–31 December 2019), <http://www.marka. org.tr/ Uploads/Files/MARKA_ 2019_Calisma_Programi-Ozeti.pdf> (Accessed in 05.06.2020).

State Planning Organization (DPT), (2000). Eighth Five-Year Development Plan, Regional Development Specialization Commission Report, <http:// www.sbb.gov.tr/wp-content/uploads/2018/11/08_BolgeselGelisme.pdf> (Accessed in 05.06.2020).

State Planning Organization (DPT) (2008). Ninth Development Plan (2007–2013) Regional Development Specialization Commission Report). <http:// www.sbb.gov.tr/wp-content/uploads/2018/11/09 _Bolgesel Gelisme.pdf> (Accessed in 05.06.2020).

The Law No 5449 on the Services of Development Agencies (2006). Dated 25.01.2006, <https://www.resmi gazete. gov.tr/eskiler/2006/02/20060208-1. htm> (Accessed in 05.06.2020).

The Ministry of Development, (2018a). General Directorate of Regional Development and Structural Adjustment), July 2018, Republic of Turkey Ministry of Development), Publication Number: 2989.

The Ministry of Development (2018b). Development Agencies Support Management Guide, General Directorate of Regional Development and Structural Adjustment, Ankara <http://www.marka.org.tr/sayfa/13/77/ mevzuat> (Accessed in 10.06.2020).

The Regulation on Development Agencies Project and Activity (2008). Development Agencies Project and Activity Support Regulation <https://www.mevzuat.gov.tr/ File/GeneratePdf? mevzuatNo= 12584& mevzuatTur=Kurum VeKurulus Yonet meligi&mevzuatTertip=5> (Accessed in 05.06.2020).

Turkey Accession Partnership Document, (2001). (Council Decision of 8 March 2001 on Accession Partnership with the Republic of Turkey in place the principles, priorities, intermediate objectives and conditions (2001/235/AT). <https://www.ab.gov.tr/katilim-ortakligi-belgeleri_46226.html> (Accessed in 05.06.2020).

Turkish Court of Accounts (2019). 2018 Development Agencies General Audit Report, October, 2019.<https://www.sayistay.gov.tr/tr/ Upload/ 62643830/ files/ raporlar /genel_raporlar/kalkinma_ajanslari/2018_Kalkinma.pdf> (Accessed in 05.06.2020).

TurkStat, (2015). Rankings and index values of well-being index for provinces, 2015, <http://www.tuik.gov.tr/PreTablo.do?alt_id=1106#> (Accessed in 10.06.2020).

TurkStat, (2016a). News Bulletin. Number: 24561, 22 January 2016, well-being index for provinces, 2015, <http://www.tuik.gov.tr/PreHaberBultenleri.do?id=24561> (Accessed in 10.06.2020).

TurkStat, (2016b). Explanations on well-being index for provinces, <http://www.tuik.gov.tr/PreTablo.do?alt_id=1106#> (Accessed in 10.06.2020).

Internet Sources

Karacadağ Development Agency, (2019). "2019 Yılı Teknik Destek Programı, eylül-ekim dönemi değerlendirme sonuçları" (2019 Technical Support Program, September-October period evaluation results)-Asil Liste (Noble List) <https://www.karacadag.gov.tr/duyuru/1267/2019-yili-teknik-destek-programi-eylul--ekim-donemi-degerlendirme-sonuclari-aciklandi/>, pp.1–2, (Accessed in 26.06.2020).

Karacadağ Development Agency, (2019). "2019 Yılı Teknik Destek Programı Temmuz-Ağustos Dönemi Değerlendirme Sonuçları" (2019 Technical Support Program July-August Period Evaluation Results)-Asil Liste (Noble List), <https://www.karacadag.gov.tr/duyuru/1262/2019-yili-teknik-destek-programi-temmuz--agustos-donemi-degerlendirme-sonuclari/>, pp.1–2, (Accessed in 26.06.2020).

Karacadağ Development Agency, (2019). "2019 Yılı Teknik Destek Programı Mayıs-Haziran Dönemi Sonuçları Açıklandı" (2019 Technical Support Program May-June Results Announced)- Asil Liste (Noble List), < https://www.karacadag.gov.tr/duyuru/1253/2019-yili-teknik-destek-programi-mayis-haziran-donemi-sonuclari-aciklandi/>, pp.1–2, (Accessed in 26.06.2020).

Karacadağ Development Agency, (2019). "2019 Yılı Mali Destek Programları Sonuçlandı" (Financial Support Programs for 2019 Concluded), <https://www.karacadag.gov.tr/duyuru/1259/2019-yili-mali-destek-programlari-sonuclandi/>, (Accessed in 26.06.2020).

Karacadağ Development Agency, (2019). "T.C. Karacadağ Kalkınma Ajansı, Program Yönetim Birimi, 2019 Yılı Tarıma Dayalı Sanayide Entegre Kaynak Verimliliği Mali Destek Programı Asil Proje Teklifleri Listesi" (Republic of Turkey Karacadağ Development Agency, Program Management Unit, 2019 Integrated Resource Efficiency Financial Support Program in Agro-based Industry Noble Project Proposals List, <https://www.karacadag.gov.tr/Duyuru/ Dosya/www.karacadag.gov.tr_1259_FF2E65FY_ ekv_ asil_ liste.pdf>, pp.1–2, (Accessed in 26.06.2020).

Karacadağ Development Agency, (2019). "T.C. Karacadağ Kalkınma Ajansı, Program Yönetim Birimi, 2019 Yılı Sanayi Altyapısı Mali Destek Programı Asil Proje Teklifleri Listesi" (Republic of Turkey Karacadağ Development Agency, Program Management Unit, 2019 Industrial Infrastructure Financial Support Program Noble Project Proposals List), <https://www.karacadag.gov.tr/Duyuru/Dosya/www .karacadag .gov.tr_1259_MC2R78NW_sanayi_asil _liste. pdf>, pp. 1–3, (Accessed in 26.06.2020).

Karacadağ Development Agency, (2019). "T.C. Karacadağ Kalkınma Ajansı, Program Yönetim Birimi, 2019 Yılı Okul Öncesi Eğitim Standartlarının Artırılması Mali Destek Programı Asil Proje Teklifleri Listesi" (Republic of Turkey Karacadağ Development Agency, Program Management Unit, Financial Support Program for Increasing Preschool Education Standards in 2019 List of Noble Project Proposals) <https://www.karacadag. gov.tr/Duyuru/Dosya/www.karacadag.gov.tr_1259_SO3A77GM_ egitim_ asil_liste.pdf>, pp.1–4, (Accessed in 26.06.2020).

Karacadağ Development Agency, (2018). "2018 Yılı Teknik Destek Programı Kasım-Aralık Dönemi Sonuçları Açıklandı" (2018 Technical Support Program November-December Results Announced)- Asil liste (Noble List), <https://www.karacadag.gov.tr/haber/897/2018-yili-teknik-destek-programi-kasim-aralik-donemi-sonuclari-aciklandi/>, (Accessed in 26.06.2020).

Karacadağ Development Agency, (2018). "Asil Liste TRC2/18/TD: Teknik Destek Programı (Noble List TRC2/18/TD: Technical Support Program) (2018 Yılı Kasım-Aralık Dönemi/ 2018 November-December Period)", <https://www.karacadag.gov.tr/Haber/Dosya/www. karacadag.gov.tr_897_IM9X71JO_td_asil_liste.pdf >, pp.1–2, (Accessed in 26.06.2020).

Karacadağ Development Agency, (2018). "2018 Yılı Teknik Destek Programı Eylül-Ekim Dönemi Değerlendirme Sonuçları" (2018 Technical Support Program September-October Period Evaluation Results), <https://www.karacadag.gov.tr/duyuru/1180/2018-yili-teknik-destek-programi-eylul-ekim-donemi-degerlen dir me-sonuclari/ >, pp.1–2, (Accessed in 26.06.2020).

Karacadağ Development Agency, (2018). Asil Liste TRC2/18/TD: Teknik Destek Programı (Noble List TRC2/18/TD: Technical Support Program) (2018 Yılı Eylül-Ekim Dönemi/2018 September-October Period)", <https://www.karacadag.gov.tr/Duyuru/ Dosya/www.karacadag. gov.tr_1180_BS5U55OX_td_asil_liste.pdf>, (Accessed in 26.06.2020).

Karacadağ Development Agency, (2018). "2018 Yılı Teknik Destek Programı Temmuz-Ağustos Dönemi Sonuçları Açıklandı" (2018 Technical Support Program July-August Period Results Announced), <https://www.karacadag.gov.tr/duyuru/1164/2018-yili-teknik-destek-programi-temmuz-agustos-donemi-sonuclari-aciklandi/>, pp. 1–2. (Accessed in 26.06.2020).

Karacadağ Development Agency, (2018). "Asil Liste TRC2/18/TD: Teknik Destek Programı (Noble List TRC2/18/TD: Technical Support Program) (2018 Yılı Temmuz Ağustos Dönemi/ 2018 July August Period)", <https://www.karacadag.gov.tr/Duyuru/Dosya/www. karacadag. gov.tr_1164_WK0R69 NA_ asil_ liste_temmuz_agustos.pdf >, (Accessed in 26.06.2020).

Karacadağ Development Agency, (2018). "2018 Yılı Teknik Destek Programı Mayıs-Haziran Dönemi Sonuçları Açıklandı" (2018 Technical Support Program May-June Results Announced), <https://www.karacadag.gov.tr/duyuru/1160/2018-yili-teknik-destek-programi-mayis-haziran-donemi-sonuclari-aciklandi/">, (Accessed in 26.06.2020).

Karacadağ Development Agency, (2018). "Asil Liste TRC2/18/TD: Teknik Destek Programı (Noble List TRC2/18/TD: Technical Support Program)(2018 Yılı Mayıs-Haziran Dönemi/ 2018 May-June Period)", <https://www.karacadag.gov.tr/Duyuru/Dosya/www.karacadag. gov.tr_ 1160_RI2D07SD_asil_liste_mayis_ haziran.pdf>, (Accessed in 26.06.2020).

Karacadağ Development Agency, (2018). "2018 Mali Destek Programları Sonuçlandı"(2018 Financial Support Programs Conclude), <https://www.karacadag.gov.tr/duyuru/1156/2018-mali-destek-programlari-sonuclandi/>, (Accessed in 26.06. 2020).

Karacadağ Development Agency, (2018). "Turizm Rotaları Ve Akıllı Kentler Mali Destek Programı Asil Proje Teklifleri Listesi" (Tourism Routes and Smart Cities Financial Support Program Noble Project Proposals List), <https://www.karacadag.gov.tr/Duyuru/Dosya/www.karacadag. gov.tr_1156_ MK0P37TY_ek_1_turizm_asil_2018web.pdf>, (Accessed in 26.06.2020).

Karacadağ Development Agency, (2018). "2018 Yılı Sanayi Altyapısı Mali Destek Programı Asil Proje Teklifleri Listesi" (2018 Industrial Infrastructure Financial Support Program Noble Project Proposals List, <https://www.

karacadag.gov.tr/Duyuru/Dosya/www. karacadag. gov.tr_ 1156_ YR4F 20KY_ek_1_sanayi_asil_2018web.pdf>, (Accessed in 26.06.2020).

MARKA, (2020). “2020 Yılı Teknik Destek Programı Başvuru Sonuçları” (2020 Technical Support Program Application Results), <http://www.marka.org.tr/sayfa/745/747/2020-yili-teknik-destek-programi-basvuru-sonu%C3%A7lari> (Accessed in 25.06.2020).

MARKA, (2020). “2020 Yılı Teknik Destek Programı Ocak-Şubat Dönemi Başvuru Sonuçları” (2020 Technical Support Program Application Results for January-February Period), <http://www.marka.org.tr/haber/detay/2663/2020-yili-teknik-destek-programi-ocak-subat-donemi-basvuru-sonu%C3%A7lari> (Accessed in 25.06.2020).

MARKA, (2019). “2019 Yılı Mali Destek Programları Başvuru Sonuçları (2019 Financial Support Programs Application Results)”, <http://www.marka.org.tr/sayfa/657/727/2019-yili-mali-destek-programlari-basvuru-sonu%C3%A7lari> (Accessed in 25.06.2020).

MARKA, (2019). “T.C. Doğu Marmara Kalkınma Ajansı 2019 Yılı Proje Teklif Çağrısı İmalat Sanayiine Yönelik Mesleki Eğitimin Geliştirilmesi Mali Destek Programı Asil Proje Listesi” (Republic of Turkey East Marmara Development Agency 2019 Call for Proposals Financial Support Program for Improving Vocational Education for Manufacturing Industry Noble Project List), <http://www.marka.org.tr/ uploads/files /2019_MDP_SONUCLAR/MESLEK%2019%20-%20AS%C 4%B0L .pdf>, pp. 1–2, (Accessed in 25.06.2020).

MARKA, (2019). “T.C. Doğu Marmara Kalkınma Ajansı 2019 Yılı Proje Teklif Çağrısı Üretim Altyapılarının Geliştirilmesi Küçük Ölçekli Altyapı Mali Destek Programı Asil Proje Listesi” (East Marmara Development Agency 2019 Call for Proposals Improvement of Production Infrastructures Small Scale Infrastructure Financial Support Program Noble Project List), <http://www.marka.org.tr/uploads/files/2019 _MDP_SONUCLAR/%C3%9CRET%C4%B0M%2019%20-%20 AS%C4%B0L.pdf>, (Accessed in 25.06.2020).

MARKA, (2019). “T.C. Doğu Marmara Kalkınma Ajansı 2019 Yılı Proje Teklif Çağrısı Kültür Ve Turizm Küçük Ölçekli Altyapı Mali Destek Programı Asil Proje Listesi” (Republic of Turkey East Marmara Development Agency 2019 Call for Proposals Culture and Tourism Small-Scale Infrastructure Financial Support Program Noble Project List) <http://www.marka.org.tr/uploads/ files/2019_MDP_SONUCLAR/KTK%C3%96A%2019%20-%20 AS%C4%B0L.pdf>, (Accessed in 25.06.2020).

MARKA, (2019). "2019 Yılı Teknik Destek Programı Başvuru Sonuçları" (2019 Technical Support Program Application Results), <http://www.marka.org.tr/sayfa/657/664/2019-yili-teknik-destek-programi-basvuru-sonu%C3%A7lari>, (Accessed in 25.06.2020).

MARKA, (2019). "2019 Yılı Teknik Destek Programı Ocak-Şubat Dönemi Başvuru Sonuçları" (2019 Technical Support Program Application Results for January-February Period), <http://www.marka.org.tr/haber/detay/2621/2019-yili-teknik-destek-programi-ocak-subat-donemi-basvuru-son u%C3%A7lari>, (Accessed in 25.06.2020).

MARKA, (2019). "2019 Yılı Teknik Destek Programı Mayıs-Haziran Dönemi Başvuru Sonuçları" (2019 Technical Support Program Application Results for May-June Period), <http://www.marka.org.tr/haber/detay/2635/2019-yili-teknik-destek-programi-mayis-haziran-donemi-basvuru-sonu%C3%A7lari>, (Accessed in 25.06.2020).

MARKA, (2019). "2019 Yılı Teknik Destek Programı Temmuz-Ağustos Dönemi Başvuru Sonuçları" (2019 Technical Support Program Application Results for July-August Period), <http://www.marka.org.tr/haber/detay/2644/2019-yili-teknik-destek-programi-temmuz-agustos-donemi-basvuru-sonu%C3%A7lari>, (Accessed in 25.06.2020).

MARKA, (2019). "2019 Yılı Teknik Destek Programı Eylül-Ekim Dönemi Başvuru Sonuçları" (2019 Technical Support Program Application Results for September-October Period), <http://www.marka.org.tr/haber/detay/2649/2019-yili-teknik-destek-programi-eylul-ekim-donemi-basvuru-sonu %C3%A7lari>, (Accessed in 25.06.2020).

MARKA, (2019). "2019 Yılı Teknik Destek Programı Kasım-Aralık Dönemi Başvuru Sonuçları" (2019 Technical Support Program Application Results for November-December Period), <http://www.marka.org.tr/haber/detay/2655/2019-yili-teknik-destek-programi-kasim-aralik-donemi-basvuru-sonu%C3%A7lari>, (Accessed in 25.06.2020).

MARKA, (2018). "2018 Yılı Mali Destek Programları Başvuru Sonuçları" (2018 Financial Support Programs Application Results),< http://www.marka.org.tr/sayfa/621/624/2018-yili-mali-destek-programlari-basvuru-sonu%C3%A7lari> (Accessed in 26.06.2020).

MARKA, (2018). "T.C. Doğu Marmara Kalkınma Ajansı, 2018 Yılı Proje Teklif Çağrısı, İmalat Sanayiine Yönelik Mesleki Eğitimin Geliştirilmesi Mali Destek Programı, Başarılı Proje Listesi" (Republic of Turkey East Marmara Development Agency, 2018 Call for Proposals, Improving Vocational Education for Manufacturing Industry Financial Support Program, Successful Project List), <http://www.marka.org.tr/ Uploads/Files/2018_MDP_SONUCLAR/MESLEK.PDF>, pp. 1–2, p. 2, (Accessed in 26.06.2020).

MARKA, (2018). "T.C. Doğu Marmara Kalkınma Ajansı, 2018 Yılı Proje Teklif Çağrısı, Üretim Altyapılarının Geliştirilmesi Küçük Ölçekli Altyapı Mali Destek Programı, Başarılı Proje Listesi" (Republic of Turkey East Marmara Development Agency, 2018 Call for Proposals, Development of Production Infrastructures Small Scale Infrastructure Financial Support Program, Successful Project List), <http:// www.marka.org.tr/Uploads/Files/2018_MDP_SONUCLAR/%C3%9CRET%C4%B0M.PDF>, (Accessed in 26.06.2020).

MARKA, (2018). "T.C. Doğu Marmara Kalkınma Ajansı, 2018 Yılı Proje Teklif Çağrısı, Turizm Mali Destek Programı, Başarılı Proje Listesi" (Republic of Turkey East Marmara Development Agency, 2018 Call for Proposals, Tourism Financial Support Program, Successful Project List), <http://www.marka.org.tr/Uploads/Files/ 2018_MDP_ SONUCLAR /TUR%C4%B0ZM.PDF>, (Accessed in 26.06.2020).

MARKA, (2018). "2018 Yılı Teknik Destek Programı Başvuru Sonuçları" (2018 Technical Support Program Application Results), <http://www.marka.org.tr/sayfa/621/644/2018-yili-teknik-destek-programi-basvuru-sonu%C3%A7lari>, (Accessed in 26.06.2020).

MARKA, (2018). "2018 Yılı Teknik Destek Programı Temmuz-Ağustos Dönemi Başvuru Sonuçları" (2018 Technical Support Program Application Results for July-August Period), <http://www.marka.org.tr/haber/detay/2597/2018-yili-teknik-destek-programi-temmuz-agustos-donemi-basvuru-sonu%C3%A7lari>, (Accessed in 26.06.2020).

MARKA, (2018). "2018 Yılı Teknik Destek Programı Eylül-Ekim Dönemi Başvuru Sonuçları" (2018 Technical Support Program Application Results for September-October Period), <http://www.marka.org.tr/haber/detay/2610/2018-yili-teknik-destek-programi-eylul-ekim-donemi-basvuru-sonu %C3%A7lari>, (Accessed in 26.06.2020).

MARKA, (2018). "2018 Yılı Teknik Destek Programı Kasım-Aralık Dönemi Başvuru Sonuçları" (2018 Technical Support Program Application Results for November-December Period), <http://www.marka.org.tr/haber/detay/2617/2018-yili-teknik-destek-programi-kasim-aralik-donemi-basvuru-son u%C3%A7lari>, (Accessed in 26.06.2020).

Dr. Mehmet Ali Polat

2.9 Effects of Foreign Direct Investments on High Technology Export: Data Analysis for Selected Developing Countries and Turkey

Abstract: High technology products are the products with high added value, competitive advantage in foreign trade and low demand flexibility. Therefore, developed countries that allocate great resources to R&D expenditures and innovation studies have a great advantage in foreign trade. Foreign direct investments and R&D expenditures are of great importance for developing countries, which have problems with foreign trade deficit and current account deficit, to produce and export more high-tech products.

In this chapter, the effects of foreign direct investments and R&D expenditures on high technology product exports in 9 developing countries were analyzed by panel data analysis using data from the 2007–2019 period. In the long-term analysis results; It has been determined that the increases in foreign direct investment stock and R&D expenditures positively affect the high technology product exports of these countries. In other words, foreign direct investments to these countries and the R&D expenditures of these countries will positively affect the high technology product export rate in the exports of the countries' manufacturing industry products. Therefore, it can be said that countries should pay special attention to these factors. In the short-term analysis, it was observed that foreign direct investment stock and R&D expenditures increased the exports of high technology products. It is noteworthy that these effects are higher than the long-term effects. The causality relationships between the series were examined with the VECM causality test and it was observed that there was a long-term, not short-term, causality relationship from foreign direct investment stock and R&D expenditures to the share of high-tech products in exports of manufacturing industry products. It has only been determined that there is a weak short-term causality relationship from foreign direct investments to R&D expenditures.

Keywords: High-tech export, Foreign direct investment, Research and development, Developing countries, Panel data analysis.

Introduction

High-tech product concept with the increase of global competition; It has become very important in developing new products, creating new production processes that provide cost advantages and exporting. In economies with high growth potential, the continuity of competitive advantage depends on the increase in the share of advanced technology products in total exports (Sara et al., 2012: 88). In this context, foreign direct investments, which are among the actors of globalization, are a driving force that accelerates the economic growth of developing countries, especially due to the realization of technology transfer (Dubickis and Gaile-Sarkanea, 2015: 966). In terms of developing countries, foreign direct investments allow the establishment of companies with higher technology than domestic companies, thanks to technology transfer. In this context, host countries specialize by using technology transfer obtained through foreign direct investments and can increase their production and then their exports (Pack and Saggi, 1997; Cantwell and Felicia, 1999; Ayhan, 2018).

In today's economies, exporting high-tech products is an important policy for countries to increase their competitive advantage. Direct foreign investments, which have the ability to stimulate the national economy and make growth sustainable, affect the production of high-tech products such as spacecraft, computers, medical and biological compounds, electronic products, scientific and precision instruments, and specialty chemicals in the developing countries they go to and support exports (Keeble and Wilkinson, 2000: 296; Srholec, 2007: 228; Şahbaz et al., 2014).

In this study, after the introduction part, a literature review has been made that examines the impact of foreign direct investments on exports. Since the aim of the article is to examine the dynamic relationship between foreign direct investments and exports, in the section after the literature review, the effects of foreign direct investment stock and R&D expenditures on high technology product exports in 9 developing countries were analyzed using panel data analysis method using the data of the 2007–2019 period. In the conclusion part of the study, some findings and policy recommendations were made within the framework of empirical findings.

1 Literature Review

Exports of high-tech products have become one of the frequently discussed phenomena in the literature, as it seriously affects the competitiveness of countries in the global market (Tebaldi, 2011: 344) Studies in the literature show that foreign direct investments increase the exports of high technology products.

Hejazi and Safarian (1999) measured the impact of foreign direct investments on international technology transfer and high technology product exports in their studies. As a result of their studies, they have observed that foreign direct investments are very effective in international technology transfer and high technology product exports. Kathuria (2001) examined the efficiency of foreign direct investment that has shaped the Indian economy in his study.

As a result of his work; It has been determined that the presence of foreign direct investments in the country leads to higher productivity increases and high technology product exports for domestic companies. Keller and Yeaple (2003), based on the period of 1987–1996, examined the effect of foreign direct investments on international technology diffusion in the US economy. As a result of his work, they stated that foreign direct investments are effective in domestic industries and, in this context, export of high technology products. Liu and Wang (2003) examined the impact of foreign direct investments in China's industrial sectors within the scope of total factor productivity in their study. As a result of their studies, they stated that it is essential for foreign direct investments to enter the country within the scope of providing advanced technology entrance to China and increasing the exports of China in this context. Liu and Trevor (2007) used panel data analysis method to find important facts in China's high-tech exports. As a result of their studies, they stated that the R&D studies carried out by multinational foreign direct investments played an important role in China's high technology product exports. Keller (2009) examined the effect of high-tech foreign capital on the international trade of that country in his study. As a result of his work; He stated that the most important channel in a country's high technology product exports is foreign direct investment. Tebaldi (2011) stated in his study that foreign direct investment is one of the most important factors that increase high technology product exports in a country. Abedini (2013) researched the driving force behind high-tech exports with econometric analysis in his study. As a result of his empirical work for this purpose, he stated that high technology product exports mostly stem from foreign direct investments. Gökmen and Turen (2013) applied panel data analysis method based on the period 1995–2010 in 15 European countries in their studies to examine the effect of foreign direct investments on high-tech exports. As a result of his work, they determined that foreign direct investments have a positive effect on high technology product exports. Newman et al. (2015) examined the relationship between foreign direct investments and the productivity of domestic firms in the host country. As a result of his work, they stated that domestic firms in the host countries that transfer technology through foreign direct investments increase their productivity and in this context, they also affect exports positively. Li et al. (2016) examined the effects of foreign direct investments in China on domestic technological development and, in this context, on high-tech product exports. As a result of their studies, they stated that the high technology brought by foreign capital to China positively affected domestic production and in this context, exports also increased. Kizilkaya et al. (2017) analyzed high technology product exports, which is an important factor in the economic growth of developing countries, based on the 2000–2012 period in 12 countries. As a result of his work, they have reached the fact that foreign direct investments increase the exports of high technology products.

2 Econometric Analysis

2.1 Data Set

In this study; In order to analyze the effects of foreign direct investments on high technology product exports, the data belonging to the 2007–2019 period of the countries in Tab. 2.9.1 were used.

According to the data in Tab. 2.9.1; while high-tech products constitute 64.64% of manufacturing industry products exports in Hong Kong, this rate is 52.77% in Malaysia and 51.72% in Singapore. In Turkey, this ratio is only 2.32% of. The data used in the study are included in Tab. 2.9.2:

Descriptive statistics belonging to the data set in Tab. 2.9.2 are included in Tab. 2.9.3.

According to the information in Tab. 2.9.3; the series used in the analysis fluctuate around their averages. The difference between max and min values is small. The standard deviations of the data are low. This indicates that the variance problem will not be encountered as a result of the analyses to be made. The number of observations used in the analysis; T = 13, N = 9, a total of 117, which is sufficient for a reliable panel data analysis.

Tab. 2.9.1: Countries Included in the Analysis. Source: Author

Sequence No	Countries	Share of High-Tech Products in Manufacturing Industry Exports in the 2018–2019 Period (Average, %)	World Ranking 2018
1	Hong Kong	64.64	1
2	Malaysia	52.77	3
3	Singapore	51.72	4
4	Vietnamese	40.15	7
5	S. Korea	36.34	9
6	China	31.43	11
7	Thailand	23.34	16
8	Kazakhstan	22.01	20
9	Turkey	2.32	106

Tab. 2.9.2: Data Used in Analysis. Source: Author

Variable	Description	Abbreviation	Source
The dependent variable	Share of high technology products in the export of manufacturing industry products (Billion Dollars)	HTX	World Bank (2020a, 2020b)
The independent variable	Foreign Direct Investment Stock (Billion Dollars)	FDI	UNCTAD (2020)
Control Variable	Research and Development Expenses (Billion Dollars)	R&D	World Bank (2020c, 2020d)

Tab. 2.9.3: Descriptive Statistics. Source: Author

	HTX	FDI	R&D
Mean	4.88	7.82	3.76
Median	5.81	7.41	3.74
Maximum	8.10	9.90	8.07
Minimum	1.51	5.76	0.15
Std. Dev.	2.10	1.08	2.00
Skewness	-0.18	0.53	0.37
Kurtosis	1.44	2.05	2.48
Jarque-Bera	12.52	9.88	3.96
Probability	0.00	0.01	0.14
Sum	571.1	915.1	440.4
Sum Sq. Dev.	513.9	134.2	462.2
Observations	117	117	117

1.2 Econometric Model

In this study, following the studies of (eung (2010), Mitic and Ivic (2016), Gamariel and Hove (2019), Yavuz and Uysal (2020), the following econometric model was established.

$$HTX_{it} = \theta_0 + \theta_1 FDI_{it} + \theta_2 R\&D_{it} + \varepsilon_{it} \quad (1)$$

Here HTX_{it}; the ratio of high technology products in the export of manufacturing industry products, FDI_{it}; the ratio of foreign direct investment stock to gross domestic product (GDP), $R\&D_{it}$; the ratio of research and development expenditures to GDP and ε_{it}; shows a series of error terms with econometrically smooth White noise process. As a result of the analysis, $\theta_1 > 0$ and $\theta_2 > 0$ are expected to have a positive effect on the export of high technology products of the countries due to direct foreign investment stock and R&D studies.

1.3 Methodology

In this study, the stationarities of the series were analyzed by Levin, Lin and Chu (2002, LLC), Im, Pesaran and Shin (2003, IPS), Maddala and Wu (1999) Fisher ADF and Fisher PP panel unit root tests. The cointegration relations between the series were examined by Pedroni (2004) test, and the long and short-term relationships between the series were analyzed by Panel FMOLS (Fully Modified Ordinary Least Squares) and Panel DOLS (Dynamic Ordinary Least Squares) methods. The long-term and short-term causality relationships between the series have been revealed by the VECM causality test.

1.4 Panel Unit Root Test

In this study, the stationarities of the series were examined by LLC, IPS, Fisher ADF and Fisher PP panel unit root tests. In panel unit root tests, the degree to which the value of the series in the current period is affected by the value of the previous period is examined (Gujarati and Porter, 2010: 744). For this purpose, the following equation is used:

$$y_{it} = \rho_i y_{it-1} + \delta_i X_{it} + \epsilon_{it} \tag{2}$$

Here i = 1,2,. . ., N cross sections (regions for this study), t = 1,2,. . ., T time dimension, X_{it}; external variables, ρ_i; autoregressive unit root parameter and ϵ_{it}; Refers to a series of error terms with a white noise process (econometrically smooth). When the unit root parameter is $\rho_i = 1$ in equation (2), the series is not stationary. Spurious regression problem may be encountered in analyzes to be made with such series (Granger & Newbold, 1974). Since the autocorrelation problem can usually be encountered in Equation (2), this model is expanded as follows:

$$y_{it} = \rho_i y_{it-1} + \sum_{j=1}^{m} \beta_{ij} \Delta Y_{it-j} + \delta_i X_{it} + \epsilon_{it} \tag{3}$$

Test statistic used in LLC panel unit root test:

$$\Delta y_{it} = \rho y_{it-1} + \sum_{j=1}^{m} \beta_{ij} \Delta y_{it-j} + \delta_i X_{it} + e_{it} \tag{4}$$

It is obtained by the equation. In equation (4), m; is the optimum lag length, and can be determined with the help of Schwarz Information Criterion (Schwarz Information Criterion: SBC) or Akaike Information Criterion (AIC). In the LLC test, it is accepted that the unit root parameter (ρ) is the same for all horizontal sections (firms in this study). Im, Pesaran and Shin (2003) stated that this assumption may not always be realistic and stated that Equation (5), which allows the unit root parameter to be different between horizontal sections, should be used in unit root testing:

$$\Delta y_{it} = \rho_i y_{it-1} + \sum_{j=1}^{m} \Delta y_{it-j} + \delta_i X_{it} + e_{it} \tag{5}$$

It should be noted that in Equation (5), different from Equation (4), *Pi* is used. Thus, individual unit root parameters can be obtained for each cross section. Test statistics in Fisher ADF and Fisher PP methods developed by Maddala and Wu (1999) are obtained with the help of Equation (6):

$$Z = \frac{1}{\sqrt{N}} \sum_{i=1}^{N} \Phi^{-1}(y_i) \rightarrow N(0, 1) \tag{6}$$

The difference of these two methods; It stems from the way probability values of unit root test statistics calculated for each cross section are calculated. In this study, the stationarities of the series were tested by LLC, IPS, Fisher ADF and Fisher PP panel unit root tests and the results obtained are presented in Tab. 2.9.4.

According to the findings in Tab. 2.9.4; while there is no exact finding about the stationarity in the level values of the series, it is seen that the series become absolutely stationary in the first differences. In this case, it would be more reasonable to assume that the series are I (1).

1.5 Panel Cointegration Test

In this study, the existence of a cointegration relationship between series was examined with the Pedroni (2004) panel cointegration test. Pedroni (2004) panel cointegration test is based on the following equation:

$$y_{it} = \alpha_i + \delta_i t + \beta_{1i} x_{1i,\ t} + \beta_{2i} x_{2i,\ t} + \ldots + \beta_{Mi} x_{Mi,\ t} + \varepsilon_{i,t} \tag{7}$$

Here t = 1,. . ., T; i = 1,. . ., N; m = 1,. . ., M. In this test, y and x must be series that are not stationary at the level but become stationary when their differences are taken from the same degree (Wooldridge, 2013). The Pedroni (2004) test is

Tab. 2.9.4: Results of Panel Unit Root Tests. Source: Author

	LLC		IPS		Fisher ADF		Fisher PP	
	Intercept	**Trend and Intercept**	**Intercept**	**Trend and Intercept**	**Intercept**	**Trend and Intercept**	**Intercept**	**Trend and Intercept**
HTX	-2.37***	-4.01***	0.54	-1.96**	13.58	31.68**	17.10	32.92**
	(0.00)	(0.00)	(0.70)	(0.02)	(0.75)	(0.02)	(0.51)	(0.01)
FDI	-8.56***	-0.84	-3.45***	0.82	47.74***	18.02	58.73***	44.87***
	(0.00)	(0.19)	(0.00)	(0.79)	(0.00)	(0.45)	(0.00)	(0.00)
R & D	-4.48***	-1.56*	-0.36	1.27	35.98***	15.21	37.64***	13.25
	(0.00)	(0.05)	(0.35)	(0.89)	(0.00)	(0.64)	(0.00)	(0.77)
ΔHTX	-8.04***	-7.26***	-6.79***	-3.61***	73.16***	48.70***	95.66***	67.97***
	(0.00)	(0.00)	(0.00)	(0.00)	(0.00)	(0.00)	(0.00)	(0.00)
ΔFDI	-2.47***	-5.25***	-3.47***	-4.07***	47.50***	47.51***	83.04***	88.86***
	(0.00)	(0.00)	(0.00)	(0.00)	(0.00)	(0.00)	(0.00)	(0.00)
$\Delta R\&D$	-5.26***	-11.30***	-3.61***	-5.82***	47.31***	61.46***	59.03***	72.61***
	(0.00)	(0.00)	(0.00)	(0.00)	(0.00)	(0.00)	(0.00)	(0.00)

Note: Optimum lag lengths are determined using Akaike Information Criteria. ***, ** and *; It expresses stagnation at 1%, 5% and 10% significance level, respectively.

based on the systematic of Engle and Granger (1987) test. So, while the x and y series are not stationary at the level, the error term series obtained from the regression analysis to be made with these series is tested whether it is stationary or not. When the error term series is stationary, it is decided that the series are cointegrated. Therefore, when the error term series is opened and written in accordance with the AR (1) process, we obtain the following equation.

$$\varepsilon_{it} = \rho_i \varepsilon_{i,t-1} + u_{i,t} \tag{8}$$

Since the autocorrelation problem may be encountered in this model, when the delayed values of the difference of the dependent variable are added to the model as explanatory variable;

$$\varepsilon_{it} = \rho_i \varepsilon_{i,t-1} + \sum_{j=1}^{p_i} \psi_{ij} \Delta \varepsilon_{i,t-j} + v_{i,t} \tag{9}$$

The null hypothesis of the Pedroni panel cointegration test: "$|\rho_i| = 1$ for all i. In other words, there is no cointegration relationship between series for all horizontal sections forming the panel "(Greene, 2002). Pedroni (2004) developed seven different test statistics in order to test the existence of cointegration relationship between the series forming the panel. In the study, Pedroni (2004) panel cointegration test was applied and the results obtained are presented in Tab. 2.9.5.

According to the results in Tab. 2.9.5; there is a cointegration relationship between the series in the model. In this case, according to Engle and Granger

Tab. 2.9.5: Panel Cointegration Test Results. Source: Author

	Test Stats.	***Weighted Test Stats.***
Panel v-Statistic	0.26 (0.39)	0.30 (0.37)
Panel** rho **-Statistic	0.11 (0.54)	-0.21 (0.41)
Panel PP-Statistic	-1.46* (0.07)	-2.85*** (0.00)
Panel ADF-Statistic	-1.40* (0.07)	-3.96*** (0.00)
Grup** rho **-Statistic	0.99 (0.83)	-
Grup PP-Statistic	-5.69*** (0.00)	-
Grup ADF-Statistic	-4.85*** (0.00)	-

Note: *** and **; expresses the existence of a cointegration relationship at 1% and 5% significance level, respectively. Values in parentheses are probability values of Pedroni (2004) test. Optimum lag lengths are determined according to Akaike Information Criteria.

Tab. 2.9.6: Long-Term Analysis Results. Source: Author

	Panel FMOLS	*Panel DOLS*
FDI	**0.51*** (0.00)**	**0.50* (0.06)**
R & D	**0.54*** (0.00)**	**0.55*** (0.00)**
R^2	0.83	0.84
$\bar{R}^2$	0.81	0.82
S.E. of Regression	0.89	0.87
Long – run Variance	0.51	0.70
Sum Squared Resid	78.54	82.06

Note: ***; It states that the relevant parameter is statistically significant at the 1% significance level. Values in parentheses are t-test probability values. Optimum lag lengths are determined according to Akaike Information Criteria.

(1987), no spurious regression problem will be encountered in long-term analyzes to be made using the level values of these series and the findings to be obtained will be reliable.

1.6 Long Run Analysis

In this study, long-term analysis was done by using the level values of the series by Panel FMOLS and Panel DOLS methods. These methods are robust estimators that take into account the cointegration vector in regression analysis and are resistant to autocorrelation and variance problems (Othman and Masih, 2015). In the study, long-term analyzes were performed using Equation (10):

$$HTX_{it} = \theta_0 + \theta_1 FDI_{it} + \theta_2 R\&D_{it} + \varepsilon_{it} \tag{10}$$

Results obtained from long-term analyzes are presented in Tab. 2.9.6.

According to the results in Tab. 2.9.6; Increases in FDI stock and RD expenditures also positively affect the high-tech exports of countries. Findings obtained by both methods are close in magnitude. In that case, it can be stated that the FDIs to be carried out for the said countries and the R&D activities to be carried out by these countries will positively affect the rate of high-tech product exports in the exports of the manufacturing industry products of the countries, so these factors should be given special importance.

Tab. 2.9.7: Short-Term Analysis Results. Source: Author

	Panel FMOLS	*Panel DOLS*
ΔFDI	**0.57*** (0.00)**	**0.40** (0.04)**
$\Delta R\&D$	**0.62*** (0.00)**	**0.65*** (0.00)**
ECT_{t-1}	**-0.31*** (0.00)**	**-0.21** (0.01)**
R^2	0.13	0.13
$\bar{R}^2$	0.08	0.03
S.E. of Regression	0.69	0.63
Long – run Variance	0.16	0.41
Sum Squared Resid	37.89	38.78

Note: ***; It states that the relevant parameter is statistically significant at the 1% significance level. Values in parentheses are t-test probability values. Optimum lag lengths are determined according to Akaike Information Criteria.

1.7 Short Run Analysis

In the study, short-term analyzes were performed by using the first difference of the series and error correction term (ECT_{t-1}) with the help of the following equation, again by FMOLS and PDOLS methods.

$$\Delta HTX_{it} = \gamma_{i0} + \gamma_1 \Delta FDI_{it} + \gamma_2 \Delta R\&D_{it} + \gamma_3 ECT_{t-1} + u_{it} \tag{11}$$

As a result of the estimation of this model, if the coefficient of the error correction term is statistically significant, it is decided that the error correction mechanism of the model works (Anderson, Qian and Rasche, 2006). Short-term analysis in the study was carried out with the PDOLS method and the results obtained are presented in Tab. 2.9.7.

According to the results in Tab. 2.9.7, in the countries included in the analysis, FDI stock and R&D expenditures had a positive and statistically significant effect on high technology product exports in the short term. It is noteworthy that these effects are higher than long-term effects. Since the coefficient of the error correction term is negative and statistically significant in both methods, the error correction mechanisms of the model work. In other words, the deviations that occur in the short term between the series acting together in the long-term also disappear and the series converge to the long-term equilibrium relationship again.

1.8 Panel Causality Test

Since the cointegration relationship between the series was determined, the causality relationships between the series were examined with the causality test based on the error correction model (Vector Error Correction Model: VECM). This method was obtained by rearranging the Granger (1969) causality test under the condition of cointegration (Persson, 2015). The null hypothesis of this test; "There is no causality relationship". Equations used in this test:

$$'HTX_{it} = \alpha_0 + \sum_{j=1}^{p} \alpha_{1j}\,'HTX_{it-1} + \sum_{j=1}^{p} \alpha_{2j}\,'FDI_{it-1} + \sum_{j=1}^{p} \alpha_{3j}\,'R\&D_{it-1} + \alpha_4 ECT_{t-1} + \vartheta_{it} \tag{12}$$

$$'FDI_{it} = \beta_0 + \sum_{j=1}^{p} \beta_{1j}\,'FDI_{it-1} + \sum_{j=1}^{p} \beta_{2j}\,'HTX_{it-1} + \sum_{j=1}^{p} \beta_{3j}\,'R\&D_{it-1} + \beta_4 ECT_{t-1} + \omega_{it} \tag{13}$$

$$'R\&D_{it} = \delta_0 + \sum_{j=1}^{p} \delta_{1j}\,'R\&D_{it-1} + \sum_{j=1}^{p} \delta_{2j}\,'HTX_{it-1} + \sum_{j=1}^{p} \delta_{3j}\,'FDI_{it-1} + \delta_4 ECT_{t-1} + \omega_{it} \tag{14}$$

In the study, the results of determining the optimum lag length required for VECM causality test are presented in Tab. 2.9.8.

According to the results in Tab. 2.9.8, optimum lag is 1. The serial correlation test results of the VAR (1) model are listed in Tab. 2.9.9.

According to the results in Tab. 2.9.9, serial correlation problem will not be seen in the VAR (1) model and the causality test to be performed using this model. The heteroskedasticity test results of the VAR (1) model are shown in Tab. 2.9.10.

According to the results in Tab. 2.9.10, the heteroskedasticity problem will not be seen in the VAR (1) model and the causality test to be performed using this model. The results of the VECM causality test performed using the VAR (1) model are shown in Tab. 2.9.11.

Tab. 2.9.8: Results of Optimal Lag Length Determination. Source: Author

Lag	*LR*	*FPE*	*AIC*	*SC*	*HQ*
0	NA	0.0001	-0.6395	-0.5374*	-0.5993
1*	25.8260*	0.0001*	-0.7915*	-0.3833	-0.6309*
2	3.8361	0.0001	-0.5743	0.1401	-0.2933
3	9.3780	0.0001	-0.4655	0.5550	-0.0641
4	9.1810	0.0001	-0.3634	0.9633	0.1584
5	9.7828	0.0002	-0.2858	1.3470	0.3564

Note: * indicates lag order selected by the criterion, LR: sequential modified LR test statistic (each test at 5% level), FPE: Final prediction error, AIC: Akaike information criterion, SC: Schwarz information criterion, HQ: Hannan-Quinn information criterion

Tab. 2.9.9: Serial Correlation LM Tests Results. Source: Author

Null hypothesis: No serial correlation at lag h						
Lag	*LRE* stat*	*df*	*Prob.*	*Rao F-stat*	*df*	*Prob.*
1	7.131940	9	0.6234	0.792608	(9, 219.2)	0.6235
Null hypothesis:No serial correlation at lags 1 to h						
Lag	*LRE* stat*	*df*	*Prob.*	*Rao F-stat*	*df*	*Prob.*
1	7.131940	9	0.6234	0.792608	(9, 219.2)	0.6235

Note: *Edgeworth expansion corrected likelihood ratio statistic.

Tab. 2.9.10: Heteroskedasticity Test Results. Source: Author

Chi-sq	*df*	*Prob.*
17.21215	84	0.2450

Tab. 2.9.11: VECM Causality Test Results. Source: Author

	Short Term Causality (Affecting Variables)			***Long-Term Causality***
Affected Variable	ΔHTX	ΔFDI	$\Delta R\&D$	ECT_{t-1}
ΔHTX	-	0.0005 (0.98)	0.14 (0.70)	-0.35*** (0.00)
ΔFDI	0.32 (0.57)	-	1.02 (0.31)	0.005 (0.27)
$\Delta R\&D$	0.006 (0.97)	2.80* (0.09)	-	0.01 (0.63)

Note: *** and * show that there is a causality relationship at the 1% and 10% significance level, respectively.

According to the findings in Tab. 2.9.11; From FDI and R&D to HTX, there is not a short-term, but a long-term causality relationship. It only seems that there is a weak short-term causality relationship from FDI to R&D. On the other hand, no causality relationship could be determined in the short-term or long-term from HTX and R&D to FDI. That is to say, foreign investors pay attention to different criteria (institutional characteristics and other macroeconomic sizes of the countries) in country selection.

Results and Conclusions

High technology products are the products with high added value, competitive advantage in foreign trade and low demand flexibility. Therefore, developed countries that allocate great resources to R&D expenditures and innovation studies have an important advantage in foreign trade. Foreign direct investments and R&D expenditures are very important for developing countries with foreign trade deficit and current account deficit problems to produce and export more high-tech products.

In this study, the effects of foreign direct investment stock and R&D expenditures on high technology product exports in 9 developing countries were analyzed by panel data analysis using the data of the 2007–2019 period. The stationarity of the series was tested by LLC, IPS, Fisher ADF and Fisher PP panel unit root tests, and it was decided that all series were I (1). The existence of cointegration relations between the series was examined with the Pedroni (2004) panel cointegration test, and it was found that the series were cointegrated. Long- and short-term analyzes between series were carried out by Panel FMOLS and Panel DOLS methods. In the long-term analysis results; It has been determined that increases in foreign direct investment stock and increases in R&D expenditures positively affect the high technology product exports of these countries. In other words, it can be easily said that foreign direct investments to these countries and the R&D activities to be carried out by these countries positively affect the export rate of high-tech products in the exports of the manufacturing industry products of the countries, therefore, it can be easily said that countries should pay special attention to these factors. At this point, it becomes easier to understand how countries such as Hong Kong and Malaysia have developed. So, like Turkey, the foreign trade deficit and current account deficit are living accordingly and so often living in countries in economic crisis, it is essential to focus on the production and export of high-tech products. In the short-term analysis results, it was observed that foreign direct investment stock and R&D expenditures increased the exports of high technology products. It is noteworthy that these effects are higher than long-term effects. It was determined that the coefficient of the error correction term is negative and statistically significant, that is, the error correction mechanism of the model works. The causality relationships between the series were examined by VECM causality test; it has been observed that there is not a short-term, but a long-term causality relationship from foreign direct investment stock and R&D expenditures to the share of high-tech products in exports of manufacturing industry products. It is only determined that there is a weak short-term causality relationship from foreign direct investment stock to R&D expenditure. On the other hand, no causality relationship has been found in the short-term or long-term from the share of high technology products and R&D expenditures to foreign direct investment stock in the exports of manufacturing industry products. That is to say, foreign investors pay attention to different criteria (institutional characteristics and other macroeconomic sizes of countries) in country selection.

Based on the results obtained from this study; It can be stated that foreign direct investments increase the capacity of developing countries to produce high-tech products and in this context, Far Eastern countries such as Hong Kong and Malaysia have come to the position to export high-tech products. Exports of high-tech products such as Turkey, also should be noted that the low country to attract more foreign direct investment in order to ensure economic stability and the need to provide necessary facilities to foreign investors. In addition, it should not be forgotten that it will be in the interest of their own countries to increase the technological production levels of their countries by providing all kinds of support to the R&D studies of both domestic and foreign investors. Especially their focus to export produce high-tech and high value-added products in order to overcome chronic current account deficits and low economic growth problems to be living in Turkey, if it difficult to achieve their own facilities, will help it/contribution that will allow to invite foreign investors to the country would be enormous benefits are evaluated.

References

Abedini, J. (2013). Heterogeneity of Trade Patterns İn High-Tech Goods Across Established And Emerging Exporters: A Panel Data Analysis. *Emerging Markets Finance and Trade*, 49(4), 4–21.

Anderson, R., Qian, H. and Rasche, R. (2006). Analysis of Panel Vector Error Correction Models Using Maximum Likelihood, the Bootstrap, and Canonical-Correlation Estimators. https://files.stlouisfed.org/files/htdocs/

econ/anderson/AnalysisOfVEC Models_15Feb2006.pdf, (Date of Access: 24 July 2020).

Ayhan, F. (2018). The Effects of Political and Economic Risk on FDI: A Theoretical Survey in Global Trends of Modernization in Budgeting and Finance (Ed.: Denis USHAKOV), Pp.: 44–63. IGI Global, Hershey: USA. ISBN: 9781522577607.

Baltagi, B. H. (1995). *Econometric Analysis of Panel Data*. John Wiley & Sons Ltd. England.

Cantwell, J. and Felicia, F. (1999). Firms as the Source of İnnovation and Growth: The Evolution of Technological Competence. *Journal of Evolutionary Economics*, 9(3), 331–366.

Cheung, K. C. (2010). Spillover Effects of FDI via Exports on Innovation Performance of China's High-Technology Industries. *Journal of Contemporary China*, 19(65), 541–557.

Dubickis, M. and Gaile-Sarkane, E. (2015). Perspectives on Innovation and Technology Transfer. *Procedia - Social and Behavioral Sciences*, 213, 965–970.

Engle, R. and Granger, C. W. J. (1987). Co-Integration and Error Correction: Represention, Estimation and Testing. *Econometrica*, 55(2), 251–276.

Gamariel, G. and Hove, S. (2019). Foreign Direct Investment and Export Competitiveness in Africa: Investigating the Channels. *Journal of African Trade*, 6(1–2), 30–46.

Gökmen, Y. and Turen, U. (2013). The Determinants of High Technology Exports Volume: A Panel Data Analysis of EU-15 Countries. *International Journal of Management, Economics and Social Sciences*, 2(3), 217–232.

Granger, C. (1969). "Investigating Causal Relation by Econometric Models and CrossSpectral Methods", *Econometrica*, 37, 427–438.

Granger, C. W. J. and Newbold, P. (1974). Spurious Regressions in Econometrics. *Journal of Econometrics*, 2(2), 111–120.

Greene, W. H. (2002). *Econometric Analysis*. (Fifth Edition). Prentice Hall, New Jersey.

Gujarati, D. N. and Porter, D. C. (2010). *Econometrics*. McGraw-Hill, New York.

Hejazi, W. and Safarian, A. E. (1999). Trade, Foreign Direct Investment, and R&D Spillovers. *Journal of International Business Studies*, 30 (3), 491–511.

Im. K. S., Pesaran, M. H. and Shin. Y. (2003). Testing for Unit Roots in Heterogeneous Panels. *Journal of Econometrics*, 115, 53–74.

Kathuria, V. (2001). Foreign Firms, Technology Transfer and Knowledge Spillovers to Indian Manufacturing Firms: A Stochastic Frontier Analysis. *Applied Economics*, 33, 625–642.

Keeble, D. and Wilkinson, F. (2000). *High-technology clusters, networking and collective learning in Europe*. Ashgate Publishing.

Keller, W. (2009). International Trade, Foreign Direct Investment, and Technology Spillovers. *NBER Working Paper*, No. 15442.

Keller, W. and Yeaple, S. R. (2003). Multinational Enterprises, International Trade, and Productivity Growth: Firm-Level Evidence from the United States. *NBER Working*, Paper No. 9504.

Kizilkaya, O., Sofuoglu, E. and Ay, A. (2017). Yüksek Teknolojili Ürün İhracatı Üzerinde Doğrudan Yabancı Sermaye Yatırımları ve Dışa Açıklığın Etkisi: Gelişmekte Olan Ülkelerde Panel Veri Analizi. [The Effect of Foreign Direct Investment and Openness on High Technology Product Export in Developing Countries]. *Dogus University Journal,* 18(1), 63–78.

Levin. A., Lin. C. F. and Chu, C. (2002). Unit Root Tests in Panel Data: Asymptotic and Finite-Sample Properties. *Journal of Econometrics*, 108, 1–24.

Li, J., Strange, R., Ning, L. and Sutherland, D. (2016). Outward Foreign Direct Investment and Domestic Innovation Performance: Evidence from China. *International Business Review*, 25, 1010–1019.

Liu, X. and Wang, C. (2003). Does Foreign Direct Investment Facilitate Technological Progress: Evidence from Chinese Industries. *Research Policy*, 32(6), 945–953.

Liu, X. and Trevor, B. (2007). Innovation Performance and Channels for International Technology Spillovers: Evidence from Chinese High-Tech Industries. *Research Policy*, 36(3), 355–366.

Maddala, G. S. and Shaowen, W. (1999). A Comparative Study of Unit Root Tests with Panel Data and New Simple Test. *Oxford Bulletin of Economics and Statistics*, 61, 631–652.

Mitic, B. and Ivic, M. (2016). The Impact of Foreign Direct Investment on Export Performance: Case of European Transition Economies. *Independent Journal of Management & Production* (IJM&P), 7(3), 771–785.

Newman, C., Rand, J., Talbot, T. and Tarp, F. (2015). Technology Transfers, Foreign Investment and Productivity Spillovers. *European Economic Review*, 76, 168–187.

Othman, A. N. and Masih, M. (2015). Do profit and loss sharing (PLS) deposits also affect PLS financing? Evidence from Malaysia based on DOLS, FMOLS and system GMM techniques. *Munich Personal RePEc Archive*, MPRA Paper No. 65224.

Pack, H. and Saggi, K. (1997). Inflows of Foreign Technology and Indigenous Technological Development. *Review of Development Economics*, 1(1): 181–198.

Pedroni, P. (2004). Panel Cointegration: Asymptotic and Finite Sample Properties of Pooled Time Series Tests with an Application to the PPP Hypothesis, *Econometric Theory*, 20(3), 597–625.

Persson, R. (2015). The short and long-term interdependencies between stock prices and dividends: A panel vector error correction approach. Uppsala University, Department of Business Studies.

Sara, T. S., Jackson, F. H. and Upchurch, L. T. (2012). "Role of Innovation in HiTechExports of a Nation", International Journal of Business and Management, 7(7): 85–93.

Srholec, M. (2007). High-Tech Exports from Developing Countries: A Symptom of Technology Spurts or Statistical Illusion?. *Review of World Economics/ Weltwirtschaftliches Archiv*, 143(2): 227–255.

Şahbaz, A., Yanar, R. and Adıgüzel, U. (2014). Ar-Ge Harcamaları ve İleri Teknoloji Mal İhracatı İlişkisi: Panel Nedensellik Analizi. [The Relationship between R&D Expenditure and High-Technology Export: Panel Causality Analysis]. *Journal of Çukurova University Institute of Social Sciences*, 223(1), 47–60.

Tebaldi, E. (2011). The Determinants of High-Technology Exports: A Panel Data Analysis. *Atlantic Economic Journal*, 39(4), 343–353.

UNCTAD (2020). Foreign direct investment: Inward and outward flows and stock, annual. https://unctadstat.unctad.org/wds/TableViewer/tableView.aspx, (Date of Access: 14.07.2020).

Wooldridge, J. M. (2013). *Introductory Econometrics: A Modern Approach.* (Fifth Edition). Cengage Learning, Boston.

World Bank (2020a). High-technology exports (%of manufactured exports). https://data.worldbank.org/indicator/TX.VAL.TECH.MF.ZS?view=chart, (Date of Access: 14 July 2020).

World Bank (2020b). High-technology exports (current US$). https://data.worldbank.org/indicator/TX.VAL.TECH.CD?view=chart, (Date of Access: 14 July 2020).

World Bank (2020c). Research and development expenditure (%of GDP). https://data.worldbank.org/indicator/GB.XPD.RSDV.GD.ZS?view=chart, (Date of Access: 14 July 2020).

World Bank (2020d). GDP (current US$). https://data.worldbank.org/indicator/NY.GDP.MKTP.CD?view=chart, (Date of Access: 14 July 2020).

Dr. Salih Ziya Kutlu and Emine Firat

2.10 Regional Development in Turkey: An Evaluation on Development Plans

Abstract: Regional development is one of the main problem areas in the world as well as in Turkey. Turkey, has implemented various policies to solve interregional and intraregional development problems. In this process from General Inspectorates to Development Agencies, many projects were tried to be implemented. Development Plans, which started to be created with the development of the central planning approach and the establishment of the State Planning Organization (SPO) in the post-1960 period, have become one of the basic factors in ensuring regional development. The increasing of regional disparities, changes in regional development concept and Turkey's relations with the European Union, has led to a change in the regional policies implemented in the country. Meanwhile, in this chapter, the concept of regional development, how the concept of region discussed in Turkey and the initiatives to establish the district administration are mentioned. The aim of the chapter is to determine how development plans affect regional development policies. Therefore, after the explanations about the region, how the notion of regional development is handled in Development Plans has been examined and evaluated. It was concluded that the factors included in the development plans were sufficient to ensure regional development, but the implementation could not be achieved at the desired grade due to reasons such as economic insufficiencies, political power changes, problems arising from legal regulations and the regions inability to attract investors at the desired grade.

Keywords: Region, Development, Regional development, Development plans, development agency.

Introduction

Countries should adopt regional policies, regional plans, etc. in order to eliminate the development differences between regions that have become more evident in the 20th century refers to various applications. In the post-1970 period, the use of concepts such as competitiveness, knowledge-intensive production, cooperation between regional actors/stakeholders, promotion of the region and attracting investment has increased the importance of the concept of the region (Özer, 2007: 390).

As well as in the world, regional development disparities issues of intra-regional and constitutes one of the main problem areas in Turkey. Turkey has implemented various policies planned development period in order to solve regional and intra-regional development issues. However, although the issue has been included in development plans, especially VII. It is seen that there are deficiencies in the preparation, implementation, monitoring and evaluation of regional policies in the period until the Five-Year Development Plan. It can be said that the economic situation of the country has an effect on the emergence of this situation (SPO, 2008: 21)

The aim of the study is to determine how development plans affect regional development policies. For this purpose interregional and intraregional developmental problems living in Turkey, will examine the policies it implements on the issue before the planned period. Then, the period after 1963, which is called the planned period, will be examined in terms of development plans, and it will be expressed how the approach to regional development in the country has evolved and which policies are implemented in this regard. In the conclusion part, evaluations about development plans are included.

1 The Concept of Regional Development

The concept of regional development is defined as a development process that enables the determination of the areas with the current development potential of the region and the realization of the policies to be implemented in these areas within the framework of the vision and mission determined with the participation of all actors in the region in order to increase the welfare level of the region and ensure its development (Ildırar 2004: 16). Regional development according to another definition; These are the policies applied to increase the socio-economic development of the region in cases where traditional regional development policies and central policies are insufficient and where the differences in development gradually increase, using social, economic and public mechanisms by using the unique potentials of the regions (Pike, Rodriguez-Pose, and Tomaney, 2016). According to another definition, these are practices determined to reduce regional inequalities in order to ensure the development of economic activities such as employment and welfare in the region (OECD, 2020).

It has been observed that the practices of traditional regional development policies that take decisions from the center and allocate a high proportion of public resources fail, cannot reduce regional development disparities and reduce social cohesion (OECD, 2020). In the light of the new regional development policy, considering the definitions of the concept of regional development, it is clear that long-term goals should be determined, the establishment of multi-stakeholder structures in which participation is essential, and a planning that includes strategies (Uzay, 2005: 16–17). The common aspects in the definitions regarding the concepts of regional development and regional planning are important in terms of expressing how the concepts are handled today. Common aspects of definitions;

- Implementation with the aim of reducing the development differences between the regions,
- Activating areas of the region with potential for development,
- Trying to increase the competitiveness and capacity of the region,
- It can be specified as having a process open to the participation of local actors.

In order to ensure regional development, a multi-stakeholder planning process must be experienced. The plans should include different elements such as strengths and weaknesses of the region, problems to be solved, future targets, human resources potential of the region, underground and above ground resources (Karaca, 2018: 42). Thanks to the cooperation realized at the regional level, the region will gain a more competitive structure in the changing global economic system (Frisken and Norris, 2001: 468).

Economic policies prepared at the national level generally focus on targets such as macroeconomic conditions, reduction of budget deficits, lowering inflation and liberalization of trade, ignoring regional and local characteristics. However, achieving national economic and social development is directly related to local development. Instead of central policies, there are benefits such as establishing policies at regional level, ensuring close coordination between different actors, using resources more efficiently, and having information about regional problems and development potentials (Šabić and Vujadinović, 2017: 464).

Among these policies, the most preferred ones are establishing development plans for certain regions and establishing special development administrations responsible for the development of the region (Ergun, 1993: 72). Tennessee Valley Authority (TVA), which was established in the United States of America (USA) in 1933 and continues its activities today, is one of the successful examples of regional development. While the area of responsibility of TVA was among the least developed regions of the country at the time of its establishment, after the establishment of TVA, productivity and welfare increase was achieved in public investments in the region (Kline and Moretti, 2014: 276–277).

TVA is considered as the first example of regional development agencies, one of the most preferred regional development tools today. This understanding, which emerged in the USA in the 1930s, started to be used more and more in Europe after the Second World War (Özer, 2007: 396). In European countries, with the localization of institutions responsible for regional development, it is thought that more positive developments will be experienced in economic growth, quality of public services and democratic participation of citizens (Šabić and Vujadinović, 2017: 464–465). The organization responsible for regional development in Portugal until 1995 is the Regional Planning Commission (CCR), which is included in the hierarchical structure of the center. In the period after 1995, development agencies were established as a completely autonomous structure from the state and reflecting the understanding of public-private partnership (Syrett and Silva, 2001: 174–177). Similarly, in Poland, it cannot be mentioned in the existence of an institution responsible for regional development until 1993. Until this period, there are mostly practices in central and sectoral development issues in the country. However, with the development of relations with the European Union after 1993 and the legal legislation adopted in 1999, an agency structure that helps the implementation of government aid programs and projects and provides business advice and consultancy to regional or local initiatives was established (Ferry, 2007; 453–456). It attaches special importance to regional policies in the European Union (EU). The importance given to Cohesion Policies in the EU budget and the European Regional Development Fund (ERDF) established in 1975 are the most important indicators of this situation. The aims of the EU to give importance to regional policies are to spread the gains obtained by economic integration throughout the union, to increase the productivity of the union, to encourage different social, economic and regional development models (Bachtler and Begg, 2017: 152).

2 Pre-Planned Period Development Approach

Turkey pre-planned periods of development policy can be examined in two periods: 1923–1950 and 1950–1960. The reference point for the İzmir Economic Congress in making this distinction, and an end to Turkey's multi-party life is passing (Marşap, 2008: 86). In the period between 1923–1950, the fact that the country was newly established, not only a part of the country but the whole of it had a problem of underdevelopment, brought about the failure to adopt the approach of dividing the country into regions and producing policies on regional development (SPO, 2000: 24). The policies implemented in this period; primarily to establish the political and administrative structure of the newly established country; creating a national society and economy; distribution of the population to other centers of the country other than Istanbul; especially the transportation of the industry outside the Marmara region to the Inner Aegean and Central Anatolia and the enrichment of the country's railway network (Göymen, 2005: 1)

With the Encouragement-i Industry Law enacted on March 28, 1927, the private sector was tried to be developed, but there was no implementation in the plan regarding the balanced distribution of investments across the country. In the first periods of the Republic, the level of development expected from liberal policies could not be achieved, and with the 1929 Economic Depression, liberal policies were abandoned in the country and statist policies started to be adopted. Two five-year industrial plans were prepared between 1933 and 1939, when statist economic policies were dominant. Among these plans, the 1st Five-Year Industrial Plan was implemented, but due to the start of the World War II, 2nd Five Year Industrial Plan could not be implemented. The main goal of these plans is to ensure the development of the region and the country through the industrial enterprises to be established by the state in various parts of the country (Çetinkaya, Dağlı, Yaman and Çapık, 2018: 23).

During the period between 1923 and 1950, General Inspectorates were established and with the decision of the Council of Ministers in 1945, the General Inspectors were informed that they should also be involved in regional development. However, this decision was implemented in a very limited way (Özaslan and Ünlü, 2015: 69).

In the period between 1950 and 1960, with the transition to multi-party life, the political power in the country changed and the Democrat Party adopted a new economic understanding that focused on more liberal policies instead of statist policies (Kanca, 2012: 48).

3 Regional Development After the Planned Period

The establishment of the State Planning Organization (SPO) in 1960 and the development plans that started to be prepared since 1963 caused this period to be called the planned period. SPO was closed in 2011 and its duties were transferred to the Ministry of Development and the plans were prepared by this ministry. With the transition to the Presidential Government System in 2018, the structure of the ministry was changed again. In this process, the Ministry of Development was abolished and the Presidency Strategy and Budget Directorate was established by merging this ministry and the General Directorate of Budget and Financial Control under the Ministry of Finance. Today, the task of preparing development plans belongs to the Presidency Strategy and Budget Directorate.

When the planned period is evaluated in general, it is seen that regional development is tried to be achieved through "Five-Year Development Plans, Integrated Regional Development Plans, Rural Development Projects, Investment Incentives, Priority Development Regions, Organized Industrial Zones and Small Industrial Sites" (Keskin and Sungur, 2012: 282). When the development plans are evaluated, it is seen that the titles such as regional development, regional development and regional planning are included in the plans and policies aimed at reducing interregional and intraregional development disparities are included in almost all of the plans. This situation shows that the issue of regional development, which was not given enough importance due to the pre-1960 social and economic conditions, became one of the main elements of the planned period (Sevinç, 2011: 44).

3.1 The First Five-Year Development Plan (1963–1967)

The First Five-Year Development Plan was published in the Official Gazette dated 03.12.1962 and numbered 11272 and entered into force. The plan includes a section titled "Regional Planning and Development". In the relevant section, the expected benefits of regional planning are listed as reducing interregional development disparities, solving problems of overpopulation and urbanization, providing a balanced distribution of public services across the country, and ensuring effective use of potential resources (SPO, 1963: 471).

Among the objectives of the plan for the regional policy are the distribution of the population across the country in a balanced manner, the transfer of resources primarily to the regions with development potential, and the faster development of the underdeveloped regions (SPO, 1963: 471). Regions that need to be developed in the plan are divided into three as Potential Development Regions, Underdeveloped Regions and Metropolitan Regions (Metropolitan Region). It has been stated that a detailed inventory study will be carried out in order to determine the current situation of Potential Development Regions and the Antalya region has been evaluated within this scope. Eastern and Southeastern Anatolia Regions were defined as Underdeveloped Regions, and it was stated that an inter-ministerial committee would be established at the center in order to ensure the development of these regions, changes would be made in the public personnel policy to increase the attractiveness of the region, and tax incentives would be prepared to actively participate in the development of the private sector. The East Marmara Region and especially Istanbul are defined as Metropolitan Regions (SPO, 1963: 473–475).

In the plan, it was stated that the main problem areas that may be encountered during regional planning are the lack of authorized administrative structures in regional planning, the lack of sound information about the current situation of the regions and the lack of qualified personnel in the field of regional planning (SPO, 1963: 476). When the plan is evaluated in general, it can be said that it has a positive perspective towards the regional planning approach. Regional plans were considered as an integral part of national plans, and it was seen that regional plans were necessary for the effective implementation of the national plan. The Eastern Marmara Planning Project prepared within this scope is the first regional plan prepared in the country (Keleş, 2013: 345).

3.2 Second Five-Year Development Plan (1968–1972)

The Second Five-Year Development Plan was published in the Official Gazette dated 21.08.1967 and numbered 12679 and entered into force. The headings of "Regional Development, Urbanization and Settlement Problem" and "Regional Planning" were included in the plan.

In the plan, the concepts of "industrialization, modernization in agriculture and urbanization" were seen as the main elements for national and regional development (SPO, 1968: 263) and it was stated that regional planning would be carried out with the cooperation of public-private sector organizations under the direction of SPO (SPO, 1968: 272) This situation shows that regional planning and development issues will be handled in a holistic manner within the plan period.

In the plan, the concept of development pole was adopted (Zeybek, 2013: 41), it was stated that service investments and economic investments in city centers with high development potential in underdeveloped regions will be increased, and appropriate strategies will be prepared for the private sector to invest in these areas (SPO, 1968: 263).

The lack of understanding in addressing the economic and social dimensions of urbanization in eliminating regional imbalances in Turkey has been regarded as a major shortcoming. The practice of directing investments to less developed regions with the incentive measures targeted in the First Five-Year Development Plan was limited to only a few examples, and the establishment of regular industrial zones could not be realized (SPO, 1968: 265).

As the policies to be applied in the second BYKP (Five -Year development Plan); centers with development potential in underdeveloped regions will be supported; Projects will be prepared to make public economic investments in underdeveloped regions; For the private sector, it was stated that incentives such as credit facilities, tax reductions, cheap energy, industrial zones with a prepared infrastructure will be created and regional opportunities will be introduced to investors (SPO, 1968: 268–269).

3.3 The Third Five-Year Development Plan (1973–1977)

The Third Five-Year Development Plan was published in the Official Gazette No. 14374 on 27.11.1972 and entered into force. (SPO, 1973: 1). The plan did not include a title such as region, regional development, regional development, and regional planning, but instead the concept of "Priority Regions for Development" was used. This situation can be expressed as an indicator of a change in understanding.

This situation can be expressed as an indicator of a change in understanding. The aim here is to address the interregional development problem together with the concept of balanced urbanization and to ensure more efficient use of economic resources. It has been stated that especially local governments should work effectively in revealing the potential resources in less developed regions (SPO, 1973: 122).

In the plan, the existence of developed problems between and within the region was expressed, and a ranking was made at the provincial level according to the development index to be formed as a result of determining the natural and human resources that have the potential to develop. The practice of preparing special development plans for the development of certain regions was abandoned because it contradicts the integrity principle. (SPO, 1973: 948–949).

3.4 Fourth Five-Year Development Plan (1979–1983)

The Fourth Five-Year Development Plan was published in the Official Gazette dated 12.12.1978 and numbered 16478 and entered into force. (SPO, 1979: 3) In the plan, the titles of "Regional Development" and "Priority Regions for Development" are included together. In the introduction part of the plan, it was stated that regional development opportunities should be taken into consideration for national development, and interregional and intraregional development differences are one of the important problems of the country (SPO, 1979: 3–4). This approach can be seen as an indication that the regional issue is given importance in the plan period.

In the plan, in the general evaluation made for the planned period, it was stated that despite all the efforts made to eliminate the interregional imbalances, the interregional development differences gradually increased rather than decreased. As the main reasons for this situation, the institutionalization required for creating a regional plan is lacking; that only a few exemplary plans were made in the less developed regions; It was stated that healthy data could not be obtained since the prepared plans did not cover the whole of the regions and the sector (SPO, 1979: 72–75).

It is aimed to use all opportunities for the development of underdeveloped regions and to prioritize integration with the space in planning decisions; Local capital in underdeveloped regions was asked to be an important factor in development with their investments in these regions (SPO, 1979: 292–293). In the plan period, the laws enacted regarding the increase of the Income and Corporate Tax reduction rate, exemption from various taxes, duties and charges, and spending 1/10 of the Public Partnership Fund in these regions can be seen as important developments (Keleş, 2013: 360–361).

3.5 Fifth Five-Year Development Plan (1985–1989)

The Fifth Five-Year Development Plan was published in the Official Gazette No. 18467 on 23.07.1984 and entered into force. There is a section titled "Regional Planning" in the plan (SPO, 1985: IV). Returning to the concept of regional planning is an expression of the importance given to the concept of region in this plan period as in the 4th Five-Year Development Plan. Regions to be planned for regional planning will be selected according to 16 different criteria such as the economic situation of the regions, their development potential on the basis of the sector and the existence of large-scale projects, regardless of the administrative boundaries, unlike the previous plan periods. Regions to be created within this scope will be named as "Functional Regions" and "Regional Development Schemes" will be created for these regions, which include both available resources and alternative solutions on sectoral and spatial basis in order to ensure harmony and balance in the development of the region (SPO, 1985: 161–162).

Practices to be put forward to ensure regional development in the plan period; credit opportunities in underdeveloped regions that are exempt from tax, dues and fees; tax benefits; "Project Offices" to be established to support and guide entrepreneurs; "Profit Partnership Documents" to be prepared for the private sector in developing regions; It is defined as "Specialized Organized Industrial Zones" that can be established when necessary. In addition, it was stated that the "Environmental Impact Assessment" report should be prepared in public investments and private sector investments that may affect the environment (SPO, 1985: 162–163). Handling the issue of regional planning together with the concept of environment is an indication that the issue is handled with a more holistic perspective and that it is desired to prevent possible adverse events related to the environment while ensuring regional development. One of the most important developments in the Plan period is the Decree Law No. 388 on the Establishment and Duties of the Southeastern Anatolia Project (GAP) Regional Development Administration (GAP, 09.09.2020), published in the Official Gazette No. 20334 dated November 6, 1989. With the decree, it was aimed to plan and carry out regional development through an institution organized within the hierarchical structure of the center. This situation has been seen as one of the concrete steps taken in regional development.

3.6 Sixth Five-Year Development Plan (1990–1994)

The Sixth Five-Year Development Plan was published in the Official Gazette dated 06.07.1989 and numbered 20217 (SPO, 1990: IV). The title of regional and local development was included in the plan and it was stated that one of the main objectives of the plan was to reduce regional and local development differences (SPO, 1990: 1).

Unlike other plans, it was stated in the plan that for the first time, a regional policy in line with the European Community regional policies will be established and the data prepared for the regions will be prepared in accordance with international standards (SPO, 1990: 318).

Irregular urbanization in the country has increased interregional and intraregional development differences. Therefore, it is stated that "sub-metropolitan cities, medium-sized centers, central cities of less developed regions and central rural settlements" will be determined and their development will be encouraged, especially in order to reduce the industrial and population density in certain regions. It was stated that "metropolitan area administrations" would be established in order to make a more comprehensive, integrated and consistent planning study (SPO, 1990: 318).

3.7 Seventh Five-Year Development Plan (1996–2000)

The Seventh Five-Year Development Plan was published in the Official Gazette numbered 22354 on 25.07.1995 (SPO, 1995). The subject in the plan has been examined under the subtitle of "Regional Development and Physical Planning" under the main heading of "Ensuring Regional Balances"

In the plan period, it was stated that regional development and physical planning studies will be focused on in order to reduce regional development differences, increase welfare in Priority Development Regions and make the issue of migration regular (SPO, 1995: 16). In the plan, especially the importance of local governments in regional development and the need for restructuring was mentioned (SPO, 1995: 130).

Socio-economic development targets for Regions with Development Priority and Eastern and Southeastern Anatolia Regions are explained in the Plan and the measures to be implemented are included. As the measures to be taken, it has been stated that the Repair Project will be prepared specifically for the Eastern and Southeastern Anatolia Regions, areas such as agriculture and handicrafts will be developed in regions that are not suitable for the development of agriculture-based industry and industry, transportation opportunities will be increased and settlement center planning will be made. As in other plan periods, the practice of supporting the regional development center, lower tier settlement center and central village settlements continued in order to ensure efficient use of resources and balanced distribution of the population (SPO, 1995: 174–175). In the plan, it was mentioned about the Southeastern Anatolia Project and its importance for the socio-economic development of the region and that the Zonguldak-Bartın Regional Development Project will be completed as soon as possible (SPO, 1995: 176).

3.8 The Eighth Five-Year Development Plan (2001–2005)

The Eighth Five-Year Development Plan was published in the Official Gazette dated 05.07.2000 and numbered 24100 (SPO, 2000). There is a heading named "Regional Development Targets and Policies" in the plan.

In the plan, it was emphasized that with the globalization process in the world, regional development plans and policies have become more and more important. New regional development approach and regions/cities such as concepts of competitiveness has brought Turkey to the adoption of new regional policies. The European Union and the Organization for Economic Co-operation and Development (OECD) likewise in Turkey for regional policy principles of "sustainability, interregional integration, provision of social and economic stability, improving the quality of life, equal opportunities, cultural development and participation" principles such as regional development has determined as the basic principles in the implementation of policies (DPT, 2000: 59–63). In the plan, it was emphasized that the economic contribution provided by the Southeastern Anatolia Project will be provided in social development with the GAP Social Action Plan prepared. It has been stated that this development will continue with the Entrepreneur Support and Guidance Centers (GIDEM) and Multi-Purpose Community Centers (ÇATOM) to be established within the scope of GAP. In the plan period, there are Eastern Anatolia Project Master Plan

(DAP), Eastern Black Sea Regional Development Plan (DOKAP), Yeşilırmak Havza Development Project, Eastern Mediterranean Region Development Project and Marmara Region Plan (SPO, 2000: 65–67).

Emphasizing the need for more comprehensive and participatory plan for regional development and planning represents one of the new applications for Turkey. At this point, the importance of local projects to be realized in cooperation with especially local administrations, public institutions and non-governmental organizations for development was mentioned (SPO, 2000: 63–67). Another remarkable innovation in the plan is that the State Planning Organization can establish centers where it needs (SPO, 2000: 63–67). These centers can be seen as an expression of the need for a more effective management understanding in the processes of plan preparation, implementation and monitoring.

One of the most important developments in the Plan period is the concrete steps taken regarding the Zonguldak region, which was mentioned in the First Plan, that the problems that may occur in the future due to the existence of large industrial facilities should be planned. In this period, planning studies of the Zonguldak-Bartın Regional Development Project were completed and put into practice.

3.9 Ninth Development Plan (2007–2013)

The Ninth Development Plan was published in the Official Gazette numbered 26215 on 01.07.2006 (SPO, 2006). The plan includes the title of "Ensuring Regional Development". The strategies determined under this title are "Activating the Regional Development Policy at Central Level, Ensuring Development Based on Local Dynamics and Internal Potential, Increasing Institutional Capacity at Local Level and Ensuring Development in Rural Area" (SPO, 2006: 91–93).

The strategies determined under this title are "Activating the Regional Development Policy at Central Level, Ensuring Development Based on Local Dynamics and Internal Potential, Increasing Institutional Capacity at Local Level and Ensuring Development in Rural Area" (SPO, 2006: 91–93). In this process, efforts were made at central and local levels to benefit from the European Union structural funds. In 2002, a three-level Classification of Statistical Territorial Units (İBBS – NUTS) was made and a database comparable with the EU was created. The law on the establishment of development agencies in NUTS Level 2 regions was enacted in 2006. The Preliminary National Development Plan covering the years 2004–2006 was prepared and local administration laws were renewed and the duties and responsibilities of local administrations regarding development were redefined (SPO, 2006: 46–48). The understanding of participation in the Eighth Plan period was discussed in a wider perspective in the ninth plan period, and it was emphasized that public-private-civil cooperation would be emphasized in the construction phase of the regional plans to be prepared through development agencies and in the construction of projects that use local potential. Participation of NGOs in the process will be encouraged especially in less developed regions (SPO, 2006: 91–93).

The most important development in the name of regional development during the plan period is that the Regional Development Agencies, which were stated in the Preliminary National Development Plan, started to be established in 2006 at the NUTS 2nd Level based on the law numbered 5449. Development agencies started operating in all 26 regions as of 2009, thus eliminating the lack of administrative structure responsible for regional development in the country. In addition to eliminating the lack of administrative structure, agencies have become one of the complementary elements of national development with their regional plans.

Another development that took place during the Ninth Plan period was the transfer of the headquarters of the GAP Regional Development Administration in Ankara to Şanlıurfa as of March 2, 2009 (GAP, 09.09.2020). With this decision, the headquarters of the administration operating in the region has been moved to the area where it works, as in development agencies.

3.10 The Tenth Development Plan (2014–2018)

The Tenth Development Plan was published in the Official Gazette dated 02.07.2013 and numbered 28699 (Ministry of Development, 2013). The title of "Regional Development and Regional Competitiveness" has been included in the plan.

After 2000, Turkey's regional development policy, regional development Increasing Competitiveness in addition to the reduction objective differences and socio-economic integration of intra-regional and been redefined to include the objective of strengthening the interregional (Ministry of Development, 2013: 119). Become a popular practice in the world of regional development and new understanding in this process and also said to be a significant impact on Turkey's European Union membership process began.

In the ninth Plan period, the Regional Development High Council and the Regional Development Committee were established in order to ensure regional development; Establishment of 26 development agencies at NUTS 2 level has been completed. Apart from GAP, DAP, DOKAP and Konya Plain Project

(KOP) regional development administrations have been established. Regional plans were prepared by development agencies and regional differences were taken into account in the plans prepared; GAP Action Plan was prepared; The Attraction Centers Support Program was implemented in order to increase the efficiency of the important cities in the central and eastern parts of the country; The investment incentive system was revised and investments in transportation throughout the country were diversified (Ministry of Development, 2013: 119–122). Although successful implementations were carried out during the ninth Plan period, the problem of interregional and intraregional development disparities continued. The main shortcomings of this plan period and the issues that should be given particular importance in the 10th Plan period were stated as comparative analysis of the regional competitiveness of the regions, increasing participation and decentralization practices in decision-making and implementation processes, and ensuring a more effective coordination among institutions (Ministry of Development, 2013: 122–123). In the 10th Plan period, the Regional Development National Strategy (BGUS) mentioned in the 9th plan was prepared. In the strategy, the concept of regional development has been accepted as a part of the national development policy, and it is aimed to actively participate in the decision-making processes of public-private-civil actors at regional level (Ministry of Development, 2014: 7). Implementation of BGUS; the regions close to the border to develop cross-border cooperation; development of important centers in the country in terms of transportation, especially on the North-South corridor; Increasing the capacity of non-governmental organizations to make projects and expanding the geographical indication application were determined. These practices aim to reduce regional development disparities, ensure a balanced distribution of wealth across the country, and increase competitiveness by using regional potentials (Ministry of Development, 2013: 123–125)

Preparation of BGUS can be seen as one of the most important developments of this plan period. The need for a strategy that reveals the current situation of the regions and determines long-term regional development goals has ended with this document. In addition, the document prepared in accordance with the EU regional development goals and policies has been an important source for development agencies whose establishment was completed in 2009 and regional development administrations, whose number reached 4 in the ninth Plan period.

3.11 Eleventh Development Plan (2019–2023)

The Eleventh Development Plan entered into force after being published in the Official Gazette dated 23.07.2019 and numbered 30840. The concept of

"Regional Development" was included in a subtitle in the plan (Strategy and Budget Directorate, 2013: 123–125).

10th Regional development plans prepared by development agencies were implemented during the plan period; the implementation of the Attraction Centers Program continued. Supporting the Infrastructure of Villages (KÖYDES) and Water and Sewerage Infrastructure Program (SUKAP) were implemented and Social Support Programs were implemented (Strategy and Budget Directorate, 2013: 26).

In the eleventh plan, it is required to use the principles of innovation, cooperation and governance in reducing interregional and intra-regional development disparities. For this purpose, strengthening the institutional structure on the basis of governance; revising the legal legislation on regional development administrations and development agencies; establishing an official statistical infrastructure to measure the development differences between regions; Updating the Socio-Economic Development Ranking Research; Renewal of the Social Support Program offered by development agencies; Continuation of the Growth Centers Support Program and increasing the amount of international resources used by development agencies will be implemented (Strategy and Budget Directorate, 2013: 157–158).

4 Evaluation of Development Plans on Regional Development

Although concepts such as regional development, regional development and regional planning were included in the development plans, regional plans were made in various periods and administrative structures responsible for regional development were established, interregional and intra-regional development problems still exist in the country. When the regional development levels of NUTS 2 regions between 2001 and 2014 is interpreted, it is seen that the development difference between the regions in the upper and lower ranks gradually increases (Kizil, 2016: 50). In an assessment to be made on the basis of provinces, while there is a sufficient development in the field of health throughout the country in the field of social development, it is stated that adequate development cannot be achieved in the eastern and southeastern provinces in the field of education; In terms of economic development, it is seen that other Eastern and Southeastern Anatolian provinces except Gaziantep, Malatya, Elazığ and Hatay are not at the desired level (Özdemir and Altıparmak, 2005: 109).

The Socio-Economic Development Ranking of Provinces and Regions (SEGE-2011) published by the Ministry of Development, General Directorate of Regional Development and Structural Adjustment in 2013 and the

Socio-Economic Development Ranking Survey of the Provinces and Regions published in 2019 by the Ministry of Industry and Technology General Directorate of Development Agencies SEGE – The 2017 reports show that although the development gap between the most developed region and the least developed region has decreased, the desired progress has not been achieved in reducing regional development disparities. As can be seen in Table.2.10.1, during the period when the reports were prepared, 6 regions in the upper ranks and 4 regions in the lower ranks remained the same. When the overall ranking is considered, it is seen that most of the regions are in the same order and at the same level of development. Only TR83 Samsun, Tokat, Çorum, Amasya region fell by 1 rank in the SEGE-17 reporting period and took place within the 3rd Tier development zone. This situation implies that the desired progress could not be achieved due to the intervention of other factors, although the development plans focused on regional development.

Tab. 2.10.1: Socio-Economic Development Ranking According to NUTS 2

NUTS Level II Code	Cities of Regions	SEGE - 11			SEGE - 17		
		Index Value	Order	Level	Index Value	Order	Level
TR10	İstanbul	4,5154	1	1	4,051	1	1
TR51	Ankara	2,8384	2	1	2,718	2	1
TR31	İzmir	1,9715	3	1	1,926	3	1
TR41	Bursa, Eskişehir, Bilecik	1,2667	4	1	1,281	5	1
TR61	Antalya, Isparta, Burdur	1,2305	5	1	1,359	4	1
TR42	Kocaeli, Sakarya, Düzce, Bolu, Yalova	1,0528	6	1	1,227	6	1
TR32	Aydın, Denizli, Muğla	0,8257	7	2	0,884	7	2
TR21	Tekirdağ, Edirne, Kırklareli	0,7736	8	2	0,802	8	2
TR62	Adana, Mersin	0,5211	9	2	0,380	11	2
TR22	Balıkesir, Çanakkale	0,5133	10	2	0,498	10	2
TR52	Konya, Karaman	0,4951	11	2	0,618	9	2
TR33	Manisa, Afyon, Kütahya, Uşak	0,2437	12	2	0,283	13	2
TR81	Zonguldak, Karabük, Bartın	0,1934	13	2	0,286	12	2
TR72	Kayseri, Sivas, Yozgat	0,1130	14	2	0,168	14	2
TR83	Samsun, Tokat, Çorum, Amasya	0,0000	15	2	-0,015	15	3

(*continued on next page*)

Tab. 2.10.1: Continued

NUTS Level II Code	Cities of Regions	SEGE - 11			SEGE - 17		
		Index Value	**Order**	**Level**	**Index Value**	**Order**	**Level**
TRC1	Gaziantep, Adıyaman, Kilis	-0,0547	16	3	-0,059	16	3
TR90	Trabzon, Ordu, Giresun, Rize, Artvin, Gümüşhane	-0,0756	17	3	-0,104	17	3
TR71	Kırıkkale, Aksaray, Niğde, Nevşehir, Kırşehir	-0,1248	18	3	-0,137	18	3
TR82	Kastamonu, Çankırı, Sinop	-0,2190	19	3	-0,287	21	3
TRB1	Malatya, Elazığ, Bingöl, Tunceli	-0,2448	20	3	-0,285	20	3
TR63	Hatay, Kahramanmaraş, Osmaniye	-0,2729	21	3	-0,197	19	3
TRA1	Erzurum, Erzincan, Bayburt	-0,3751	22	3	-0,459	22	3
TRC2	Şanlıurfa, Diyarbakır	-1,1466	23	4	-1,220	23	4
TRC3	Mardin, Batman, Şırnak, Siirt	-1,3284	24	4	-1,468	25	4
TRA2	Ağrı, Kars, Iğdır, Ardahan	-1,3611	25	4	-1,424	24	4
TRB2	Van, Muş, Bitlis, Hakkâri	-1,4927	26	4	-1,506	26	4

Source: Ministry of Development, (2013). Socio-Economic Development Ranking of Provinces and Regions (SEGE-2011), Ankara, p. 74; Ministry of Industry and Technology, (2019). Socio-Economic Development Ranking Survey of Provinces and Regions SEGE-2017, Ankara, p.17.

Conclusions

When development plans both in Turkey and in conjunction with efforts to establish a regional development authority in the country, region increasingly on the concept seems to be a growing interest. Acknowledging the existence of interregional and intra-regional development differences in the process brought along the use of headings such as regional development, regional development and regional planning in the plans.

It can be said that the accession negotiations with the European Union have also developed the approach to the concept of regional and regional development in the country. Especially when the plans prepared in the post-2000 period are examined, it is seen that the European Union is trying to produce policies in accordance with the regional policies. In addition, firstly the adoption of the law on NUTS and then the establishment of development agencies in 2006 can be expressed as one of the clearest indicators of this.

One of the elements instead of traditional regional development approach that improves the outlook for the regional development concept in Turkey increasingly becoming a popular concept that periods beginning after 1970 "Regional Development" is understanding. While the traditional understanding of regional development represents a structure where there are administrations that are administratively and financially dependent on the center and where decisions regarding the regions are taken from the center; The concept of New Regional Development adopts a new understanding strengthened by the concept of regional competition, in which more participatory processes take place, regional potential is used and not only domestic but also foreign capital is tried to be attracted to the region.

Considering Turkey in particular the concept of regional development, development plans being implemented since 1963, clutch overlooked in some periods although (example III. Five-Year Development Plan), is seen as increasingly important. The main reasons for this can be listed as follows;

- Considering regional development as complementary to national development.
- Observing that there are interregional and intraregional development differences in the country.
- Using the development potential of the regions more efficiently with small scale plans, not national ones.
- The specific conditions of the regions are not fully reflected in national plans.
- Relationship with the European Union after 2000.

  In the future, it is predictable that the concept of regional development will take place more widely in development plans and that administrative structures established with the task of ensuring regional development will gain more importance. The existence of the concept of interregional competitiveness that gets stronger with globalization, the need for regions to discover their own potential to develop, and the popularization of the concepts of governance and participation are the factors that strengthen this situation.

As a result, the existence of elements included in development plans to ensure regional development is important. It is a positive point of view that the issue should be handled comprehensively, especially in post-2000 plans. However, despite all these positive developments, the existence of interregional and intra-regional development differences still shows that this situation is due to different reasons. These reasons can be specified as economic insufficiencies, changes in political power, problems arising from legal regulations and the regions not attracting investors at the desired level, etc.

References

Bachtler, J. and Begg, I. (2017). Beyond Brexit: Reshaping Policies for Regional Development in Europe. Papers in Regional Science, 97, 151–170.

Çetinkaya, S., Yaman, H., Dağlı, İ. and Çapık, E. (2018). Bölgesel Politikaların Kalkınma Planlarındaki Yeri ve Zamana Bağlı Dönüşümü [The Place of Regional Policies in Development Plans and Time Conversion]. Süleyman Demirel University Journal of Visionary, 9(22), 21–31.

Ergun, E. (1993). Bölgelerarası Dengesizliklerin Giderilmesinde Bölgesel Örgütlenmelerin Önemi: "Tennessee Valley Authority".[The Importance of Regional Organizations in Overcoming Interregional Imbalances: "Tennessee Valley Authority]. Journal of Public Administration, 26(1), 73–77.

Ferry, M. (2007). From Government to Governance: Polish Regional Development Agencies in a Changing Regional Context, East European Politics and Societies, 21, 447–474.

Frisken, F. and Norris, D. F. (2001). Regionalism Reconsidered. Journal of Urban Affairs, 23(5), 467–478.

GAP Bölgesel Kalkınma İdaresi Başkanlığı [GAP Regional Development Administration. History, http://www.gap.gov.tr/gap-bki-tarihcesi-sayfa-37.html 09.09.2020.

Göymen, K. (2005). Türkiye 'de Bölge Politikalarının Evrimi ve Bölgesel Kalkınma Ajansları [Turkey's Evolution of Regional Policy and Regional Development Agencies], Conference Proceedings of Partnerships for Local Development, İstanbul.

Ildirar, M. (2004). Bölgesel Kalkınma ve Gelişme Stratejileri [Regional Development and Development Strategies]. Ankara: Nobel Publication.

Kanca, O. C. (2012). 1950–1960 Arası Türkiye'de Uygulanan Sosyo-Ekonomik Politikalar [Socıo-Economic Policies Applied ın Turkey between the Years of 1950–1960]. Mustafa Kemal University Journal of the Institute of Social Sciences, 9 (19), 47–63.

Karaca, M. (2018). Türkiye'de Bölgesel Kalkınma Politikalarının Kurumsal Analizi: Kalkınma Ajansları Örneği [Instıtutıonal Analysıs of Regional Development Policies ın Turkey (Published Doctoral Thesıs). İnönü University Social Sciences Institute, Malatya.

Keleş, R. (2013). Kentleşme Politikası (Urbanization Policy). Ankara: İmge Publishing.

Keskin, H. and Sungur, O. (2010). Bölgesel Politika Ekseninde Yaşanan Dönüşüm: Türkiye'de Kalkınma Planlarında Bölgesel Politikaların Değişimi [Transformation in Regional Policy: Changes in Regional Policies in Development Plans in Turkey]. Süleyman Demirel University Faculty of Arts and Sciences Journal of Social Sciences, (21), 271–293.

Kizil, C. (2016). Türkiye'de 2001–2004 Döneminde Uygulanan Bölgesel Kalkınma Politikası Çıktılarının Bölgesel Gelişmişlik Endeksi ile Analizi [The Analysis of Regional Development Policy Outputs in 2001–2004 Period]. Journal of Economic Policy Researches, 3 (2), 33–53.

Kline, P. and Moretti, E. (2014). Local Economic Development, Agglomeration Economies, and the Big Push: 100 Years of Evidence from the Tennessee Valley Authority. The Quarterly Journal of Economics, 129 (I. 1), 275–331.

Marşap, G. (2008). Yeni Kamu Yönetimi Anlayışı Çerçevesinde Yerellik İlkesi Açısından Türkiye'de Bölge Kalkınma Ajansları [Locality Principle and Regional Policies in the New Public Management Understanding, In the Model of Regional Development Agencies], Master Thesis, Gazi University Social Sciences Instıtute, Ankara.

OECD (2020). Regional Development, http://www.oecd.org/gov/, (Date of Access: 24.08.2020).

Özaslan, A. and Ünlü, H. (2015). Türkiye'de Bölgesel Kalkınma Politikalarında Değişim ve Kalkınma Ajansları [Transformation ın Regional Development Policies and Regional Development Agencies in Turkey]. Mehmet Akif Ersoy University Journal of Social Sciences Institute, 7(13), 64–83.

Özdemir, A. İ. ve Altıparmak, A. (2005). Sosyo-Ekonomik Göstergeler Açısından İllerin Gelişmişlik Düzeyinin Karşılaştırmalı Analizi [Comparative Analysis of the Development Level of the Provinces in Terms of Socio -Economic Indicators]. Erciyes University Faculty of Economics and Administrative, 24, 97–110.

Özer, Y. E. (2007). Küresel Rekabet -Bölgesel Kalkınma Ajansları ve Türkiye [Global Competition Regional Development Agencies and Turkey]. Review of Social, Economic & Business Studies, 9(10), 389–408.

Pike, A., Rodriguez-Pose, A. ve Tomaney J. (2016). Local and Regional Development. London: Routledge.

Republic of Turkey Ministry of Development (2013). Socio-Economic Development Ranking Survey of Provinces and Regions. Ankara.

Republic of Turkey Ministry of Development (2013). The Tenth Development Plan, Ankara.

Republic of Turkey Ministry of Development (2014). Regional Development National Strategy 2014–2023], Ankara.

Republic of Turkey Ministry of Industry and Technology (2019). İllerin ve Bölgelerin Sosyo-Ekonomik Gelişmişlik Sıralaması Araştırması SEGE-2017 [Socio-Economic Development Ranking Survey of Provinces and Regions], Ankara.

Republic of Turkey State Supervisory Authority (2014). Evaluation of Development Agencies in Turkey Research and Practice Review Report. Ankara.

Sevinç, H. (2011). Bölgesel Kalkınma Sorunsalı: Türkiye'de Uygulanan Bölgesel Kalkınma Politikaları [Problematic of Regional Development: Regional Development Policies Applied in Turkey]. Journal of Entrepreneurship and Development, 6(2), 35–54.

SPO (1963). The First Five-Year Development Plan. The Establishment of the State Planning Organization Publications: Ankara.

SPO (1968). Second Five-Year Development Plan. The Establishment of the State Planning Organization Publications: Ankara.

SPO (1972). The Third Five-Year Development Plan. The Establishment of the State Planning Organization Publications: Ankara.

SPO (1975). Seventh Five-Year Development Plan. The Establishment of the State Planning Organization Publications: Ankara.

SPO (1979). Fourth Five-Year Development Plan. The Establishment of the State Planning Organization Publications: Ankara.

SPO (1984). Fifth Five-Year Development Plan. The Establishment of the State Planning Organization Publications: Ankara.

SPO (1989). Sixth Five-Year Development Plan. The Establishment of the State Planning Organization Publications: Ankara.

SPO (2000). The Eighth Five-Year Development Plan. The Establishment of the State Planning Organization Publications: Ankara.

SPO (2000). The Eighth Five-Year Development Plan Regional Development Specialization Commission Report (2001–2005]. The Establishment of the State Planning Organization Publications. Ankara.

SPO (2003). Economic Report. The Establishment of the State Planning Organization Publications Nu: 2003–77. Ankara.

SPO (2006). Ninth Development Plan. The Establishment of the State Planning Organization Publications: Ankara.

SPO (2008). Ninth Development Plan Regional Development Specialization Commission Report. The Establishment of the State Planning Organization Publications: Ankara.

Strategy and Budget Department of the Republic of Turkey (2019). Eleventh Development Plan. Ankara.

Syrett, S. ve Silva, C. N. (2001). Regional Development Agencies in Portugal: Recent Development and Future Challenges. Regional Studies, 35:2, 174–180.

Šabić, D. and Vujadinović, S. (2017). Regional Development and Regional Policy. Collection of Papers - Faculty of Geography at the University of Belgrade, 65(1a), 463–477.

Uzay, N. (2005). Bölgesel Gelişmişlik Farklarının Giderilmesi ve Bölgesel Kalkınma Ajansları (Eliminate the Regional Development Differences and Regional Development Agencies), Ankara: Seçkin Publishing.

Zeybek, E. (2013). Regional Development Policies Implemented in Turkey and 2003–2011 Period Economic Development. Unpublished Master Thesis, Uşak: Uşak University, Institute of Social Sciences.

Dr. Peyman Uysal

2.11 Paradigm Shift in Rural/Regional Development: Endogenous Development and Territorial Capital[1]

Abstract: It is seen that sectoral development strategies have been replaced by regional development strategies as a result of structural change in developed, democratic, capitalist and industrialized countries, especially in rural areas in Europe. Uncovering internal development potentials in order to utilize the non-agricultural economic potential in rural/regional areas instead of agricultural development, which has been accepted as the dominant development paradigm in rural/regional development in many developed and developing countries, especially in the European Union countries since the 1990s in the context of endogenous development understanding has become widespread. On the other hand, development, can be seen as a process in which the endogenous and unique development potentials of rural areas/spaces are revealed in line with the decisions of the local people and the state is a partner in the process through development policies that support these decisions. In this section, paradigm shift in favor of endogenous development in rural/regional development and components of capital and their importance in endogenous development are examined.

Keywords: Rural development, Regional development, Endogenous development, Territorial development, Territorial capital.

Introduction

The economic, social, cultural and environmental problems caused by the phenomenon of migration from rural to urban such as the problems in rural areas caused by leaving the countryside (environment, loss of cultural heritage, aging and feminization in the remaining population, etc.) and the point of view to reveal the rural potential in obtaining the potential growth of economies, have been taking a considerable attention of many developed and developing countries since 1990s. Especially European Union countries has been focussing on rural/regional development instead of agricultural development and the understanding of evaluating non agricultural economic potential in the

1 This chapter is prepared from author's unpublished PhD Thesis entitled "Social Innovation in Rural Development in Turkey".

rural/regional areas. In this process, the establishment of regional development agencies and the grant support it provides for non-agricultural (rural tourism, etc.) and evaluation/processing of agricultural products in rural areas have also triggered local actors in rural areas to cooperate around the project. Today, a great search for development has begun in rural areas.

Changes in the development paradigm are frequently discussed in current studies in the economic literature on the subject, and when the literature is examined, it is observed that centrally driven development policies gradually leave development policies that are described as endogenous (internal) in economic jargon such as decentralized development/local development/regional development. One of the reasons for this paradigm change is the inability of central governments to find solutions such as climate change, water scarcity, deterioration in income distribution and environmental caused by the globalizing economic activities. Another reason is the understanding that the development dynamics and potentials of a local community or region are different from the development dynamics and potentials of other local communities or regions. The problems faced by each local community or region on the path to development may differ from each other, as well as in terms of capital accumulations (financial or human capital) and production factors. Therefore, a development policy that will be formed under the direction of the central government cannot be effective in every region at the same level and may even negatively affect the welfare of the people of the region. For this reason, it has become more and more widely accepted that development policies should be built and implemented based on a bottom-up understanding instead of creating and implementing a top-down approach.

Advocates of the new endogenous development phenomenon state that endogenous potentials must be mobilized to develop rural areas. In the studies conducted in line with this view, it is stated that the new endogenous regional development process depends on the success of individuals in developing sustainable structures and enabling all kinds of innovation, creativity, new ideas and visions. For example, Cooke emphasized in his 1998 study that the differences in development levels between regions cannot be explained solely by physical and financial resources, but that these differences are due to different organizational abilities of regional actors and their success in putting these skills into practice, as well as resource differences. In other words, coordination, communication and collective knowledge production between the actors in the regions are essential for success in regional development.

1 A New Paradigm in Rural/Regional Development: Endogenous Development

Endogenous development understanding has been positioned as the opposite idea to the traditional (modernist) understanding. The basic hypothesis of the endogenous development approach is that improvements in the socio-economic welfare levels of disadvantaged areas can be achieved by defining and mobilizing the collective resources of the space in question. In other words, in the new development approach, not only quantitative and monetary factors but also qualitative and structural determinants such as cultural, social, political and ecological values, social costs and long-term effects are taken into account (Bassand, 1986). In the late 1970s and early 1980s, doubts arose about the effectiveness of traditional development policy tools, and regional development experts sought an alternative to the dominant regional development paradigm at that time (Helmsing, 2001). Walter Stöhr and John Friedman can be given as two examples (Nemes, 2005). Walter Stöhr and John Friedman can be given as two examples (Nemes, 2005). With the selective territorial closure theory proposed by Stöhr as an alternative to the traditional development paradigm in his 1978 work, in which regions are positioned almost autonomously, Friedman (1981) planned a combination of agriculture and industry as economic activity, the size of which is determined by economies of scale and scope rather than the state. Development theory based on agricultural policies, in which an area is designed according to its own development potential, are two important examples of this alternative search. Although the theories differ substantially in general terms, their emphasis on local actors, local resources and local potentials may provide evidence that these theories form the foundations of the endogenous development paradigm. In both theories, the importance of local actors to take initiative in investment decisions and to participate in policy definition and implementation processes is underlined. In addition, according to both theories, the development of a space can only be possible through the companies and actors in the space coming together and making investment decisions in order to develop the local economy and the society (Friedman & Weaver, 1979; Stöhr & Taylor, 1981). The main features of the endogenous development concept are expressed in the 1998 study of Lowe and his friends.

- The unique natural, human and cultural capital of a region forms the basis of sustainable development,
- Local government units and local companies in the region create the dynamic power of the area,

- In addition to agricultural and industrial production, production of various services within the region is necessary for endogenous development,
- The focal point of development in rural areas is to build institutional and structural capacity in the said area and to prevent social exclusion.

Endogenous development approach, in a sense, refers to the creation of capital accumulation by using the unique potentials of spaces (Vazquez-Barquero, 2006). In other words, it is a set of development activities based on local savings and investments. While private and public resources can be managed from other centers, endogenous development deals with the diffusion of innovations within the local productive system. Here, the development potential of the space is directly related to the functioning of the institutional infrastructure. Based on the hypothesis that a space should be understood as a network of interests of the community living in that space, endogenous development can be positioned as a territorial approach to the process of economic growth and structural change (Massey, 1984). As a result of the examination of the literature on endogenous development, it is seen that there are many definitions brought to the concept of endogenous development. When these definitions are evaluated as a whole, the common elements that appear to be covered by each definition are as follows (Mühlinghaus & Walty, 2001):

1) Endogenous Potentials: The concept of endogenous development expresses the existence of local potentials and capabilities that are not addressed by traditional regional development policies. Endogenous development is based on the activation of these potentials and capabilities. Endogenous potentials can be defined as the sum of development opportunities within a limited area and time frame. These opportunities can be the natural resources of the space, as well as the human and social skills of the community members living in the space, either individually or together.
2) Regional Economy: The necessity of increasing regional economic decentralization within the scope of endogenous development approach is frequently mentioned in studies on the subject. In the studies, it is stated that the economic autonomy of the region will have a positive contribution to reducing the dependence on external effects, and the way to achieve this goal is shown as increasing cooperation within the region, substituting products and services provided from outside the region and exporting competitive products outside the region.
3) Sustainable Development: Endogenous development does not aim at economic development alone, but a holistic development, including economic, social and environmental development.

4) Participation: Endogenous development focuses on local needs and problems. The necessity for local people to participate in policy decisions and implementation processes is the most underlined point of endogenous development.
5) Regional/Territorial Identity: It is stated that endogenous development policies will be much more successful when individuals living in a region or space can identify themselves with the area they live in. It is argued that this phenomenon, which can be defined as regional or territorial identity in the endogenous development approach, will bring individuals closer to the community they live in and to other individuals of the community. This identity, which was initially defined at the individual level, will bring with it a sense of belonging and community identity, and thus, cooperation and communication within the region or space will increase. Local initiatives that can be defined as activities based on cooperation and innovation at the local level are a form of direct participation and emerge as a result of the combination of regional/territorial identity and participation elements in the endogenous development approach. Thanks to this combination, local community members can be both actors and decision makers in development activities.

1.1 Territorial Approach to Endogenous Development

Territorial development can be seen as a process in which the endogenous and unique development potential of rural areas/spaces is revealed in line with the decisions of the local people and the state is a partner in the process through development policies that support these decisions. In other words, rural development includes both a planned development through state intervention and a development that can be achieved as a result of positive social changes, provided that it is supportive.

In other words, rural development includes both a planned development through state intervention and a development that can be achieved as a result of positive social changes, provided that it is supportive. The spread of new production systems in agriculture (organic, good agriculture, fair trade, local products-geographical signs, etc.), industrialization of rural areas (industry, tourism, etc.), strengthening of the relationship/connection between rural and urban areas (especially through labor; Rural-urban workers), progress in decentralization of governance, widespread use of non-governmental organizations in rural areas, and increasing demand for environmental services (clean and natural environment, wildlife, etc.) lead to the spread of the territorial approach as a rural development model (Janvry) and Sadoulet, 2007).

It can be said that the common point of the policies put into practice as a result of the search for new rural development approaches in recent years is that they aim at a holistic development rather than sectoral development. It is striking that in the new paradigm, the concept of territorial is often used instead of the concept of regional. The features that make the concept of space different from any geographical area in the study of Camagni in 2008:

- Localized externalities system,
- System of localized activities, skills, know-how and traditions;
- System of localized close relations that allows capital formation and thus increases the static and dynamic productivity of local factors,
- Cultural elements and system of values that give meaning and emotion to local practices and define local identities,
- Defined as the system of rules and practices that define the local government model (Camagni, 2008).

State intervention in rural development is deemed necessary in issues such as reducing poverty, eliminating social inequality in the rural population and development differences between different rural areas within the same region. Considering the fact that ensuring a balanced income distribution is the duty of the state in constitutions, it can be said that the role of the state in development is important in the distribution of income obtained as a result of production in rural areas. In the territorial development approach, it is aimed to reveal and use the endogenous and unique development potential of rural areas in partnership with the local people and the state (central and local administrations) through state policies that aim to establish the infrastructure for the creation of the environment that will enable rural development. The conclusion that emerges from this is that state intervention is required in all development approaches, whether sectoral or territorial, but the most important difference is the difference between the levels of intervention.

1.2 Territorial Capital and Its Components

The concept of territorial capital was first used in the report prepared by the OECD in 2001 within the scope of regional policies (OECD, 2001).

According to the definition of the OECD on territorial capital in the said report, *"each region has its own territorial capital stock that distinguishes itself from the others and allows some investments to adapt better to the region and provide higher returns in terms of using the region's assets and potential more effectively"*. Territorial capital is simply a necessary measurement tool to reveal the structure of the space where it exists and to make various analyzes. Although the capital of a region was tried to be measured based on concrete, easy-to-measure concepts such as regional GDP, which can be defined as the contribution of economic activities carried out in that region to the GDP until a short time ago, today it is not only concrete factors but also abstract factors in the composition of regional/territorial capital. It turned out to have an effect. Barca states in a report he prepared in 2009 that regional gross domestic product cannot be the only measurement tool that can reveal regional differences, and even the comparisons made in this respect alone are far from providing healthy results. As a matter of fact, although their contributions to the gross domestic product are equal to each other, there are regions where there is great difference between the living standards and welfare levels of the human communities they host. From this point of view, the development process is far from being a process where only concrete factors are effective (Toth, 2011).

Bourdieu states in his study of 2004 that the effects of some distribution channels and resource allocation mechanisms, which are necessary for the transformation of income increase into wealth increase on the path from economic growth to development, may be as important as concrete factors (Bourdieu, 2004). In other words, it can be thought that territorial capital is a combination of all concrete and intangible factors that are effective in the processes of creating economic growth in a region or the existing economic growth resulting in economic development. Territorial capital approach is a holistic approach in which territorial functions and relations are taken into account, and it aims to explain territorial processes by considering the dynamics of the regions (Toth, 2011). The innovation brought by the concept of territorial capital to the economic literature is its effort to examine intangible assets that are highly influential in the development process, which were not evaluated by previous approaches, and to make these assets measurable in sociological and economic terms. According to the approach, although they are described as abstract, abstract entities can also be measured like concrete entities (Toth, 2011).

Marshall, one of the founders of the Cambridge school, is the economist who first emphasized the territorial side of abstract sources. Although Marshall did not use the concept of abstract asset (commodity), he stated that there are factors that make up the economic environment that make economic activities possible with the concept of pending commodity. According to Marshall, these factors include institutional networks, laws, local researchers, traditions and customs, cultural characteristics, moral judgments of producers and politicians, practices peculiar to the local economy and the ability of local people to transform their interests into value. The concept of territorial capital was used for

Tab. 2.11.1: Sources of Territorial Capital

Concrete factors	Non-commercial interdependencies	Abstract Factors
Geographical location, production equipment, climate, traditions, natural resources, quality of life, proximity to industrial areas and cities to reduce transaction costs, agglomeration economies	Understandings, customs and informal rules that enable economic actors to work together, or the joint implementation of ideas developed in clusters of small and medium-sized enterprises operating in the same sector, solidarity and cooperation (social capital)	Results achieved when institutions, rules, practices, researchers and policy makers come together to enable creativity and innovation.

Source: OECD, 2001

the first time within the scope of regional policy in a 2001 report of the OECD. In this report, it is mentioned that each region has a unique composition of territorial capital that distinguishes it from other regions and enables it to use its assets and potentials more effectively, which allows it to obtain higher returns as a result of certain investments (OECD, 2001). Factors included in this report and shown as sources of territorial capital are given in Tab. 2.11.1.

As can be seen from Table 1, OECD divided the factors that make up the territorial capital into three groups as concrete factors, non-commercial interdependencies and abstract factors. Toth argues that territorial capital has a two-component structure, namely concrete and abstract factors. According to Toth, tangible resources refer to assets consisting of the sum of produced capital, financial capital and investment capital. Abstract resources, on the other hand, consist of the combination of intellectual capital, human capital, spiritual capital, creative capital, knowledge capital, organizational capital, relational capital, cultural capital, and social capital (Toth, 2011). Some factors can be mentioned about how the territorial capital phenomenon emerged and why it is considered important. The first of these factors is the increasingly complex structure of the world economy, the increasing difficulty of the implementation of central policies due to the intensification of globalization, resulting in the change of perspective towards approaches emphasizing local values, endogenous resources and territorial assets. In addition, the widespread use of case-based, speculative and in-depth analyzes rather than complex technical analyzes during the evaluation of policies and approaches has paved the way for the emergence of the concept (Toth, 2011). Another effective factor in revealing the importance of territorial capital is the understanding that the planned policies implemented within the scope of the EU integration policy are not effective enough in reducing inequality between the regions within the union. Territorial capital is positioned as a very important source of added value in the light of the studies that are frequently discussed in the Union meetings and aiming to reveal the reasons for the ineffectiveness of the policies and it has been accepted as a type of capital that will create positive effects not only for the regions that are disadvantaged in development but also for all regions. As an important strategy agenda that determines the framework of the European Union's regional policies, a consensus has been reached that territorial capital is essential to achieve the goals set in the EU 2020 Report within the scope of the Europe 2020 platform. Camagni, in his 2012 study, argues that the roots of the territorial development phenomenon were laid with supply-oriented traditional development theories that were valid in the 1960s in earlier periods. As a result of the supply-oriented traditional development policies pointed out by Camagni, intensive market-oriented agriculture caused a decrease in the number of farmers in the world population and caused difficulties in issues such as the employment of individuals excluded from agricultural production and environmental pollution caused by industrial agriculture (Jankovic, 2012). As a result of these problems that emerged as a side effect of industrial agriculture, rural areas are no longer under the control of farmers (Van der Ploeg et al., 2000). Agricultural dominance has decreased in rural areas (Murdoch et al., 2003) and agricultural hegomoni has decreased (Marsden, 1998).

In this case, rural heterogeneity has emerged and the need for differentiated rural policies sensitive to the characteristics and potentials of the regions has arisen. The necessity of establishing political relations other than centrally planned policies in rural areas first emerged in this period (Murdoch, 2003). The need for new regional and rural development policies emerging in rural areas requires the adaptation of existing central institutions to the regions, the establishment of new institutions, increasing the capacities of existing regional institutions and increasing the efficiency of activities. At this point, it emerges that regional/rural development is clearly related to the concept of space. In his 2012 study, Jankovic defines space as a geographical area that is not defined by administrative boundaries, but has a relatively homogeneous and integrated economic structure and socio-cultural identity against other spaces or regions. Moreover, these differences constitute the competitive advantages of the place in question.

The components of territorial capital, which Camagni put forward a theoretical taxonomy in his 2008 study, are given in Tab. 2.11.2. When you go from left

Special goods	Private fixed capital stock Monetary externalities (hard) Transit goods (C)	Relational special services – external links of companies – Transfer of R&D results – By-products of universities (I)	Human Capital – Entrepreneurship – Creativity – Special knowledge skills – Monetary Externalities (F)
Social goods and impure public goods	Property networks Joint goods - Land (pasture etc.) -Cultural heritage (B)	Collaborative networks - Strategic partnerships in R&D and knowledge - Public-private partnerships - Natural and cultural resources management (H)	Relational capital – Collaboration ability – Ability to operate together – Collective powers (E)
Public goods	Sources – Natural – Cultural – Capital for social expenses – Infrastructure (A)	Clustering and regional economies Access to empowering tools Connection R&D agencies (G)	Social capital - Institutions - Behavior models and values - Trust and reputation - Societies (D)
	Tangible Goods	Mixed Goods	Intangible Goods

Competition

Materiality

Tab. 2.11.2: Theoretical Taxonomy of Components of Territorial Design.
Source: Camagni, 2008

to right in the table, goods that are described as capital move from concreteness to abstractness. When the table goes from bottom to top, competition increases.

Cell of the table (A) includes traditional public goods consisting of social expenditure capital, natural and cultural public resources and environmental resources required to meet public expenses such as infrastructure expenditures.

This type of capital underlies the attractiveness of the space and expresses externalities that support the profitability of local activities. The cell referred to in Table (B) consists of concrete intermediate goods such as property networks in the transportation, communication and energy sectors where competition is moderate. Some of the capital mentioned here belongs to the public and the other to the private sector.

The cell indicated as (C) in the table contains private fixed capital and capital consisting of transition goods. Private fixed capital is regarded as an indicator of the territorial equipment that will benefit from the advantages of expansion in world trade demand. Social capital, which is named in the table (D) and is on the side of abstract goods, is defined by Camagni as the glue that holds societies together. In his study, Camagni defined social capital as a phenomenon formed by the coming together of norms, trust level and social networks (societies) in accordance with Putnam's definition of social capital. Unlike Putnam, Camagni included institutions in this structure. According to Camagni, social capital will only gain functionality when the relational capital in the (F) region in the table is combined with the elements of cooperation and ability to operate together. Camagni emphasizes the effect of the combination of social capital and relational capital on the formation of human capital in the (F) region of the table and underlines that the elements of entrepreneurship and creativity, which are the elements of human capital, can take action when they come together with social capital and relational capital.

The (G), (H) and (I) regions of the table are the parts in which the types of capital that can be described as either fully abstract or concrete capital are specified. In these sections, there are cluster economies, connectivity and reciprocity, respectively; and also types of capital defined as co-operative networks and relational special services. Camagni interprets this table, which includes all types of capital, in the context of Fig. 2.11.1, which shows the scope of traditional territorial capital and the scope of innovative territorial capital, which he calls the innovative cross, which will pave the way for innovations.

When the innovative territorial capital composition, which consists of components that are outside the scope of the traditional square, expressing the traditional territorial capital composition, it is seen that the human and social capital parts are excluded. In addition, private fixed capital stock and resources representing concrete production factors are not considered as innovative territorial capital components. The reason why these factors, each considered as a production factor in classical economic theory, remain outside the scope of innovative territorial capital, of course, does not mean that these factors are insignificant. Beyond the existence of production factors within the scope

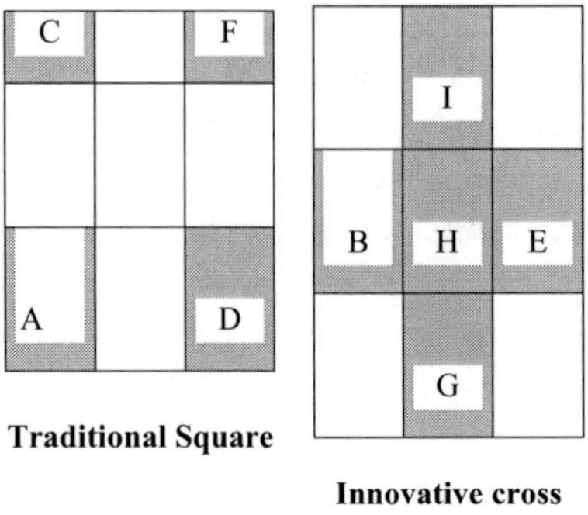

Fig. 2.11.1: Traditional and Innovative Components of Territorial Capital.
Source: Camagni, 2008

of innovative territorial capital, how the property rights of these production factors are defined gains importance. In addition, in the formation of human capital and human capital, rather than separate levels of effective social capital, it is also important to what extent these two types of capital can be transformed into relational capital, which consists of elements such as cooperation, ability to act together and collective powers to increase participation.

Discussion and Conclusion

The facts of economic growth and development, which started to be given great importance after the Second World War, were very effective in bringing together the countries that came out of the war and gained their new independence after the war for a common purpose. The development activities that were originally planned and implemented on the basis of theory have now been replaced by the implementation of policies whose outputs are more clearly predictable, scaled, and thus have evidence that they will provide positive outputs. When the development paradigms that have been valid until today are examined as a whole, it is observed that the integrated development and participatory development approaches, which were primitive at first, have been shaped and evolved according to needs and conditions over time. The first proposed rural development approaches emerge as the approaches that make a division of labor between rural areas and cities and hold rural areas responsible for agricultural production and cities for industrial production and innovation development in accordance with this division of labor. When it was revealed that these approaches, which advocate the dual structure, could not achieve their intended outputs and deepened the problems in rural areas rather than solving them, more holistic policies began to be needed on rural development. Even though the holistic development approach was put forward in response to this need, these policies, which were implemented with a top-down management style, that is, only state-driven, could not put an end to the dissolution in rural areas. Until the view that individuals living in rural areas should take part in problem diagnosis, solution and decision processes, sufficient progress could not be achieved in rural development until it was accepted that individuals with a problem can best be diagnosed and produce solutions. In the historical process, it is clearly understood today that the individuals of the rural community, whose opinions were sought only in the diagnosis of the problems, should now take part in all stages of the development process and that only participation-oriented development efforts can produce sustainable results.

Another important issue in the development of rural areas is the fact that not all rural areas can be developed at the same level by using the same policies. Undoubtedly, rural areas have many common features. However, it is certain that the areas in question and the individuals living in those areas have many characteristics that distinguish them from others. The endogenous development paradigm and the territorial development approach that can be defined as the embodiment of the endogenous development paradigm in rural areas has opened the way for a wide range of opportunities for rural development. The territorial approach, which argues that the characteristics and potentials that make rural areas out of being geographical areas and turn them into spaces should be revealed, revealed a type of capital that entered the literature as territorial capital. It contains capital types that can be transformed into each other within the scope of territorial capital, which can become a production factor when evaluated correctly, are used in production processes but do not decrease as a result of production such as physical capital. Territorial capital can generally be divided into three sub-components. The first component consists of concrete factors such as the existing geographical location in the rural area, production equipment, climate, traditions, natural and historical resources. The second component, on the other hand, consists of the results obtained by bringing together the institutions, rules, practices, researchers and policy makers, which are called abstract factors, to make innovations possible. The third component is the social capital component. Social networks stated in the literature that social capital is a component other than trust and norms enable individuals to come together and to work together by allowing them to come together and unite around common interests and problems. Until today, many development activities/projects in accordance with the holistic rural development approach adopted as the dominant rural development approach in the development plans of the countries have been presented. However, there are two important points that draw attention in rural development projects developed in recent years. The first of these is the determination that state guidance is gradually decreasing in the planning of development studies and the participation of all existing actors in rural areas in the stages of problem diagnosis, idea development, execution, decision and evaluation is emphasized more than ever. The second striking point is the change in the ideas that the agricultural sector of the state should be supported in order to develop rural areas and rural areas can only be developed in this way. The agricultural sector is, of course, still the most important source of income for the majority of individuals living in rural areas. However, in order to improve the living conditions in rural areas at this point, it will be at least as beneficial to mobilize the internal development potentials of the areas in question, which can only be used in production processes other than agricultural production, as territorial capital. Cooperatives, producers unions, non-governmental organizations and local entrepreneurs representing people living in rural areas and local government units working in rural areas can work together, meet and interact with each other and enable territorial capital with elements such as trust, norms and social networks. Social capital potential, which is one of the most important components, is the most important factor for successful rural development studies. Encouraging activities in the field of rural development, which can be described as social innovation, bringing new and sustainable solutions to the existing local problems and causing changes in attitudes and behaviors in the communities where they are realized as a final result, will result in sustainable development in rural areas. In this context, both the state and the private sector should support projects to increase the social capital levels of rural areas. Promoting sustainable activities will result in sustainable development in rural areas. In addition, it is important for policy makers, academics and investors representing the private sector to raise awareness of individuals living in rural areas about the internal development potentials (natural, historical and cultural capital) that distinguish rural areas from others and to raise awareness of how and how to unleash these potentials in the most effective way.

References

Barca, F. (2009). "An Agenda for A Reformed Cohesion Policy: A Place-Based Approach to Meeting European Union Challenges and Expectations,"

Independent Report, Prepared at the Request of the European Commissioner for Regional Policy, Danuta Hübner, European Commission, Brussels.

Bassand, M., Brugger, E. A., Bryden, J. M., Friedman, J. ve Stuckey, B. (1986). *Self-Reliant Development in Europe. Theory, Problems, Actions* Gower, Brookfield, Vermont.

Bourdieu, P. (1986). "The Forms of Capital" in: J. Richardson (Ed) *Handbook of Theory and Research for the Sociology of Education*, Pages: 241–258, Westport, CT, New York: USA: Greenwood Publishing.

Boxelaar, L., Paine, M. and Beilin, R. (2007). "Sites of Integration in a Contested Landscape", *Rural Society*, 17(3), 258–272.

Brooks, K. (2007). "Social Capital: Analysing the Effect of a Political Perspective on the Perceived Role of Government in Community Prosperity", *Rural Society*, 17 (3), 231–247.

Camagni, R. and Capello, R. (2012). "Regional Competitiveness and Territorial Capital: A Conceptual Approach and Empirical Evidence from the European Union". *Journal of Regional Studies*, 47(9), 1383–1402.

Camagni, R., Capello, R., Chizzolini, B. and Fratesi, U. (2008). "Regional Competitiveness: Towards a Concept of Territorial Capital", in *Modelling Regional Scenarios for the Enlarged Europe*, Springer Berlin, pp. 33–48.

Coleman, J. S. (1988). "Social Capital in the Creation of Human Capital". *The American Journal of Sociology*. 94, 95–120.

Coleman, J. D. (1990). *Foundations of social theory*. Cambridge, MA: Harvard University Press

Çekiç T. İ. and Ökten, A. (2009). "Sosyal Sermaye Perspektifinden Kırsal Kalkınma Sorunsalına Yeniden Bakış [Revisiting the Rural Development Problem from a Social Capital Perspective]". *Megarojournal*. 4(3): 203–213.

Çetin, M. (2006). "Bölgesel Kalkınmada Sosyal Ağların Rolü: Silikon Vadisi Örneği [The Role of Social Networks In The Regional Development: The Case of Silicon Valley]", *Dokuz Eylul University Faculty of Economics and Administrative Sciences Journal*, 21(1): 1–25.

Friedmann, J. (1981). "The Active Community: Toward a Political Territorial Framework for Rural Development in Asia", *Economic Development Cultural Change*, 29, 235–261.

Friedmann, J. and Weaver, C. (1979). "Territory and Function: The Evolution of Regional Planning", University of California Press, Berkeley and Los Angeles, 1979.

Fukuyama, F. (1999). "Social Capital and Civil Society". IMF Conference in Second GenerationReforms,www.imf.org/external/pubs/ft/seminar/1999/reforms/fukuyama.htm (erişim tarihi: 16.07.2020).

Giorgas, D. (2007). "The significance of social capital for rural and regional communities", *Rural Society*, (2007) 17(3), 206–214.

Grootaert, C. (1998). "Social Capital: The Missing Link?". The World Bank Social Development Family Environmentally and Socially Sustainable Development Network, Social Capital Initiative Working Paper.

Grootaert, C. ve Bastelaer, T. (2002). *The Role of Social Capital in Development: An Empirical Assessment.* Cambridge University Press, New York.

Helmsing, B. (2001). "Local Economic Development: New Generations of Actors, Policies and Instruments", A Summary Report prepared for the UNCDF Symposium on Decentralization Local Governance in Africa, 59–78.

Jankovic, D. (2012). "Territorial Approaches to Regional Rural Development". *Economics of Agriculture*, 4, 675–688.

Janvry, A. ve Sadoulet, E. (2007). "Toward a territorial approach to Rural Development". *Electronic Journal of Agricultural and Development Economics, Agricultural Development Economics Division (ESA) FAO*, 4 (1), 66–98 (www.fao.org/es/esa/eJADE, Date of Access: 12.05.2020).

Loury, G. (1977). "A Dynamic Theory of Racial Income Differences". *Women Minorities and Employment Discrimination* Philyllis, (Edit. Wallace ve Annette LaMond), 153–188, Lexington, MA, Heath.

Lowe, P., Ray, C., Ward, N. and Woodward, R. (1998). "Participation in Rural Development: A Review of European Experience". Centre for Rural Economy, University of Newcastle, Newcastle, England.

Marsden, T. (1998). *Economic Perspectives.* In B. Ilbery (editor), "The geography of rural change", Harlow, Longman, UK.

Massey, D. (1984). *The Territorial Division of Labour: Social Structures and the Geography of Production*. Oxford, Macmillan.

Milani, C. (2004). "Local Development and Social Capital Theory". International Society for Third Sector Research, 6th International Conference, July 11–14th, Ryerson University and York University, Toronto, Canada.

Mitchell, R. (2007). "Social Capital and the Rural Church", *Rural Society*, 17 (3), 273–285.

Moseley, M. J. (2003). *Rural Development: Principles and Practice.* London, Thousands Oaks, Sage publications.

Muhlinghaus, S. and Walty, S. (2001). "Endogenous Development in Swiss Mountain Communities". *Mountain Research and Development*, 21 (3), 236–242.

Murdoch, J., Lowe, P., Ward, N. and Marsden, T. (2003). *The Differentiated Countryside.* Routledge, London.

Nemes, G. (2005). "Integrated Rural Development: The Concept and Its Operation". Institute of Economics Hungarian Academy of Sciences. Discussion Papers 2005/6.

OECD. (2001). *Territorial Outlook*. Paris, OECD Publications.

Onyx, J., Edwards, M. and Bullen, P. (2007). "The Intersection of Social Capital and Power: An Application to Rural Communities". *Rural Society*, 17 (3), 215–230.

Perman, R., Ma, Y. and McGilvrav J. (1996). *Natural Resource and Environmental Economics*. Longman, London.

Ploeg, J. D. (2000). "Revitalising Agriculture: Farming Economically as a Starting Ground for Rural Development". *Sociologia Ruralis*, 40 (4), 497–511.

Putnam, R. (1995). "Bowling Alone: America's Declining Social Capital". *Journal of Democracy*, 6 (1), 65–78.

Stöhr, W. B. and Taylor, F. (1981). *Development From Above or Below? The Dialectics of Regional Planning in Developing Countries*, Chichester, UK: John Wiley.

Tóth, B. I. (2011). "Changing Endogenous Development: The Territorial Capital". *Journal of Urry*, J. *(1995). Consuming Places*, Routledge, London.

Van der Ploeg, J. D. (2008). *The new peasantries, struggles for autonomy and sustainability in an era of empire and globalization*. London, Earthscan.

Vazquez-Barquero, A. (2007). "Endogenous Development: Analytical and Policy Issues." Eds.: Allen J. Scott and Gioacchino Grafoli, In Development on the Ground: Clusters, Networks and Regions: *Emerging Economies*. 23–43. New York: Routledge Taylor& Francis Group.

Vennesland, B. (2004). "Social Capital and Networks in Forest Based Rural Economic Development". *Scandinavian Journal of Forest Research*, 1432, 82–89.

List of Figures

List of Tables